LB.

WITHDRAWN

Culture and Society in Lucian

Culture and Society in Lucian

C. P. JONES

Harvard University Press
Cambridge, Massachusetts
London, England   1986

This book is printed on acid-free paper, and its binding materials
have been chosen for strength and durability.

Library of Congress Cataloging in Publication Data

Jones, C. P.
   Culture and society in Lucian.

   Bibliography: p.
   Includes index.
   1. Lucian, of Samosata—Criticism and interpretation.
2. Civilization, Greco-Roman, in literature. 3. Athens
(Greece) in literature. 4. Rome in literature.
I. Title.
PA4236.J66   1986   887'.01   86-3099
ISBN 0-674-17974-9 (alk. paper)

Preface

"THE INIMITABLE LUCIAN," as Gibbon called him, has never lacked admirers, even when the Greek literature of the Roman Empire was most neglected. In the past twenty-five years or so that literature has enjoyed a revival, and he has benefited from a number of studies both general and particular. The present book, however, arose out of a dissatisfaction with a strong current in the criticism of this author, namely, the tendency to regard him as an "artist" hermetically sealed in a world of books and literary reminiscences. This view is connected to another one, which sees the Greek literature of the imperial period as indifferent to the present, the victim of a voluntary amnesia.

By contrast, the view which I argue here is that Lucian is a keen observer of the society and culture of his time. Several of these terms require definition. I assume that Lucian "observes" if his "observations" accord either with those of other writers of his day, or with contemporary documents such as inscriptions or papyri. Among writers I have given special attention to Galen for several reasons. To measure Lucian against Aelius Aristides, say, would be to run the risk of being charged with circularity, since it might be said that Lucian and Aristides were both equally literary and nothing was shown by coincidences between them. Galen was a doctor, and though well read and influenced by his reading he cannot be imagined to be lost in literature. Moreover, he was a writer with a temperament similar to Lucian's: sharp, often unkind, but informed and interested. One of his observations concerns a contemporary called "Lucianus," who played a hoax on a philosopher and certain teachers of literature; since this person is now agreed to be Lucian, there is also a bond of acquaintance, however slight or indirect, between the two. By

[v]

"society" I mean the social class in which Lucian moved and for which he presumably wrote, together with its customs and attitudes; I shall try to define this class more narrowly in what follows. By "culture" I mean both the condition of being "cultured" and what was required to attain that condition, especially the literary taste and knowledge. By Lucian's "time," or "contemporary," I understand roughly the latter half of the second century of the Christian era, though I shall cite examples both earlier and later than that period.

Any study of Lucian faces certain dangers. One is the scarcity of chronological signposts, which has led some to attempt to dispense with chronology altogether, others to draw up elaborate tables based largely on impression and conjecture. Where a work seems to me to allow an approximate date, I have said so, but I have not used chronology as a principle of organization; I have summarized my conclusions in Appendix B. Another difficulty is the lack of an agreed canon; Lucian's critics have tended to include or exclude this work or that in light of their preconceived notions of him. I have tried to be orthodox, but where the authenticity of a work is in serious question I have argued my decision in Appendix C. Yet another difficulty is that of organization. Lucian's works are so varied that any grouping is bound to appear artificial. I am conscious that some of my choices are awkward, but my main concern is that each chapter, and within each chapter each section, should lead logically to the next. The greatest danger is perhaps that of simple tactlessness; some critics of Lucian seem immovably ponderous, others twitch with the expectation of amusement. Though I have tried to respect Lucian's appeal to the "Attic nose," I am conscious that my picture of him may seem rather more earnest than is usual; but the flippant, colloquial pamphleteer which he is often imagined to be (especially as presented in current English translations) does not do him justice. Lucian aimed to amuse, but the subjects he chose were often ones taken very seriously by his contemporaries.

Probably the most influential work on Lucian in the last half-century has been Jacques Bompaire's *Lucien écrivain* (1958). This book for a long time made the literary, artistic view of Lucian into orthodoxy. Although I have often cited it in disagreement, it would be churlish not to acknowledge my debt to its learning and the provocation of its arguments. The heterodox view presented here is not novel, but has many forebears. Jonas Palm's *Rom, Römertum und Im-*

perium in der griechischen Literatur der Kaiserzeit (1959) has strongly influenced my view of Lucian, as of Plutarch and Dio Chrysostom. Glen Bowersock's *Greek Sophists in the Roman Empire* (1969) has at last provided a historical framework for the Greek resurgence of the second and third centuries; though I disagree with some details of his account of Lucian, his book gave the original impulse to my own study of the author. Barry Baldwin's *Studies in Lucian* (1973) also took Bowersock's book as its point of departure; though his view of Lucian is similar to mine, I would not have written this book if I had not thought there was more to say. I had already begun it when I saw Jennifer Hall's *Lucian's Satire* (1981); though I find her approach to Lucian very sympathetic, I decided on reflection that there was still room for a study of Lucian as an observer of his society, but on many points, especially ones connected with the literary background of his satires, I have been content to refer to her. My immediate stimulus was conversations about Lucian which I was privileged to have with the late Louis Robert in Paris in the spring of 1979, when he expounded the ideas subsequently published in the eighteenth chapter of his *À travers l'Asie Mineure* (1980), "Lucien en son temps"; I hope he would have seen in this book some lineaments of that formation.

The occasion of my stay in Paris was an invitation kindly extended by the École Normale Supérieure des Jeunes Filles through its Directrice Adjointe, Mlle. Simone Follet, and I take this opportunity of expressing my gratitude for those three fruitful and instructive months. I did most of the work on this book as a Member of the Institute for Advanced Study, Princeton, in 1982–83; for a second time I have to thank the Institute for its hospitality and for offering perfect conditions, at once tranquil and stimulating. During that year I was very generously funded by the Connaught Committee of the University of Toronto as a Connaught Senior Fellow in the Humanities, and I am grateful to my university for that, for a grant toward the typing of my manuscript, and for the less tangible benefits of a happy environment and the no less precious gift of time. I owe a similar debt to my department, and particularly to Carol Ashton for learning so well the ways of Clytaemnestra. Above all I thank Glen Bowersock, for his support during my year at Princeton, for reading and discussing my manuscript, and for twenty-five years of friendship.

[vii]

Contents

Abbreviations

Authors, including Lucian

Greek authors are cited in accordance with Liddell-Scott-Jones, *A Greek-English Lexicon* and Lampe, *A Patristic Greek Lexicon,* Latin in accordance with the *Oxford Latin Dictionary.* When referring to Lucian's works in the text, I have usually translated their titles, whereas in the notes and appendixes I have used the Latin abbreviations of Liddell-Scott-Jones. There follows a list of these abbreviations, with the full Latin titles and (where used) the translation.

Abd.	*Abdicatus*
Alex.	*Alexander (Alexander or the False Prophet* or *Alexander)*
Am.	*Amores (Loves)*
Anach.	*Anacharsis*
Apol.	*Apologia (Self-Defense)*
Asin.	*Asinus*
Astr.	*Astrologia*
Bacch.	*Bacchus (Dionysos)*
Bis acc.	*Bis accusatus (Double Indictment)*
Cal.	*Calumniae non temere credendum (On Slander)*
Cat.	*Cataplus*
Charid.	*Charidemus*
Cont.	*Contemplantes*
Cyn.	*Cynicus*
D. Deor.	*Dialogi Deorum (Dialogues of the Gods)*
Dear. Iud.	*Dearum Iudicium (Judgment of the Goddesses)*
Dem. Enc.	*Demosthenis Encomium*
Demon.	*Demonax*

Deor. Conc.	Deorum Concilium (Assembly of the Gods)
Dips.	Dipsades
D. mar.	Dialogi marini (Dialogues of the Marine Gods)
D. meretr.	Dialogi meretricii (Dialogues of the Courtesans)
D. Mort.	Dialogi Mortuorum (Dialogues of the Dead)
Dom.	De Domo (Hall)
Electr.	Electrum (Amber)
Epigr.	Epigrammata
Eun.	Eunuchus (Eunuch)
Fug.	Fugitivi (Runaways)
Gall.	Gallus (Cock)
Halc.	Halcyon
Harm.	Harmonides
Herc.	Hercules (Heracles)
Herm.	Hermotimus
Herod.	Herodotus
Hes.	Hesiodus
Hipp.	Hippias
Hist. conscr.	Quomodo Historia conscribenda sit (On Writing History)
Icar.	Icaromenippus
I. conf.	Iuppiter confutatus (Zeus Refuted)
Im.	Imagines (Portraits)
Ind.	Adversus Indoctum (Uncultured Man)
I. trag.	Iuppiter tragoedus (Tragic Zeus)
Iud. Voc.	Iudicium Vocalium
Laps.	Pro Lapsu (Apology for a Slip in Salutation)
Lex.	Lexiphanes
Luct.	De Luctu
Macr.	Macrobii
Men.	see Nec.
Merc. cond.	De Mercede Conductis (On Hirelings in Great Houses)
Musc. Enc.	Muscae Encomium
Nav.	Navigium (Ship)
Nec.	Necyomantia sive Menippus (Menippos)
Nero	Nero
Nigr.	Nigrinus
Ocyp.	Ocypus
Paras.	Parasitus
Patr. Enc.	Patriae Encomium (Praise of Native Cities)
Peregr.	De Morte Peregrini (On the Death of Peregrinus or Peregrinus)
Phal.	Phalaris

Philop.	*Philopatris*
Philops.	*Philopseudes (Lovers of Lies)*
Pisc.	*Piscator (Fisherman)*
Pod.	*Podagra*
Pro Im.	*Pro Imaginibus (Defense of the Portraits)*
Prom.	*Prometheus*
Prom. es	*Prometheus es in Verbis*
Pseudol.	*Pseudologista (Mistaken Critic)*
Rh. Pr.	*Rhetorum Praeceptor (Teacher of Rhetoric)*
Sacr.	*De Sacrificiis (On Sacrifices)*
Salt.	*De Saltatione (On the Dance)*
Sat.	*Saturnalia*
Scyth.	*Scytha (Scythian)*
Sol.	*Soloecista*
Somn.	*Somnium sive Vita Luciani (Dream)*
Symp.	*Symposium sive Lapithae (Banquet)*
Syr. D.	*De Syria Dea (On the Syrian Goddess)*
Tim.	*Timon*
Tox.	*Toxaris*
Tyr.	*Tyrannicida*
VH	*Verae Historiae (True Histories)*
Vit. Auct.	*Vitarum Auctio (Sale of Lives)*
Zeux.	*Zeuxis*

Journals, Inscriptions, Papyri, Dictionaries

For journals I have used the abbreviations of *L'Année Philologique* in the footnotes, but resolved them in the bibliography, except for certain well-known ones which are included below. For inscriptions and papyri I have used the abbreviations of Liddell-Scott-Jones, though I have also shown them below. In addition the following list shows my abbreviations for dictionaries, handbooks, encyclopedias, and the like.

AJA	*American Journal of Archaeology*
AJPh	*American Journal of Philology*
BCH	*Bulletin de Correspondance Hellénique*
BMC	*Catalogue of the Greek Coins in the British Museum*
Bull.	J. Robert and L. Robert, *Bulletin Épigraphique*, cited by the year of *REG* and the number of the item
Chrestomathie	L. Mitteis and U. Wilcken, *Gründzüge und Chrestomathie der Papyruskunde*

CIG	Corpus Inscriptionum Graecarum
CIL	Corpus Inscriptionum Latinarum
CPh	Classical Philology
CQ	Classical Quarterly
EAA	Enciclopedia dell' Arte Antica
FDelphes	Fouilles de Delphes, 3: Épigraphie
FGrHist	F. Jacoby, Die Fragmente der griechischen Historiker
GIBM	Ancient Greek Inscriptions in the British Museum
GRBS	Greek Roman and Byzantine Studies
GVI	W. Peek, Griechische Vers-Inschriften
I. Ephesos	Die Inschriften von Ephesos
IG	Inscriptiones Graecae
IGRR	Inscriptiones Graecae ad Res Romanas pertinentes
IGUR	L. Moretti, Inscriptiones Graecae Urbis Romae
ILS	H. Dessau, Inscriptiones Latinae Selectae
I. Sardis	Sardis 7: Greek and Latin Inscriptions
JHS	Journal of Hellenic Studies
JOEAI	Jahreshefte des Oesterreichischen Archäologischen Institutes
JRS	Journal of Roman Studies
LSJ	H. G. Liddell, R. Scott, and H. Stuart Jones, A Greek-English Lexicon
MDAI(A)	Deutsches Archäologisches Institut, Abteilung Athen, Mitteilungen (Athenische Mitteilungen)
MDAI(I)	Deutsches Archäologisches Institut, Abteilung Istanbul, Mitteilungen (Istanbuler Mitteilungen)
Mitteis-Wilcken, Chrestomathie	L. Mitteis and U. Wilcken, Grundzüge und Chrestomathie der Papyruskunde
OGIS	W. Dittenberger, Orientis Graeci Inscriptiones Selectae
OLD	Oxford Latin Dictionary
P. Berol.	Papyri Berolinenses
PIR	Prosopographia Imperii Romani
PLRE	Prosopography of the Later Roman Empire
P. Mag.	K. Preisendanz, Papyri Magicae Graecae
POxy.	The Oxyrhynchus Papyri
P. Ross. Georg.	Papyri Russischer und Georgischer Sammlungen
PSI	Papiri Greci e Latini (Pubblicazioni della Società Italiana)
RAC	T. Klauser et al., eds., Reallexicon für Antike und Christentum
RE	A. Pauly, G. Wissowa, and W. Kroll, eds., Real-Encyclopädie der classischen Altertumswissenschaft
REG	Revue des Études Grecques

ABBREVIATIONS

RPh	*Revue de Philologie*
SNG	*Sylloge Nummorum Graecorum,* Deutschland: Sammlung von Aulock
Syll.[3]	W. Dittenberger, *Sylloge Inscriptionum Graecarum*
TGF	A. Nauck, *Tragicorum Graecorum Fragmenta*
TrGF 2	R. Kannicht and B. Snell, eds., *Tragicorum Graecorum Fragmenta: Fragmenta Adespota*
UPZ	U. Wilcken, *Urkunden der Ptolemäerzeit*
ZPE	*Zeitschrift für Papyrologie und Epigraphik*

Culture and Society in Lucian

1 Introduction: The Modern Lucian

FOR THE CRITIC it is an easy illusion to suppose that, while his subject is affected by time and place, he himself observes from a fixed point. In fact, both observer and object are moving. The theme of this book is Lucian's place in the culture and society of his time; but it is well to remember that the criticism of Lucian is an evolving phenomenon, and that Lucian's observer is as much subject to the past as he was.

The modern era in the criticism of Lucian may be said to have begun in the continental Europe of the late nineteenth century, and more precisely in the Germany and France of the decade following 1870. A united and triumphant Germany was entering the last phase of scientific scholarship, while France, though joining in the advance of knowledge, struggled to maintain and revalue its cultural tradition. For Lucian the epoch did not augur well. The "new humanism" preferred the early to the late, the direct to the artful, and to a degree poetry to prose; and it had other, darker prepossessions which were also to prove unfavorable to a second-century satirist born on the eastern edge of the Roman Empire.

As it happened, Lucian's attacker in the first round of the debate was a scholar who had never been accepted into the academic establishment of nineteenth-century Germany, while his most eminent defender held the chair of Classical Philology in Berlin. Jacob Bernays' *Lucian und die Kyniker,* published in 1879, was almost the last work of its author. Its core was Lucian's *Peregrinus,* a satirical sketch of the Cynic philosopher who threw himself on a pyre after the Olympics of 165. Bernays saw the Cynics as preachers of monotheism, self-sufficiency, and courage in the face of corrupt authority, and Peregrinus as a kind of rabbi. To explain Lucian's hostility he introduced a number of critical phrases and ideas that were to recur in the following decades. Bernays' Lucian imitated the Greek classics with the "dexterity of an energetic and far from graceless Syrian," but he also had a "nihilistic emptiness"; and Bernays compared him to an author closely connected with his own family, Heinrich Heine, thinking not of the romantic lyricist but of the exiled author of deadly satires on German culture.[1]

Bernays' essay encountered immediate criticism, of which some of the most damaging came from Johannes Vahlen in Berlin. Vahlen acutely observed that in his eagerness to exalt Peregrinus Bernays left Lucian "practically nothing but a knack for writing, and that acquired by imitation," while he paid "too little attention to his skill and genius."[2] Vahlen's estimate of Lucian was not shared by the man who succeeded him at Berlin in 1897, Wilamowitz. This great Hellenist, for all his appreciation of the whole breadth of Greek culture, seems never to have written on any work of Lucian. Surveying Greek literature in a famous essay of 1905, Wilamowitz gave Lucian only a couple of pages, but those were enough to have a decisive effect on later opinion. For Wilamowitz Lucian was a "journalist . . . whom no one recognizes as a man of his own kind"; his formal talent was all the more remarkable in that he concealed the effort which composition cost him, carefully erasing the traces of his borrowings from others; he might attack a "minor sham-prophet" like Alexander of Abonuteichos, but never formidable targets like the Caesars; after all, " 'spirits that always deny' are basically stupid," even if now and then one of them rises to the level of an agreeable rogue.[3] Wilamowitz' final judgment on Lucian and his epoch was no less severe: "everywhere whited sepulchres . . . Lucian too is just the same, only the whitewash is different."[4]

Wilamowitz' low opinion of Lucian was shared by a colleague scarcely less redoubtable, Eduard Norden. In his all-embracing book of 1898

1. Bernays, *Lucian*, esp. 21–41 (Cynics), 42 (Syrian), 44 (nihilism), 53 (Heine). For Bernays' relationship to Heine, e.g., *Encyclopaedia Judaica* 4.673. For the comparison with Heine cf. also Helm, *Lucian* 7; Honigmann, *RE* Suppl. 4 (1924) 989. Heine's satires: Prawer, *Heine*.

2. Vahlen, *Opusc. Acad.* 1.181–182.

3. Wilamowitz in *Die gr. und lat. Litt. und Sprache*[1] 172–174 (unchanged in the third, "stark verbesserte und vermehrte," edition, 247–249); note also the unfavorable comparison of Lucian with Aristides, 164 (239).

4. *Glaube der Hellenen* 2[3] 502–504.

on ancient literary prose, he devoted half a page to Lucian, this "oriental without depth or character"; he had once, he confessed, read him with a certain pleasure, but now did so only with reluctance.[5] Norden was one of the chief exponents of a tendency of German scholarship particularly visible in the last generation before the First World War, the rage for reconstructing lost authors and works by means of surviving ones; the most famous of these edifices is perhaps Posidonios, to which Norden made a substantial contribution in 1903 with his classic edition of Vergil's sixth book.[6] Here one of Norden's concerns was the theme of the descent into the underworld (*catabasis*) in other ancient authors, and he noted the similarities between Vergil and Lucian's *Menippos,* in which such a descent is made by Menippos of Gadara, a Palestinian Cynic of the third century; from these he inferred a common source used by Vergil and Lucian.[7]

One of the *Assistenten* in Berlin at this time was the young Rudolf Helm, who in 1906 published a study of Lucian that was to be as influential as the sketch by Wilamowitz.[8] Helm's Lucian is like that of Bernays, Norden, and Wilamowitz, "an irresponsible Syrian," nihilistic, lacking in seriousness, not even worthy of the comparison with Heine, though he must be allowed some importance for the history of culture.[9] With this conception of Lucian as a crafty oriental, Helm joined the fad for reconstruction. Prompted by Norden's commentary on Vergil,[10] Helm fixed on Menippos, whom Lucian uses as a sympathetic character in several dialogues, while in another he claims to have "dug him up" and made him his confederate. By a metaphor ill-suited to this "savage dog," Helm made Menippos the

5. Norden, *Antike Kunstprosa* 1[5] 394, cited with approval by Helm, *Lucian* 8 n. 6.

6. Reinhardt, *RE* 22 (1953) 586–624; for Norden's role, 602–605.

7. Norden, *Aeneis VI* 199, cf. 250 on the *VH.*

8. Helm, *Lucian.* For Helm in Berlin, Wilamowitz, *Erinnerungen*[2] 285.

9. Helm, *Lucian* 6–7. In a generally favorable review of Helm published in 1914, W. Capelle complained that he had not gone far enough: "Nirgends finde ich . . . in Helms Buch eine Würdigung der Tatsache, dass Lukian wie sein Vorbild Menipp keine Hellenen, sondern Syrer sind [*sic*]. Daraus erklärt sich vieles in ihrem Wesen und ihrem Verhältnis zu hellenischem Glauben und Empfinden" (*BPhW* 34 [1914] 262 n. 5: similarly, recommending against the use of Lucian in schools, *ZG* 2 [1914] 606–622). Similar preoccupations underlie the somewhat later debate about Lucian's "Rassenzugehörigkeit" and, at least in some cases, the comparison with Heine: above, n. 1.

10. Note that Helm's first chapter concerns the *Menippos,* precisely the work emphasized by Norden: cf. Helm, *Lucian* 19.

Sleeping Beauty who could be awakened once the undergrowth of the Syrian imitator had been cleared away.[11]

Meanwhile a reaction had already set in, of which the effects were to be felt for a long time. Three years after Bernays, Maurice Croiset produced his *Essai sur Lucien,* a synthesis characteristic of French scholarship of the period. Croiset defended Lucian by shifting the emphasis from his content to his style, his matter to his manner. In one chapter in particular, entitled "Lucien écrivain," he planted a conception of his author that was to flower only much later, the writer concerned above all with clarity, elegance, and wit, and comparatively indifferent to the world around him. Croiset was conscious of the recent humiliation of French arms by Germany, and in his closing pages pleaded with "the heirs of the Gallic tradition" not to "darken their genius" by excluding Lucian from their culture.[12] Between the two world wars, the Berlin view of Lucian dominated continental scholarship, but at the end of this period, in 1937, Maurice Caster drew a portrait of Lucian which was largely derived from Croiset, though also influenced by Helm. For Caster as for Helm Lucian is still a Syrian, but compensates for his feelings of cultural inferiority by transforming himself into a Greek of Attic refinement.[13] One year later Caster produced a special study of Lucian's *Alexander* and gave the work a reading curiously similar to Bernays' reading of the *Peregrinus:* "it contains truth only insofar as a work of polemic is obliged sometimes to coincide with the facts."[14] From Caster there is a direct line to Bompaire's *Lucien écrivain* published twenty years later under a title borrowed from Croiset. Here the theme of imitation, already introduced by Bernays, dominates, though it is now not opposed to originality but implies the creative reinterpretation of acknowledged classics. By contrast, "actuality," the element of immediate observation, is reduced to the lowest degree possible.[15]

11. Helm, *Lucian* 16. Norden was not the first to exploit Menippos as a source of Lucian (cf. e.g., Bruns, *RhM* 43 [1888] 191–196), but the first to make Menippos' influence the inspiration of Lucian's literary activity.

12. Croiset, *Essai;* for the appeal to the "French genius," 395.

13. Caster, *Pensée* 368–369.

14. Caster, *Études* 91.

15. Bompaire, *Lucien écrivain,* e.g., 491, "La dose d'actualité varie suivant le cas . . . Mais nulle part elle ne parvient à faire perdre à la satire son allure d'exercice gratuit rejoignant le plus souvent l'époque par le seul effet du hasard et sans cesser d'être anachronique." In criticism, Delz, *Gnomon* 32 (1960) 759–761; and note also Bompaire's own second thoughts, *REG* 88 (1975) 228–229.

Naturally the German and French portraits of Lucian do not exhaust the catalog. A series of Italian studies has depicted him as a passionate adherent of philosophy or of intellectual radicalism, but this view has not found general favor.[16] Conversely, Lucian has often appealed to Protestant sympathies, and in modern times there has been an Anglo-Saxon line of moderate, commonsensical interpreters. Among these are the brothers Fowler (of whom the elder, Henry, is also the author of *Modern English Usage*) and Sir Richard Jebb, the editor of Sophocles; Francis W. Allinson's *Lucian* of 1927 is still the most balanced introduction to the author.[17] In the last quarter-century Bompaire's picture of Lucian as the self-absorbed artist has retained its influence, especially on the European continent; but now a strong protest has been voiced by Louis Robert, and in English-speaking scholarship the old strain of moderation has begun to reappear.[18]

Although Lucian's powers of observation have again begun to be appreciated, they still lack a study of their own. There can be no return to the simple view that he merely describes what he saw; too much is known about his age and its veneration of past culture. Nevertheless, too much is now also known about other features of the second century, its religious preoccupations, its scientific and scholarly curiosity, the life of the cities which were its main social units. To understand Lucian it is necessary to examine both his culture and his society.

16. Gallavotti, *Luciano;* Peretti, *Luciano;* Quacquarelli, *Retorica antica*. For criticism, note especially Momigliano's review of Peretti, *RSI* 60 (1948) 430–432 (*Quarto Contributo* 641–644).

17. H. W. Fowler and F. G. Fowler, *Lucian;* Jebb, *Essays* 164–192; Allinson, *Lucian*. On the other hand, common sense is not an attribute of Chapman, *Lucian, Plato and Greek Morals*.

18. Robert, *Asie Mineure* ch. 18; Hall, *JHS* 100 (1980) 229–232, and now in her *Lucian's Satire*.

2 Lucian in Society

TO SHOW LUCIAN as an observer of his time, it is first necessary to determine his own position in society. There is a danger of circularity, since much of the evidence is supplied by the author, and his works thus become the lens through which they themselves are viewed. But it is usually possible to guess how much allowance must be made for distortion.

Lucian was born at Samosata on the middle Euphrates. This had once been the capital of the small kingdom of Commagene, founded in the third century B.C. and incorporated in the Roman Empire in 72 A.D. Though Lucian says nothing of the kingdom or its kings, one of the indirect influences on him is their enthusiasm for Greek language and culture, attested by their benefactions to cities such as Athens and Ephesos. After the fall of the dynasty, a descendant of the last king settled in Athens, became a patron of the arts, and was sumptuously buried on the Hill of the Muses overlooking the Acropolis. Fifty years later another Commagenian of very different class and disposition was to settle in the same city.[1]

Iranian by descent, the kings of Commagene were oriented by geography and history to Syria and the south. The majority of the population seems to have been Semitic, speaking the dialect of Ar-

1. The literature on Commagene has grown with recent study of the archaeology and topography. For general guidance, Honigmann, *RE* 4 (1924) 978–990, is still useful: cf. also Dörner et al., *AW* Sondern. 6 (1975), *Kommagene*. On the archaeology and exploration, Dörner and Naumann, *Forschungen in Kommagene;* Wagner, *Seleukeia am Euphrat;* Hellenkamper in *Stud. zu den Militärgrenzen Roms* 2.461–471; Wagner, *MDAI(I)* 33 (1983) 177–224. On the kings and their foreign policy, Sullivan in *Aufstieg u. Niedergang* II. 8, 732–798; Fraser in *Stud. zur Religion u. Kultur Kleinasiens* 1.359–374; for Philopappos and his monument at Athens, *PIR²* I 151; Jones, *Plutarch* 59; Kleiner, *Monument of Philopappus.*

amaic later known as Syriac.[2] Lucian always refers to himself as "Syrian," or by a purely literary variation "Assyrian," and pretends that when he began his higher education he was "barbarian in speech": this phrase probably denotes accent or vocabulary rather than language, but it is possible that this writer of crystalline Greek began as a speaker of Aramaic.[3] The earliest manuscript of Lucian happens to be a Syriac paraphrase of his treatise *On Slander*.[4]

In what appears to be a speech delivered in Samosata he discusses men's affection for their city of origin *(patris)*: even if it is not large, and a man needs to go to a second one to complete his culture, he can never forget his first debt and earliest lessons.[5] Since Lucian went to Ionia to complete his education, he seems to refer to himself, and there is no need to doubt the warmth of his tribute. Samosata had an advantageous position at an important crossing-point of the Euphrates; its territory was small but fertile; from 72 it was the headquarters of a Roman legion, and thus a link in a chain of communications that ran between the Black Sea and northern Syria.[6] One of the earliest examples of Syriac literature is by a certain Mara bar Serapion, a Samosatene imprisoned by the Roman authorities, who cites a large number of examples drawn from classical Greek culture, one of which, a comparison of Jesus and Socrates, is also found in Lucian.[7] At the same time Commagene seems to have been isolated from the general stream of Greco-Roman culture: Lucian is the only native of the region to achieve distinction in pagan literature, though in the next century his city was to produce a controversial bishop of Syrian An-

2. The earliest Syriac inscription is from Birecik, some 120 km. down the Euphrates from Samosata: Wagner, *Seleukeia am Euphrat* 32 and n. 63; on the letter of Mara bar Serapion, below, n. 7. On Syriac and Aramaic in Roman Syria, Millar, *JRS* 61 (1971) 2–5.

3. Unless otherwise indicated, all English translations from the Greek texts are my own. "Syrian": *Bis acc.* 14, 25–34, *Ind.* 19, *Pisc.* 19. "Assyrian": *Bis acc.* 27, *Syr. D.* 1. "Barbarian in speech": *Bis acc.* 27, cf. *Ind.* 4.

4. Macleod, *Luciani Opera* 1 p. ix.

5. *Patr. enc.* 2, 6: a good analysis by Bompaire, *Lucien écrivain* 278–281.

6. Position: see the useful sketch-map in Wagner, *MDAI(I)* 33 (1983) 189; the famous crossing-point of Zeugma is now known to have been located some 110 km. south of Samosata at Seleuceia: Wagner, *Seleukeia am Euphrat* 39–56. Territory: Str. 16.2.3, 749C. An interesting description of this part of the Euphrates valley in Ellis and Voigt, *AJA* 86 (1982) 319–323.

7. For the text and a translation of the letter, contained in a single manuscript, Cureton, *Spicilegium Syriacum* 70–76; see further Millar, *JRS* 61 (1971) 4–5; Döring, *Exemplum Socratis* 143–146.

tioch.[8] While he clearly does not have the attachment to Samosata that Plutarch had to Chaeronea, he speaks with pride of its culture, its "acropolis and walls," and the benefactions conferred on it by an eminent contemporary.[9]

Lucian's birth cannot be precisely dated. It may have fallen in the later years of Trajan, when the emperor was campaigning across the Euphrates in Armenia and Mesopotamia, or in the earlier ones of Hadrian, when peace had been restored on the frontier, approximately between 115 and 125.[10] His name is derived from the Latin "Lucius," and he usually hellenizes it to "Lycinos." It may show the cultural influence of Romans implanted in Samosata, but his circumstances seem too modest for him to have been born a Roman citizen.[11] On the subject of his family and early upbringing the only evidence is provided by a work in which personal and literary reminiscence are almost inseparably fused: the *Dream*. In form this is an address to an audience of Samosatenes, as also is the *Praise of Native Cities*, and it may be presumed that an actual speech underlies the written version. The narrative kernel concerns the young Lucian's choice of a career. As a schoolboy he had shown skill in making wax figures, and when the time came to choose a career a council of family members decided to apprentice him to his maternal uncle, an "excellent carver of sacred statues."[12] On his first day at work, however, he ruined a block of marble, was thrashed by his uncle, ran home in

8. On the cultural isolation of Commagene, Fraser in *Stud. zur Religion u. Kultur Kleinasiens* 1.371–373; on Paul of Samosata, Millar, *JRS* 61 (1971) 1–17.

9. Culture: *Pisc.* 19. Acropolis and walls: *Hist. conscr.* 24 (on these, Weissbach, *RE* 1 A [1920] 2223–24; Hoepfner in *AW* Sondern. 6 [1975] 43–50). Benefactor: *Harm.* 3.

10. The *Suda* (λ 683) puts his *floruit* under Trajan, clearly in error: Rohde, *RhM* 33 (1878) 173–175 (*Kl. Schr.* 1.128–129). Otherwise the best indication is that he claims to have taken up the writing of comic dialogues at about forty, and one of these, the *Runaways*, seems to have been written not long after 165 (below, Appendix B). Hall, *Lucian's Satire* 13–16, argues from the references to Olympia and Babylon in *Bis acc.* 2 that Lucian was born about 125, but Olympia is the sanctuary of Zeus par excellence, and Babylon is merely a typical scene of warfare (*Charon* 23, *Merc. cond.* 13, *Nav.* 34). The reference to Trajan's capture of "Samosata" in Cassius Dio, 68.19.2, should rather be to "Arsamosata": thus Lepper, *Trajan's Parthian War* 7.

11. Compare the non-citizens with Roman names at Seleuceia: Wagner, *Seleukeia am Euphrat* 191 (Pouplios), 261 (Lucius), 227 (Gaianus).

12. There is a textual problem in section 2, where his uncle is described both as a ἑρμογλύφος and a λιθοξόος (cf. 3, 7): on the meaning of the second, Robert, *Hellenica* 11/12 (1960) 31. In 18 Lucian uses the rare λιθογλύφος, close in meaning to λιθοξόος, and also found in Galen's discussion of the figurative arts, below, n. 15.

tears, and cried himself to sleep. He dreamed that two female personifications appeared before him, Craft and Culture, each urging the benefits she would confer upon him. He was quickly persuaded by Culture, and as a reward she took him in her chariot, in which he flew with her across the world from east to west, "scattering something on the ground like Triptolemos" and enjoying applause everywhere. In the end Culture returned him, now dressed in purple, to his father.

The artificiality of Lucian's story is obvious. The opposition between craft and culture made explicit in the dream is present throughout the work. In the opening it is connected to another set of contrasts: culture required much time and expense, whereas Lucian's family had only meager resources, and craft promised to bring an immediate income. The connection between culture and wealth, craft and poverty is underlined by the symbolism of clothing: the personified Craft is dressed in the soiled garments of a worker, while Culture is herself decked in finery and puts a purple robe on Lucian. There is also a contrast of language: Craft speaks "barbarously," while Culture's speech is refined and learned, and Lucian riding in her chariot scatters "something on the ground," which can only be words.[13] The reader is further reminded of Lucian's art by the allusions to earlier literature: he compares his dream to one recounted by Xenophon in the *Anabasis,* and the contrast of two personifications is influenced by another passage of Xenophon, Prodicos' famous myth of the Choice of Heracles.[14]

Although Lucian has evidently passed his experiences through a prism of literature, it does not follow that they are fiction: at least when mentioning external, verifiable facts he must be supposed to have respected the knowledge already possessed by his hearers and readers. It can be accepted that he was originally of modest means, though not so modest as to put a life of culture out of the question: sculpture could be highly paid, and when discussing the skills that a young man may honorably pursue Galen puts the figurative arts only slightly lower than the purely intellectual ones.[15] What Lucian says of his chosen profession is studiously vague, but again not implausible. Although Culture does not specify his calling, she implies that it will

13. *Somn.* 8 (*Craft* βαρβαρίζουσα), 15 (Lucian's sowing: cf. 7).

14. Dream: *Somn.* 17, cf. Xen. *Anab.* 3.1.11. Personifications: Xen. *Mem.* 2.1.21–34; Waites, *HSCPh* 23 (1912) 1–46, esp. 43–46.

15. Pay of sculptors: Daremberg-Saglio s.v. *sculptura* 1150–52. Galen: *Protr.* 5, 14 (*Scr. min.* 1.107, 129).

involve oratory, travel, and applause. This was the golden age of the Second Sophistic, when highly trained speakers called "rhetors" or "sophists" enjoyed enormous influence and success. Their star turn was the "practice-speech" *(melete)*, a declamation on fictitious or historical themes, but they were often employed as lawyers and ambassadors.[16] Just as Lucian was to fly in Culture's chariot scattering speeches below him, so the great men of Philostratos and even more the numberless petty sophists of the age traveled the length and breadth of the Roman Empire.[17] If Lucian declines actually to say that he became a sophist or a rhetor, however, that may be both because of the necessary vagueness of a dream, and also because his later career, though still involving travel and oratory, took him in a new direction.[18]

Even his claim to have been guided by a "clear" dream may have a basis in reality. Certainly it recalls famous incidents of ancient literature such as the visions of Xerxes in Herodotos, and Lucian admits that his account may seem suspiciously detailed.[19] His exact contemporary Galen, however, whose observations so often coincide with his, took up medicine because of the "clear dreams" experienced by his father, and many other authors of the period, Roman as well as Greek, claim similar guidance.[20] Lucian could have embroidered his memories of an actual dream to make them more literary, though since dreams and the recollection of them tend to be influenced by cultural patterns the embellishment may be in part unconscious.[21]

The *Dream* therefore implies that, like Galen, Lucian had turned away from an intended career early in youth and taken up another which, it is strongly hinted, involved travel and public speaking. Other works suggest that his later career had several stages, and that the familiar figure of the satirist and pamphleteer is only the product of a long development.

16. Generally, Bowersock, *Sophists:* Bowie, *YClS* 27 (1982) 29–59, however, cautions that some sophists owed their prestige to inherited wealth and position as much as to their profession.

17. On sophistic travel, Bowersock, *Sophists* 17–18.

18. Below, at nn. 44, 60.

19. Hdt. 7.12–19; note also the "clear" dream of Atossa, similarly involving two personifications, in Aesch. *Pers.* 179–199. Luc. *Somn.* 17.

20. Galen, *Lib. propr.* 4 *(Scr. min.* 2.88). On dreams in second-century culture, Dodds, *Pagan and Christian* 38–53; Bowersock, *Sophists* 73–74; Nutton, *Galen: De praecog.* 159–160.

21. Cf. Dodds, *Pagan and Christian* 39.

Lucian refers to his sophistic phase in another work, equally elusive, the *Double Indictment*. Here the personified Rhetoric claims that she came across him as a young man in Ionia, made him her husband, and traveled with him through the world as far as Gaul.[22] The references to rhetoric and Ionia point to the world of the Second Sophistic, in which the chief centers were Ephesos and Smyrna, closely followed by Athens and Rome; a sophist teaching in Ionia could draw pupils from all over the Roman Empire.[23] The travels to which Lucian alludes are less a mark of the great sophist, who tended to stay in the major cities, than of the beginning one: thus Aelius Aristides, after being trained in Smyrna, launched his career at about age twenty-five by a visit to Rome, and would have proceeded to the western ocean if he had not fallen ill.[24]

Two works seem to refer to a single visit made by the young Lucian to a city of Macedonia sometimes thought to be Thessalonica, but which is more probably Beroea.[25] One and probably both are prefaces *(prooemia)*, designed to win the favor of his hearers before the principal speech, which may have been a declamation. In the *Scythian* Lucian uses the figure of the half-mythical Anacharsis—who according to tradition had come to Athens and been kindly treated by Solon—as a vehicle for himself. He too has arrived in one of the great cities of Macedonia, famous for its "size and beauty" (a frequent item of praise), and hopes to gain the favor of two of its leading citizens, father and son.[26] The *Herodotos* is very similar; here his vehicle is the Ionian historian, who used the great festival of the Olympic Games to recite his *Histories* and thus to spread his fame. Lucian on his own arrival in Macedonia had been eager to display his work to as many people as possible; but since a visit to all the cities was inconvenient, he chose the leading one on the occasion of a general meeting of the province, when his audience consisted of "the cream of every city . . . the most reputable of rhetors, historians and sophists."[27] Lucian's desire to please his hearers is evident, but so is the culture that he expects

22. *Bis acc.* 27.

23. Bowersock, *Sophists* 17.

24. Aristid. 36.91.

25. In favor of Thessalonica, Oberhummer, *RE* 6 A (1936) 147: but Beroea was the meeting place of the Macedonian κοινόν, cf. Deininger, *Provinziallandtage* 91–92. Lucian's age is implied when he compares himself to the young Anacharsis and to Telemachos at the palace of Menelaos, *Scytha* 9.

26. *Scytha* 9: for this standard expression, Robert, *Asie Mineure* 423–424.

27. *Herod.* 7–8.

from them. Lucian is often imagined even by friendly critics as an entertainer interested only in what will amuse his hearers, and by unfriendly ones as a mere journalist.[28] Yet even these works, spoken when he was still a sophist, show that amusement of the public entailed for him no sacrifice of refinement.

Lucian's reference to Gaul in the *Double Indictment* is echoed in a late work in which he recalls how his friend Sabinus, when traveling to the western ocean and Gaul long ago, had found him "receiving a very large public payment for oratory *(rhetorike)*" and "numbered among the highly paid sophists."[29] Gaul was well known as a home of rhetoric, Greek as well as Latin, and a young sophist might well have found employment in one of its cities. It was far from the great centers of rhetoric, however, Athens, Smyrna, Ephesos, even Rome, and as a place of residence seems only to have attracted lesser lights, such as Plutarch's townsman Nigros and two brother rhetors from Mopsos in Cilicia. The great Favorinus came from Arelate but did everything to avoid going back.[30] For all his high salary, Lucian may have realized that as a sophist he had no future: though if he did fail, his failure made him, for otherwise his voice would have been lost in the chatter of the Second Sophistic.

Though Lucian uses the word "rhetoric" to describe his early career, the word could also designate the profession of forensic oratory, and he also seems to have practiced in the courts.[31] According to the notice about him in the tenth-century *Suda,* "he was at first an advocate in Syrian Antioch, but after proving a failure at this turned to authorship": while this may be true, the *Suda* is not a friendly witness to an author it considered blasphemous and anti-Christian.[32]

Even without the *Suda,* however, it is clear that in middle age Lucian took a new departure. Writers who claim to have undergone con-

28. Thus Helm, *Lucian* 7, "wie ein echter Sophist haschte er nach dem Erfolg und dem Ruhme, ganz gleich wie er sein Ziel erreichen konnte"; for Lucian as a "journalist," Wilamowitz quoted in Ch. 1 at n. 3, and most recently Anderson, *BICS* 23 (1976) 64.

29. *Apol.* 15.

30. Nigros: Plut. *De tuenda san.* 131 A. Brothers from Mopsos: *IG* 14.2516; *Bull.* 1980.283. Favorinus: Bowersock, *Sophists* 35.

31. For the various senses of "rhetor," Bowersock, *Sophists* 12–14; Jones, *Dio* 9, with bibliography in 162 n. 7. Lucian as a lawyer: *Bis acc.* 32; *Pisc.* 25.

32. *Suda,* λ 683.

versions tend to give obscure or confusing accounts of them,[33] and although Lucian devotes all of one work and part of another to his own transformation the precise truth is probably irrecoverable. The *Double Indictment* is a fantasy in which, as in the *Dream,* personifications contend for the allegiance of human beings; here, however, the theme is not choice but litigation. The work begins with a series of hearings, all of which involve intellectual conversion: in the first, for example, Drunkenness contends with the Academy for the philosopher Polemo, whose conversion from a life of dissipation to one of philosophy was a favorite subject of moralists.[34] The climax of the work is the "double indictment" of the "Syrian," who clearly stands for Lucian. Rhetoric enumerates all the favors she has conferred on him while he in rebuttal accuses her of adultery;[35] he also claims that it was time for him at the age of forty to give up the lawcourts and the usual subjects of declamation. Dialogue in turn complains that the Syrian has transformed him from his philosophic appearance into a mixture of prose and verse, of comedy and the Cynic Menippos: the Syrian replies that he has turned him from an esoteric creature into one pleasing to the many.

As in the *Dream,* Lucian does not conceal the influence of literary prototypes. The theme of intellectual conversion goes back at least to Aristophanes' *Clouds,* a play to which Lucian alludes in this very passage: Cratinos in the *Flask* had represented Comedy as his estranged wife.[36] He might therefore be suspected of disguising the facts when he explains his abandonment of Rhetoric by her infidelities and his desire for a quiet life in middle age. In the *Fisherman,* a work very similar to the *Double Indictment,* his story is different: he had grown tired of forensic activity and wanted to take up philosophy, but finding its modern practitioners to be charlatans decided to expose them by means of dialogue. The *Hermotimos* gives yet a different

33. On conversion in literature and life, Nock, *Conversion;* Nock in *Pisciculi,* 165–177 (*Essays* 1.469–480); Gigon, *MH* 3 (1946) 1–21; Nock, *RAC* 2 (1954) 105–118.

34. *Bis acc.* 15–18. For Polemo's conversion by Xenocrates, the best known source is Hor. *Sat.* 2.3.250–257.

35. For the description of Rhetoric as an adulteress, Dion. Hal. *Orat. vett.* praef. 1–2 (*Opusc.* 1.3–5); cf. Lucian's similar description of false Philosophy, *Pisc.* 12.

36. Aristophanes: *Bis acc.* 33. Lucian refers to this more often than any other play of Aristophanes: Householder, *Literary Quotation* 4. Cratinus: Helm, *Lucian* 278. A comedy of the obscure Augeas also had the title of *Double Indictment* (Helm, *Lucian* 282), but the connection with Lucian is beyond conjecture.

account: Lucian had felt a sympathy for philosophy at about the age of twenty-five, but at the dramatic date he is about forty and an inveterate enemy of it.[37] Despite the contradictions, it seems reasonable to infer that he gave up an oratorical career, which he had pursued both as a forensic speaker and as a sophist, and at the age of forty or so devoted himself to literature and especially to the comic dialogue. His motive may have been less the fatigue alleged in the *Fisherman* than the disappointment at which he hints in the *Double Indictment*.[38] That he should have made the change about forty is not implausible, since this was the age conventionally regarded as a turning point *(acme)* in a man's life, and the convention must sometimes have corresponded with reality.[39]

As in his first phase, the later Lucian often spoke before audiences, and it has been demonstrated that the dialogues are carefully written in order to be read aloud by a single performer.[40] Several brief works show that his audiences brought with them a high expectation of refinement. Two prefaces, the *Heracles* and the *Dionysos,* both belong to his "old age," which may not represent much above fifty.[41] In the first he is about to give an exhibition *(epideixis)* after a long retirement but does not specify the subject.[42] The *Dionysos* seems to preface the reading of a comic dialogue at a festival in honor of the god; the deprecation with which Lucian excuses the novelty of his invention is partly ironic, but it indicates yet again that he was not concerned simply to satisfy accepted taste.[43] The *Zeuxis* is a much more elaborate exercise on the same theme. Lucian addresses an audience in a city where he is a visitor and begins by recalling a recent recital there, clearly of one of his comic dialogues, when his hearers had acclaimed

---

37. *Herm.* 13 (Lucian aged forty), 24 (attracted to philosophy about fifteen years before), 51 (an inveterate foe of it). The *Nigrinos,* in which he describes his enthusiasm for the doctrines of a Platonist, is best left out of the present discussion, since Lucian does not represent this as a conversion: cf. Hall, *Lucian's Satire* 18–19, 157–164.

38. The bitter tone of the *Teacher of Rhetoric,* esp. 26, also suggests frustrated ambition.

39. For forty as the age of the *acme,* Polman, *CPh* 69 (1974) 171–172; cf. Galen, *Anim. Pass.* 1.10 *(Scr. min.* 1.41), a man cannot correct his faults after forty, or at most fifty.

40. Bellinger, *YClS* 1 (1940) 3–40.

41. *Bacch.* 7, *Herc.* 8.

42. *Herc.* 7.

43. *Bacch.* 5; for the festival, note ὧν ποιοῦμεν, 6.

his ingenuity and innovation.[44] With similar deprecation he resorts to the device of classic exemplars: the first of these, the description of Zeuxis' *Centaur Family,* constitutes the fullest account of an ancient painting that has survived.[45] The refinement of the hearers is suggested not only by the subject matter, but by Lucian's addressing them as "friends" and "connoisseurs who view everything with a trained eye."[46]

The *Zeuxis* closely resembles the short work, probably not a speech but an open letter, addressed to a friend who had praised Lucian's invention of comic dialogue by calling him a Prometheus.[47] The work is full of erudite wit and Attic irony. Lucian compares his friend, a lawyer whose inventions are golden, with people like himself, who come before a crowd and offer mere enjoyment and frivolity. Though Lucian speaks as a public entertainer, what he offers to his audiences is again a novelty which elicits praise from the wealthy and the refined.

This impression is strengthened by references in other works. Diogenes in the *Fisherman* accuses Parrhesiades of "inviting the best people" and reading from a "thick book" his attacks on philosophy.[48] The dialogues are not the only work which Lucian presented thus. Lucian represents his friend Sabinus recollecting the success of the *Hirelings in Great Houses:* "the work was approved when read before a large crowd, as those who heard it reported, but also among the cultured who saw fit to study it at leisure."[49] It is not clear whether the crowd consisted of only friends or the general public, but once again it is implied that for Lucian culture was not inimical to success, but rather a condition of it.

If it is right that Lucian's later readings were not made for immediate gain, but resembled the literary receptions that roused the enthusiasm of the Younger Pliny and the spleen of Juvenal, that prompts the question of his means and income. In the *Dream* Culture promised to make him "admired by the best people and respected

44. *Zeux.* 1.

45. *Zeux.* 3–7, cf. Le Morvan, *REG* 45 (1932) 385–387; Kraiker, *Das Kentaurenbild des Zeuxis;* P. Moreno, *EAA* 7 (1966) 1266. For Botticelli's recreation of it in the *Calumny of Apelles,* Horne, *Botticelli* 261.

46. *Zeux.* 1, 12.

47. *Prom. es* 1–2.

48. *Pisc.* 26.

49. *Apol.* 3.

by those notable for birth and riches": this sounds like a comfortable competence, but not wealth.[50] When Lucian took a highly paid position in Egypt, he justified it by recalling to Sabinus the salary he had long ago made as a sophist in Gaul, and this too implies no great wealth in the interval.[51] His usual tone is that of Attic poverty, though this was the traditional stance of satire.[52] Although his sources of income can only be guessed, they could easily have included gifts from wealthy friends. He denies ever having been a client like those he pillories in the *Hirelings,* but that does not exclude a friendship similar to that of Martial and the Younger Pliny, or even of Horace and Maecenas.[53] The situation of the poor scholar implied by the *Saturnalia* recalls that of a Roman poet: the rich man is enjoined to pay the debts or even the rent of his friends, and generally "to know what they most need," while the poor man is to make him a present either of one of the classics or a composition of his own.[54] This kind of friendship, politely dependent and yet higher than that of the salaried client, may be presumed to be the link between Lucian and such notables as Rutilianus, the father-in-law of Alexander of Abonuteichos; another such friend was the senator at whose morning levée Lucian committed a linguistic blunder, and yet another is the prefect of Egypt who gave him a position on his staff.[55] Nor need westerners have been Lucian's only such patrons. Greek senators either in Rome or in their own cities,[56] or wealthy Greeks whose ambitions did not extend beyond their own province, must also have taken pleasure in their literary friendships: Herodes Atticus, the great sophist of Lucian's Athens, was also a patron of fellow men of letters.[57]

50. *Somn.* 11.

51. *Apol.* 15.

52. *Ind.* 4 ("us poor people"); *Nigr.* 12–14; *Sat.* passim.

53. Pliny and Martial: Pliny, *Ep.* 3.21. On literary patronage, Saller, *Personal Patronage* 28–29, 123.

54. *Sat.* 15–16. Compare the presents received by Martial at the Saturnalia, Saller, *Personal Patronage* 123.

55. Rutilianus, *Alex.* 54; levée, *Laps.,* esp. 12–13; prefect, *Apol.* 9.

56. Note that Lucian expects the wealthy man in Rome to send gifts "at the Saturnalia or the Panathenaea," *Merc. cond.* 37.

57. For Herodes' benefactions to his friends, Philostr. *VS* 49.4–14, 56.7–15; for Lucian's relations with him, below, Ch. 9 at nn. 61, 62.

Athens, still the capital of Greek culture, seems in fact to have been Lucian's preferred city in his later years. He had visited it in his youth and seems to have made it his permanent residence: the clearest evidence is his biography of the Cynic *Demonax,* most of the incidents of which date to the reign of Marcus Aurelius,[58] but Athens is also the setting of many of his dialogues. Although the place in which a work is set is not necessarily that in which it was written or first published,[59] it may be guessed that the city which supplied so much of Lucian's literary background had become his second home. The city which appears in Lucian most frequently after Athens is the political capital, Rome. This too he had visited in his early youth, but the date and length of his later stays are unknown.[60]

Most of the datable events of Lucian's life belong to the decade that followed the accession of Marcus Aurelius in 161 and can be indirectly connected with the public events of that troubled time. At the beginning of the reign war broke out in Armenia, and Marcus sent his coregent Lucius Verus to the front. Departing in 162, Verus made a slow progress though southern Italy, Greece, and along the south coast of Asia Minor, and in the next year reached Antioch, which was to be his headquarters until the conclusion of the war in 166.[61] Three works show Lucian at least on the fringes of the imperial court at Antioch: the treatise on the "dance" and the two encomia of the emperor's mistress, Pantheia of Smyrna. It is not known when or how he joined the imperial entourage, but it may well have been in Athens.[62]

For unknown reasons Lucian appears not to have awaited the outcome of the war or the return of the emperor; rather, he started westward with his family and dependents, taking not the shortest route along the southern coast but a long circuit northward. The visit to Samosata on which he delivered the *Dream,* and perhaps the *Praise of Native Cities* also, may have been part of this journey. Another

58. Below, Ch. 9.

59. Cf. the remarks of Bowie, *P&P* 46 (1970) 9 (*Studies in Anc. Soc.* 173).

60. Travels to Italy are mentioned in *Bis. acc.* 27, *Electr.* 2, *Herod.* 5; a visit to Rome, *Nigr.* 2 and passim; the *Merc. cond.* (esp. 26) suggests a considerable familiarity with the city.

61. On the war and its chronology, below, Ch. 6.

62. Below, Ch.7. There is no authority for the frequent spelling "Panthea."

stage provided material for one of his most famous works. After crossing the province of Cappadocia, where he was aided by the governor, he stopped in the small city of Abonuteichos on the Paphlagonian coast, and there met the "false prophet" whom he was later to immortalize, Alexander.[63] An encounter with another of his victims followed soon after. At the close of the Olympic Games of 165 the Cynic Peregrinus immolated himself, and Lucian, who was attending the festival for the fourth time, later described the event in a pamphlet no less ferocious than the *Alexander*.[64] In the next year, 166, Verus led his victorious armies back from the east, and to the same year belongs Lucian's essay *On Writing History,* which is in part a disguised encomium of the emperor's victories. At the time of writing Lucian had recently been in Ionia and Corinth, but these visits appear subsequent to his return from the eastern front to attend the Olympic Games of 165.[65]

It is understandable that a satirist should have little or nothing to say about the crises that marked the larger part of Marcus' rule, though since Lucian lived into the next reign they must have impinged on him. The great plague brought back by Verus' returning armies, though it certainly affected Athens and perhaps Samosata, is mentioned merely to show the cunning of Alexander or the folly of an inept historian.[66] As the Parthian war was ending, a new and more serious one broke out on the Danube and was to last for nearly a decade: yet this too Lucian mentions only to illustrate another of Alexander's frauds.[67] In these same years Athens was torn by internal strife, the central issue being the influence of the millionaire sophist, Herodes Atticus; but apart from a possible allusion in one of the comic dialogues, this receives no mention.[68] Nor does Lucian notice an event perhaps caused by the strains of the German wars, the

63. *Alex.* esp. 55–56: below, Ch. 12.
64. *Peregr.*: below, Ch. 11. Lucian's crossing with Peregrinus from (Alexandria) Troas, *Peregr.* 43, need not have occurred long before the Cynic's death since πάλαι can mean "previously," "already": cf. Hall, *Lucian's Satire* 443–444.
65. Below, Ch. 6. *Hist. conscr.* 14 (cf. 17) suggests that he was in Corinth more recently than in Ionia.
66. *Alex.* 36, *Hist. conscr.* 15; for the plague at Athens, Ch. 6 at n. 6.
67. *Alex.* 48.
68. See below, Ch. 4 at nn. 23, 24.

invasion of the Costoboci, who about 170 broke into the Balkan provinces and penetrated as far south as Eleusis.[69] He is equally silent on the last crisis of the reign, the rebellion of Avidius Cassius in 175, though since Avidius was the governor of Syria, Lucian's native Commagene was certainly involved.[70]

This same period of public uncertainty is also the time of Lucian's greatest success. His few references to himself in his later works suggest fame and confidence.[71] Probably to this same period belongs an incident mentioned by Galen: discussing the subject of interpolated or spurious works, Galen refers to "one of our contemporaries, Lucian," who fabricated a work of Heracleitos and used it to expose a well-known philosopher, and by a similar ruse made a mockery of certain "grammarians" or professional students of literature. There can be little doubt that this is Lucian, since in the extant works he parodies Heracleitos and other writers of Ionic, and makes fun of grammarians.[72] Parody and pastiche were natural by-products of the highly verbal education of the time: thus Hadrian of Tyre could imitate *extempore* all the leading sophists, and Galen was obliged to curb forgeries of his own writings.[73]

Almost nothing is known of Lucian's relatives: he mentions that his father and family accompanied him from Cappadocia to Pontus, and as Lycinos he refers to a young son.[74] His friends are more discernible. Among eminent Romans he claims to have known and even to have advised the consular Sisenna Rutilianus, the father-in-law of Alexander of Abonuteichos. The governor of Cappadocia at

---

69. For the sources on the Costoboci, Oliva, *Pannonia and the Onset of Crisis* 276–278, and Astarita, *Avidio Cassio* 62–66.

70. On the rebellion of Avidius Cassius, see Astarita, *Avidio Cassio* 91–148. The old theory that Avidius was related to the royal house of Commagene (most recently in Astarita, 18–20) has long since been exploded: Dörner and Naumann, *Forschungen in Kommagene* 47–51.

71. E.g., *Alex.* 55; *Apol.* 3; *Bacch.* 5–8; *Herc.* 7–8; *Prom. es.*

72. Strohmeier, *Philologus* 120 (1976) 117–122; for a good summary of the discussion, Hall, *Lucian's Satire* 4–6. Heracleitos: *Vit. auct.* 14. Other imitations of Ionic: *Syr. D.,* cf. *Dom.* 20, *Vit. auct.* 3. Grammarian: *Symp.* 41, with the discussion of Wilhelm, *WS* 56 (1938) 54–89.

73. Hadrian: Philostr. *VS* 90.20–23 K. Galen: *Libr. propr.* praef. (*Scr. min.* 2.91–93).

74. *Alex.* 56; *Eun.* 13.

the time of his visit to Alexander was sufficiently well-disposed to provide him with an escort of two soldiers.[75] He speaks with respect of two Greeks distinguished both in culture and in rank, Arrian and Herodes Atticus; with Herodes at least he seems to have had some personal connection.[76] Acquaintance with prominent men, whether Roman or Greek by origin, is also implied by works such as the *Saturnalia* and the *Apology for a Slip in Salutation*.

The persons to whom Lucian addresses his works seem, insofar as they are not fictions, to be literary Greeks of his own kind. At least two are philosophers, and both receive masterpieces. The Cronios addressed in the *Peregrinus* is probably a minor Platonist respectfully mentioned by later members of the school as an associate of Numenios.[77] The Celsus to whom Lucian dedicates the *Alexander* is generally agreed to be, not the Platonist against whom Origen wrote his defense of Christianity, but a man with whom Origen at first confused his opponent, an Epicurean who also received an open letter from Galen.[78] Lucian describes the Sabinus to whom he addresses the *Self-Defense* as a "kindly and philosophic man" *(chresto kai philosopho andri)*: this may be a contemporary of his who was an honored Platonist at Athens.[79] Lucian's claims to have admired the Platonist Nigrinus and the Cynic Demonax are therefore not implausible, but cohere with his known acquaintance.

At a date perhaps as late as the reign of Commodus, when he had "one foot on the ferry" of Charon, he took a step similar to one taken by other literary Greeks of the period, and entered the service of Rome by taking a position in the retinue of an unnamed prefect of Egypt. His duties included the arrangement of the prefect's judicial calendar and the minutes of his hearings, and he may have held the

75. Rutilianus: *Alex.* 30, 54, and below, Ch. 12. Governor of Cappadocia: *Alex.* 55.

76. Arrian: *Alex.* 2. Herodes: *Peregr.* 19, and below, Ch. 11.

77. The identification was first argued by Bernays, *Lucian* 3–4; cf. also Dillon, *Middle Platonists* 362, 379–380. The name "Cronios" is well attested, particularly in Ionia (Sittig, *De Graecorum Nominibus theophoris* 19); because Lucian elsewhere taxes a Greek historian for using it to translate the Roman name *Saturninus* (*Hist. conscr.* 21), it does not follow that he does the same himself here.

78. For this interpretation of the evidence, Chadwick, *Origen* xxiv–xxvi, and Hall, *Lucian's Satire* 512–513; for the contrary view, Schwartz, *Biographie* 23–24. Celsus and Galen: Gal. *Libr. propr.* 16 (*Scr. min.* 2.124).

79. *Apol.* 2; *IG* 2² 3803 (C. Iulius Sabinus); cf. Follet, *Athènes* 76 n. 7.

position of "introducer" *(eisagogeus)*, the official who brought cases into the prefect's court.[80] He claims to have taken the position out of respect for the prefect;[81] governors were allowed to dispense such appointments to dependent friends, and Lucian must have drawn the favorable attention of powerful members of Roman society, probably including the emperor.[82] He even had hopes of being "entrusted with a province," a phrase which must allude to the position of imperial procurator; this too was a position sometimes held by educated and well-connected Greeks.[83] Lucian must long since have become a Roman citizen, and if he aspired to be a procurator must have anticipated the status of a Roman knight, but it is unknown whether he received either this or the hoped-for promotion.

Nothing more is known of him, and it is possible that this enemy of superstition died in Egypt, that nursery of magic and strange gods.[84] The *Suda* reports a tale that he was torn to pieces by dogs in divine punishment for his blasphemy, but ancient slander was always ready to envisage condign deaths for evildoers, and this one had already been attributed to Euripides.[85]

Just as Lucian enjoyed a modest fame in his own lifetime, so his works continued to be read after his death. No papyrus containing one of his authentic works has yet been identified, but this may be put down to chance.[86] Nor is the silence of Philostratos in the *Sophists*

80. *Apol.* 1, cf. 4 (age, service); 13 suggests that only one emperor was in power. For Lucian's duties, 12, esp. the phrase τὰς δίκας εἰσάγειν: that this refers to the *eisagogeus* was rightly argued by Box, *CQ* 29 (1935) 39–40, cf. J. vander Leest, *GRBS* 26 (1985) 75–82, whereas Pflaum, *MEFR* 17 (1959) 281–286 (*Scripta varia* 1. 155–60) supposed that Lucian was *archistator*, a kind of military official (I retract my argument in *GRBS* 13 [1972] 486 n. 58); on the *eisagogeus*, see the useful discussion of Daris, *Aegyptus* 63 (1983) 127.

81. Schwartz, *Biographie* 12–13, peremptorily identified the prefect as C. Calvisius Sabinus, but on no evidence: Bowersock, *Sophists* 114 n. 6 (on p. 115) and Hall, *Lucian's Satire* 7–9.

82. On this kind of patronage, Saller, *Personal Patronage* 46–50, 157–158.

83. *Apol.* 12, ἔθνος ἐπιτραπῆναι, clearly a periphrasis of ἐπίτροπος. Lucian does not specify whether he hoped to be a financial or a presidial procurator, and perhaps did not know. Cf. Fronto's request to Pius on behalf of Appian, Champlin, *Fronto* 98–100; Saller, *Personal Patronage* 47.

84. On Lucian's references to Egypt, esp. *Luct.* 21, Hall, *Lucian's Satire* 43.

85. *Suda*, λ 683: for this interpretation, Baldwin, *Studies* 8–9.

86. So Turner, *Greek Papyri* 97–98. A parchment scrap of the spurious *Asinus* has been recognized by Lenaerts, *CE* 49 (1974) 115–120, and *POxy.* 52.3683 contains a colophon of the *Halcyon*, attributing it to Plato.

significant, for he does not include all the known sophists, and Lucian had been one only in the early part of his career. Athenaeus writing about 200 seems to be acquainted with him; the *Amores*, a work which shows Lucian's influence, may be not later than 250.[87] Criticizing pagan divinities in the early fourth century, Lactantius talks of "Lucian who spared neither gods nor men": this anticipates Lucian's later enrollment by Christians as an ally against the old religion.[88] The pagan Eunapios is the first author to refer to a work of his by title; "Lucian of Samosata, a man earnest in his pursuit of laughter, wrote a life of Demonax, a man of that time, and in that work and very few others was completely earnest."[89] Lucian's style and his mockery of paganism gained the stamp of approval from Christianity, and thus his works survived with almost no detectable losses and a large number of accretions. Yet his unkind portrait of the early Christians in the *Peregrinus* was a stumbling block, and two great figures of Byzantine culture exemplify the mixed feelings that he evoked. Photios, later to be the influential patriarch of Constantinople, praises Lucian warmly in his *Library,* and in language reminiscent of Eunapios calls him "serious in his mockery of the Hellenes," a word which had long since come to denote pagans: the young Photios does not even mention his attacks on Christianity.[90] Arethas, bishop of Cappadocian Caesarea in the next generation, was not so indulgent: though he rendered great services to Lucian by his care for the text and his comments, he also covered the margins of his copy with angry abuse, especially in the *Peregrinus.*[91]

Lucian is far from an outsider in his own society. As a youth he

87. Athenaeus: below, Ch. 10 at n. 13. *Amores:* Jones, *GRBS* 25 (1984) 177–178. On Lucian's *Nachleben* generally, Helm, *RE* 13 (1927) 1773–75 (where for "Euagrius" read "Eunapius").

88. Lact. *Inst.* 1.9.8, *Lucianus, qui diis et hominibus non pepercit.* Ogilvie, *Library of Lactantius* 82, follows Volkmann in thinking this an interpolation.

89. Eun. *VS* 454 (p. 348 Wright, 4 Giangrande). Eunapios may be thinking of the term σπουδογέλοιος ("earnest-humorous"), applied by Strabo to Menippos (16.2.29, p. 759 C.).

90. Phot. *Bibl.* 128 (2.102 Henry). On the date of this work, Treadgold, *Nature of the Bibliotheca of Photios* ch. 2.

91. For Arethas as a commentator on Lucian, Rabe, *NAWG* 1902, 729–735, 1903, 643–656; for his comments on the *Peregrinus*, Rabe, *Scholia* 216–220. Cf. Baldwin, *Studies* 100–102, and on Lucian in the Byzantine era generally, Mattioli, *Luciano* 9–38.

had imbibed that higher education which dominated the Greek culture of his day. He traveled widely in the east and the west, and was known to educated Greeks and Romans. Those for whom he wrote and performed were not the unlettered public but the "cultured," "those who pursue letters."[92] It is to be expected that when he talks of contemporary culture and society he does so from the vantage point of a practiced observer: not an otherworldly "artist," still less a "journalist," but a man in touch with his time.

92. *VH* 1.1; cf. *Harm.* 4.

3   Philosophy and Philosophers

LUCIAN'S TREATMENT of philosophy is at once a central feature of his works and one of the most paradoxical. When he aims his satire at targets such as religious belief or magic, he often does so by making philosophy their defender or representative; when he mocks vices like hypocrisy or venality, he often incorporates them in philosophers. Yet in other works he claims an interest in philosophy or praises individual philosophers such as the Platonist Nigrinus and the Cynic Demonax. This apparent inconsistency might be thought simply another sign that he is playing a literary game, and that what appears to be comment on the contemporary scene is merely borrowed from books.[1]

Considering his treatment of philosophy, Lucian is naturally reticent about his own experience of it. His early education can be presumed to have given him a familiarity with the basic authors and ideas; so much is implied by Culture's promise in the *Dream* to adorn his soul with the moral virtues and her citation of Socrates as an exemplar.[2] His acquaintance with the literature written by disciples of Socrates, above all Plato but also Xenophon and Aeschines, must go back at least to this stage: the same is probably true of the *Picture of Cebes,* a still extant work of popular morality which Lucian often uses, though it is not clear whether he believed the attribution to the pupil of Socrates.[3] A work which gives the impression of being early,

---

1. Thus Helm begins his appendix, "Die Philosophie in der Komödie," with the observation, "In den Satiren Lukians nimmt die Philosophenverspottung den grössten Raum ein," and ends it, "Schliesslich liefert auch er nur, was die Komiker vor ihm ausgestaltet hatten" (Helm, *Lucian* 370, 386).

2. *Somn.* 10, 12.

3. Below, Ch. 13 at n. 28.

the *Calumny,* with its famous description of Apelles' painting on the same subject, belongs to a type of half-philosophical discourse of which Lucian's contemporary Maximus of Tyre has left a complete collection; though it does not prove Lucian a serious philosopher, it indicates his familiarity with a style favored by fashionable preachers.

There may even have been periods of a more than literary interest in philosophy, though Lucian's claims are too obliquely expressed to allow certainty. In the *Hermotimos* he recalls an experience from about his twenty-fifth year, and in language clearly influenced by Cebes' *Picture* describes how he was attracted to the City of Philosophy but then turned away out of youthful folly.[4] This may, however, be a mere stratagem designed to make his mockery of the aging Hermotimos seem reasonable and almost reluctant. Among the several and conflicting accounts of his conversion about the age of forty is one that again resembles Cebes' *Picture:* for a long time, Lucian sought the house of Philosophy, but those he asked for guidance either confessed ignorance or led him to a "little lady" whose dress showed her lack of respectability. This is Lucian's parody of a standard pattern of narrative used to describe philosophical searches, for example by the Christian Justin, and again it may be in part a literary device of which the aim is to palliate his attacks on modern philosophers.[5] The *Nigrinus* describes how he visited the Platonist of the title in Rome and was converted from his false valuation of material things by Nigrinus' eloquence. This work has evoked a whole literature, both for what it suggests about the author's attitude to philosophy and because his rapture seems not to correspond to the satirical tone of Nigrinus. The best view is that the work, being addressed to a Platonist, politely recalls Plato's description of the effects of Socrates' teaching on Alcibiades and others: the content, even if not transcendental, involves a series of moral antitheses: Rome and Athens, wealth and poverty, true philosophers and false.[6] How much actual experience underlies the work cannot be judged, but there is no reason to assume none or to doubt Nigrinus' existence.[7]

---

4. *Herm.* 24. For a balanced discussion, Hall, *Lucian's Satire* 18–20.

5. *Pisc.* 11–12; the same motif also in *Nec.* 4–6, and cf. *Bis acc.* 31; Justin, *Dial.* 2. Cf. Nock in *Pisciculi* 172 (*Essays* 1.475).

6. For Hall's very good discussion, *Lucian's Satire* 157–164.

7. Thus, rightly, Hall, *Lucian's Satire* 163–164. The cognomen "Nigrinus" may denote a connection with the Avidii of Faventia, two of whom were friends of Plutarch (*PIR*[2] A 1407–10): note C. Avidius Heliodorus, rhetor and philosopher under Ha-

Nor is Nigrinus the only philosopher among Lucian's friends. The *Demonax* is a monument to an amusing old Cynic with whom he claims a long association, "the best philosopher that I have known," and beyond doubt a real person.[8] Cronios, to whom the *Peregrinus* is dedicated, is probably another Platonist of Lucian's acquaintance; the philosophic Sabinus who receives the *Self-Defense* may well be yet another.[9] The best evidence for Lucian's philosophical friendships is provided by the *Alexander*. Dedicated to an Epicurean called Celsus, the work extols the *Principal Doctrines* of Epicurus and Celsus' own writings and shows Lucian acting in league with the Epicurean community of Amastris in order to unmask the false prophet of Abonuteichos.[10] Whether Lucian felt a personal inclination to Epicureanism or any other persuasion will be considered later, but it is clear that, as would be expected of a cultured man of letters in the second century, his acquaintance with philosophy and philosophers was not merely superficial. In his own words, he was "bred up to culture and moderately conversant with philosophy."[11] Certainly he describes himself in the *Apology* as "not a wise man, if indeed anyone is, but one of the common mob, who pursued literature and received moderate praise for it, but never attained that perfect virtue of the masters." But his purpose here is to elude the charge of ethical inconsistency, and he does not imply complete ignorance of philosophy.[12] A similar position is taken by Galen, who did not follow any school and yet held that the best doctor was also a philosopher: this philosophic detachment from partisanship was probably common.[13]

Though Lucian keeps his distance, he has visible preferences among the schools. The enthusiasm that he expresses for Epicurus in the

---

drian (*PIR*[2] A 1405) and two philosophic Avidii from Thespiae, Plassart, *BCH* 50 (1926) 433 no. 63. For a papyrus referring to Peregrinus rather than to Nigrinus, below, Ch. 11 at n. 69.

8. On Demonax, his Cynicism, and the evidence for him outside Lucian, below, Ch. 9.

9. For Cronios and Sabinus, above, Ch. 2 at nn. 77 and 79.

10. *Alex.* 47 (Epicurus' *Doctrines*), 21 (Celsus' κατὰ μάγων), 25 (Epicureans of Amastris): see further below, Ch. 12.

11. *Salt.* 2.

12. *Apol.* 15. Momigliano, *RSI* 60 (1948) 432 (*Quarto Contributo* 643), compares Sen. *De Vita beata* 17.3.

13. Galen, *Med. Phil.* (*Scr. min.* 2. 1–8). Cf. Horace's famous *nullius addictus iurare in uerba magistri, Epist.* 1.1.14.

Alexander might be dismissed as another stratagem adopted for that work, except that a similar sympathy is visible elsewhere. The Epicurean Damis is the urbane rationalist and critic of religion in the *Tragic Jupiter,* while the irascible Stoic Timocles defends the cause of the gods: the Epicurean Hermon is the only philosopher in the *Banquet* to behave with any dignity or humor.[14] Here and elsewhere Lucian brings conventional charges against the Epicureans, their gluttony and hedonism, their apparent hypocrisy in observing conventional religion. But these jabs are very gentle compared to his treatment of other schools.[15]

Lucian's sympathy for the doctrines of Epicurus may also be supposed in works where they are not directly invoked. Of two short treatises which appear to be pendants, one is the discourse *On Sacrifices,* the preface of which echoes a dictum of Epicurus: "the impious man is not the one who denies the gods of the many, but the one who fastens the opinions of the many onto the gods."[16] Lucian proceeds in a manner reminiscent of Lucretius, mocking men's absurd notions about the life of the gods and the practices they adopt in worshiping them. The truculent tone also gives the work a Cynic flavor, although there is nothing in it that is peculiarly Cynical, and on matters of belief and right conduct the two schools sometimes coincided. The other work of the pair is the treatise *On Mourning.* Here too Lucian begins by mocking received ideas about the underworld and then turns to rituals of burial and mourning. With these he shows his powers of observation and description in many details: the corpse "crowned to excess," the practice of sacrificing or burying pets or other possessions of the deceased, the funeral banquet *(perideipnon)* held after three days of fasting.[17] One touch added by Lucian is a fantasy compounded of literature and actuality. He imagines a father addressing his dead son and regretting all the pleasures of life

14. Cf. esp. Caster, *Pensée* 92 (*I. trag.*), 90–92 (*Symp.*): also Schwartz, *Biographie* 145–148.

15. E.g., *Pisc.* 43, *Symp.* 9, 43. For Epicureans of Lucian's day serving as priests, cf. for example *Bull.* 1976.720.

16. D. L. 10.123 = Epicur. *Ep. ad Men.* p. 60 Usener, p. 109 Arrighetti; Luc. *Sacr.* 1.

17. *Luct.* 12 (crown), 14 (sacrifice), 24 *(perideipnon).* For funerary crowns and banquets, many examples in *Index du Bulletin Épigraphique* 1966–1973 s.vv. banquet funèbre, couronne funéraire; for sacrifices of pets, cf. Pliny on M. Regulus, *Ep.* 4.2.3.

that the youth has not lived to enjoy, until the corpse, "raising itself on its elbow," consoles him with rational arguments for the nullity of death.[18] The theme of lost enjoyment is a commonplace both of literature and of funerary inscriptions, and the notion of the dead coming to life might seem a mere reminiscence of passages in Aristophanes.[19] But inscriptions of the Roman period show a belief in the ability of the young dead to appear to their parents in dreams or visions, urging them to moderate their grief.[20]

One of Lucian's more elusive dialogues, which is often thought to be Cynic in inspiration, might rather be Epicurean. The *Anacharsis* is a dialogue between the half-mythical Scythian and the Athenian Solon on the subject of the training of the young, especially in athletics.[21] Though the Epicureans do not seem to have shown much interest in athletic display,[22] it went against their treasured precepts of the quiet life and the avoidance of renown. As in the essay *On Mourning,* Lucian shows a precise knowledge of contemporary practices. Though the dialogue is set in sixth-century Athens, his account accords with the literature and inscriptions of his own day. He refers to institutions known only from authors later than the classical period, such as apples being given as prizes at the Pythian games and the contest of the whips at Sparta. And the "labors" *(ponoi)* that he ascribes to the athletes recur frequently in later poetry and prose.[23]

By contrast with the Epicureans, their traditional enemies the Stoics are perhaps Lucian's favorite butt.[24] The *Hermotimos* represents Ly-

---

18. *Luct.* 13–20. It is notable that Lucian uses the example of "someone young and handsome": for the heightened mourning accorded to the prematurely dead, bibliography in *Bull.* 1973.458.

19. Notably Ar. *Ra.* 170–178.

20. Thus in the testament of Epicrates of Nacrason, *Bull.* 1970.512 p. 440; a Christian example in *SEG* 6.140 (improved by Wilhelm, *SDAW* 1932.818–825 [*Akademieschriften* 2.362–369]).

21. A balanced discussion in Kindstrand, *Anacharsis* 65–67.

22. I notice only Lact. *Inst.* 3.17.3 (fr. 553 Usener), *Epicuri disciplina . . . prohibet . . . pigrum exerceri.*

23. Apples at Pythia: *Anach.* 9, 13, al., Robert, *Hellenica* 7 (1949) 95–97. Contest of the whips: *Anach.* 38, Michell, *Sparta* 175–177. Πόνοι: *Anach.* 9, 10, 13, 14, al., Robert, *Hellenica* 11/12 (1960) 344–349, 13 (1965) 141. Note also Lucian's reference to the cheering of athletic audiences, *Anach.* 12, 16, cf. Robert in *L'épigramme grecque* 253 n. 3.

24. Caster, *Pensée* 19–29, esp. 27–29.

cinos persuading an elderly student of Stoicism to give up his fruitless pursuit and acknowledge the superiority of the ordinary man. Although Lycinos claims to attack the Stoics only because their school happens to be the one chosen by Hermotimos, the excuse cannot be taken seriously.[25] Similarly Lucian pretends to recount the tribulations of the Stoic Thesmopolis in the *Hirelings* only to illustrate a general lesson, but the effect is to make the Stoics typify the venal clients of rich Romans.[26] He introduces three different Stoics into the *Banquet,* the quarrelsome Zenothemis, the pederastic Diphilos, and Hetoimocles, whose letter, read out before the guests, simultaneously parodies the ugly Greek of the Stoics and exposes their materialism.[27] The prominence of this sect in Lucian cannot be fortuitous. Hermotimos explains his adherence to Stoicism thus: "I saw most people eagerly taking it up, and so I guessed it was better."[28] This was the age when Stoicism, once the source of opposition to the emperors, now claimed a follower in Marcus Aurelius. According to Cassius Dio, Marcus' predilection caused many to pretend to be philosophers in order to gain wealth, and though Dio is no friend of philosophy, his testimony may be accepted.[29] The example had been set by one of Marcus' teachers, Apollonios of Chalcedon, whose avarice drew the sarcasm of Antoninus Pius, as later of Demonax.[30] Lucian accuses the Uncultured Man of amassing books for the same purpose, of impressing Marcus and winning advancement, and hints that this person too had pretensions as a philosopher.[31] Marcus may even have contributed a few features to the portrait of Hermotimos, the elderly Stoic dutifully attending the lessons of mercenary teachers.[32]

The Peripatetics receive the least notice from Lucian of all the major schools, and yet one work is entirely devoted to them. The *Eunuch* takes its occasion from a historical event, Marcus' foundation of chairs of philosophy at Athens: if Lucian can be believed, there

25. *Herm.* 85.

26. *Merc. cond.* 33–35.

27. *Symp.* 22–27.

28. *Herm.* 16.

29. Cass. Dio 71.35.2.

30. HA *Pius* 10.4, Luc. *Demon.* 31 (apparently referring to a later visit of Apollonios to Rome). On Apollonios generally, *PIR²* A 929.

31. *Ind.* 22–23. For this person's claims to wisdom, ibid., 20, 26.

32. Note the mockery of Marcus by the philosopher Lucius, Philostr. *VS* 65.13–24.

were two for each of the major schools.[33] One of the Peripatetic holders has recently died, and Lycinos recounts with cynical amusement how the two contenders for the position make their claims, mainly on their evidence of virility. The essence of the work is the satire of philosophers betraying their professions by lust, quarrelsomeness, and greed, like the guests in the *Banquet*. It is impossible to tell how much fact lies behind the work, and the Peripatetics may be singled out only because their doctrines exposed them to the charge of avarice.[34] There may, however, be a dash of actuality in the *Hermotimos* when Lucian names a Peripatetic "Euthydemos," since a very eminent member of the school, a teacher of Galen, was called "Eudemos."[35]

Two schools receive similar treatment, the Platonists and the Pythagoreans. The Platonists are usually treated to nothing worse than mild banter, for example on the invisibility of the Ideas or the sharing of wives. A character called Ion, however, is a principal victim in two works. He is one of the most gullible of the *Lovers of Lies,* and his apparent gravity in the *Banquet* soon turns out to cover boorishness, irritability, and dishonesty. It is natural to wonder how the Platonists of Lucian's acquaintance such as Cronios would have taken such satire: a man of literature and culture, however, might have derived more amusement than annoyance from the superficial caricature of a few well-known doctrines and the misbehavior of imaginary colleagues. Lucian pays considerable attention to Pythagoras and the Pythagoreans, an index of the revival which this school was enjoying. He is often content merely to tease them, as he does the Platonists, for example, when he makes Pythagoras an avatar of the *Cock*.[36] The Pythagorean Arignotos, however, is one of the chief culprits among the *Lovers of Lies,*[37] and the *Alexander* is still more hostile: Lucian

33. Luc. *Eun.* 3; Cass. Dio 72.31.3; Philostr. *VS* 73.28–31; it seems unlikely that Tat. *Orat.* 19.1 refers to this, see Whittaker ad loc. The philosophical chairs are of course different from the rhetorical one, though perhaps founded at the same time: Avotins, *HSCPh* 79 (1975) 313–324; Hall, *Lucian's Satire* 396–402.

34. Caster, *Pensée* 55–56; Hall, *Lucian's Satire* 167.

35. *Herm.* 11; on Eudemos, *PIR*² E 109; for this suggestion, Nutton, *Galen: De praecog.* 157.

36. *Gall.* 4, 16–20. For the significance of the cock in Pythagoreanism, see now Şahin, *Hommages Vermaseren* 999–1000. On Lucian and Pythagoreanism in general, Caster, *Pensée* 40–47.

37. Note esp. *Philops.* 29.

perfunctorily salutes the Master, but emphasizes the Pythagorean coloring of Alexander's religious propaganda.[38]

Lucian's attitude toward Cynicism is the most complicated of all, as befitted a school whose manifestations were so varied. He must owe a large literary debt to Menippos, the third-century Cynic from Gadara, even if it can no longer be held that he plundered him systematically. More can be learned from his relations with living Cynics. The *Demonax* is a remarkable tribute to a revered friend, but Lucian seems concerned to minimize his Cynicism, which was in any case of the milder kind.[39] The Craton who is Lycinos' interlocutor in the *Portraits* is similarly represented as a Cynic who manages to remain polite and persuadable. By contrast, the *Peregrinus* is a frontal attack on two of the best known Cynics of the day, Peregrinus and his disciple Theagenes of Patrai; and the *Runaways* extends the caricature to include an unnamed follower of Peregrinus and takes the occasion to excoriate the whole tribe.[40] This duality of attitude probably reflects the wide range of thought and behavior that Cynicism permitted, so that a Demonax could be closer to Stoicism or Epicureanism than to the more rigorous members of his own school.[41] In the same way Epictetos in his famous discourse on Cynicism warns the aspirant against the vulgar charlatans to whom the label is commonly attached, and sets before him an ideal which is as much Stoic as Cynic.[42]

Lucian's treatment of the various schools, therefore, is more nuanced than would be expected if his knowledge came solely from books. Certainly many of his jokes are found in earlier writing, not only comedy but epigram.[43] It does not follow, however, that because his typical philosopher has a long beard and knitted eyebrows, he is cut out of paper:[44] that would only be likely if Lucian's picture differed

38. *Alex.* 4 (Pythagoras), 25, 33, 40 (Alexander's propaganda).

39. Below, Ch. 10.

40. *Fugit.* 12–21.

41. Note his mockery of Honoratus, who dressed in a bearskin, and his exchange with Peregrinus, *Demon.* 19, 21; and also the incident in which a Roman proconsul spared another Cynic out of respect for Demonax, *Demon.* 50.

42. Arr. *Diss. Epict.* 3.22.2, 10–11, 15, 50, 80.

43. Note esp. the anonymous epigram in Ath. 4.162 A = Page, *Further Greek Epigrams* 475–477.

44. Contrast Bompaire, *Lucien écrivain* 485: "Il s'agit d'un type générique, assez indépendant des étiquettes de secte . . . Les traits physiques sont toujours les mêmes . . . Bref l'observation est nulle."

greatly from that drawn by contemporaries, which is not the case. His attack on the Cynics in the *Runaways* is so similar to one in Aristides that one of the two authors has been thought dependent on the other.[45] Rather, their common charges of gluttony and boorishness read more like a common type of social generalization, a shorthand whereby one group blackens another with the faults of its most conspicuous members. So also when Lucian's contemporaries blame philosophers for their quarrelsomeness or love of gain, they must be allowed at least a measure of observation.[46]

Lucian's attitude to philosophy is not simple, but neither is it incomprehensible. His society contains a mixture of friends and enemies, friends such as the Platonist Nigrinus and the mild Cynic Demonax, enemies such as the Pythagorean Alexander of Abonuteichos and the rigorous Cynic Peregrinus. His literary poses form a similar mixture, admiration for the ancients like Plato and Menippos, praise and blame for contemporaries in which there is a blend of the borrowed and the observed. The prominence of philosophy in his work is due not only to his reading or to the demands of his audiences but also to the fact that the society and the culture of the day swarmed with philosophers as much as with sophists. Even the most conspicuous of them all, the emperor Marcus, observed to Galen that most modern philosophers were "not only fond of money, but contentious, ambitious, envious and malicious."[47]

45. Aristid. 3.663–685. Cf. Boulanger, *RPh* 47 (1923) 144–151, arguing for the influence of Aristides on Lucian; Bompaire, *Lucien écrivain* 488 n. 2, postulating a common source.

46. E.g. the emperor Pius, *Dig.* 27.1.6.7, cf. Nutton, *Galen: De Praecog.* 216–217; App. *Mithr.* 28; Tat. *Orat.* 2–3, 19.1; Diog. Oen. fr. 24 col. 1 Chilton.

47. Gal. *De Praecog.* 11.8.

4   Gods and Oracles

IF LUCIAN has a favorite topic, it is religion, understood in a broad sense to include gods old and new, cults, oracles, beliefs. Naturally, therefore, his treatment of religion has always weighed heavily with his critics. When Photios praised Lucian for his mockery of the pagans, he was thinking above all of his treatment of the Greek gods; and the more susceptible Arethas excoriated him as anti-Christian.[1] Several of his most prominent admirers since the Renaissance were drawn to him by their own antipathy to the established religion of Rome: thus Erasmus, Ulrich von Hutten, Gibbon, and Voltaire.[2] During the Enlightenment it was tempting to see his wit as clever subversion, a device to expose the enthusiasm and superstition of the times, whereas modern views are influenced by Bernays, who protested that this was to make a Voltaire out of an irresponsible Syrian.[3] Since Bernays there has been general consent that as a critic of religion Lucian is defective, whether his deficiencies are due to the self-imposed restraints of a literary artist, for whom precedent mattered more than

1. On Arethas and Photios, above, Ch. 2 at nn. 90 and 91. I defer until Chs. 11 and 12 discussion of Lucian's observations on Christianity.

2. Robinson, *Lucian* 165–197 (Erasmus), 110–115 (von Hutten), 155–157 (Voltaire); for Gibbon's sympathy, note esp. *Decline and Fall* 1.30 Bury, "We may be well assured, that a writer conversant with the world would never have ventured to expose the gods of his country to public ridicule, had they not already been the objects of secret contempt among the polished and enlightened orders of society."

3. Thus Tooke, *Lucian* 1, xv–xvii, esp. xvii, "In order the more certainly to attain his more serious purpose, he must so frequently conceal it under an appearance of frivolity, and seem to be merely amusing while he was endeavouring to instruct and improve his reader"; against, Bernays, *Lucian* 42–43.

observation, or the exigencies of an entertainer, who settles on whatever will amuse his audience.[4] It is arguable, conversely, that many of these supposed deficiencies are due to the perspective of Lucian's critics. Because he does not say anything, or at least very much, on subjects they would like to see addressed (Mithraism, Christianity, the imperial cult), they infer that he misses the most important phenomena of the day. It may be conceded that Lucian did not enter the religious scrimmages of his contemporaries but stood smiling on the sidelines. That did not prevent him from observing much that was characteristic of spiritual life—if not a Voltaire, at least a gentler Swift.

Lucian usually treats religious subjects by means of dialogue. Some of these works are mythological miniatures such as the *Judgment of the Goddesses* and the *Dialogues of the Gods,* and these are in large part literary exercises in a genre that goes back as far as Homer, though an element of satire is already present. Thus the scene in which Zeus gives birth to Athene by persuading Hephaistos to split his skull with an axe makes an instructive contrast with the beginning of Aelius Aristides' prose hymn to the same goddess.[5] Whereas Aristides solemnly explains the myth as the expression of Athene's powers and privileges, Lucian's sketch exposes its absurdity.

Lucian puts his more direct attacks into those dialogues which include both the gods and their critics, including the renegade god Momos, the personification of blame.[6] The work that has been most faulted, though not the longest or most complex, is the *Assembly of the Gods.* Here Zeus and Momos are the sole speakers, and the subject is the single one of intrusive gods. In a divine assembly called to debate the issue, Momos questions in turn the credentials of a series of gods. He takes first those long accepted among the Olympians despite their mortal mothers, Dionysos, Asclepios, and Heracles. Second, by way of Ganymede, he moves to barbarian importations,

4. Thus Caster, *Pensée,* esp. 382, "Il n'a pas utilisé tous les matériaux que le second siècle offrait à son esprit satirique"; Hall, *Lucian's Satire* 199, "Had he wanted to satirise the religious features that were really important in his age he could have found scope for his mockery . . ."

5. Luc. *D. Deor.* 13; Aristid. 37.2–4.

6. For Momos, more a literary figure than a real god, Tümpel in Roscher, *Lexikon* 2.3117–19.

Attis, Corybas, Sabazios, Mithras, and the animal-faced gods of Egypt. He then considers three pairs of heroes, Trophonios and Amphilochos, noted for their oracles, the athletes Polydamas and Theagenes whose statues were used to cure fevers, and the Trojan heroes Hector and Protesilaos. Next he condemns abstractions, such as Virtue, which philosophers had turned into divinities. And finally he proposes a motion whereby commissioners are to review the gods' credentials.[7] Without putting it to the vote Zeus promises an impartial review soon, with the final threat that "the commissioners will not care if someone has a large temple on earth and men think him a god."

Lucian has certainly drawn on earlier literature. The frame of the dialogue may well have been supplied by Menippos, since the parallels with Seneca's *Apocolocyntosis* are frequent and close.[8] Many of the arguments against intrusive gods had been made in literature before, for example by the Academic Cotta in Cicero's *De Natura Deorum,*[9] and they were no doubt stock ammunition of the schools and in the public spaces. It has also been thought that the whole substance of the work is tralatician, that on the one hand the Olympian gods and their myths were no longer taken seriously, and on the other new gods, especially oriental ones, had advanced much further than Lucian notices.

The Olympian religion, however, does not appear from the literature or the monuments of the time to have been in decline. Aristides' fervor is perhaps exceptional, but there is no sign that he was eccentric in his choice of gods, and the list of those to whom he addresses his prose hymns includes the same three with which Lucian begins here, Dionysos, Asclepios, and Heracles. Aristides' description of Asclepios' sanctuary at Pergamon, corroborated by the many inscriptions, shows the god enjoying unprecedented renown and devotion.[10] If the traditional myths were not taken seriously, it is hard to see why the Christian apologists contemporary with Lucian attacked them so fiercely.

7. At the end of section 14 there should be a colon, not a full stop, still less the end of a paragraph.

8. Helm, *Lucian* 161–162; Hall, *Lucian's Satire* 104–108.

9. Helm, *Lucian* 157–158.

10. For the cultural life of the Asklepieion of Pergamon, Habicht, *Asklepieion* 15–17; Bowersock, *Sophists* 19.

The best illustration is perhaps Aristides of Athens, who devotes much of his *Apology* to an exposure of the Greek myths, using many of the same examples as Lucian.[11] It may be relevant that both Aristides and Lucian lived in the Athens of the mid-second century, since despite its celebrated curiosity this city had a marked conservatism of cult.[12]

The spread of new cults in the Greco-Roman world, above all of oriental ones, has been a natural preoccupation of scholars seeking to explain the eventual triumph of Christianity. On this issue Lucian has been blamed both for what he includes and for what he omits. It is alleged that the gods he singles out, Attis, Corybas, Sabazios, Mithras, and Egyptian animal-gods such as Anubis, the bull of Memphis, and Zeus Ammon, had in fact been worshiped for centuries. Lucian's primary interest, however, is not in new gods, but in spurious ones, and of those whom he names, none—not even the shadowy Corybas—had lost ground since their introduction, and some were gaining fast.[13] His mention of Mithras is of especial interest. Since the god had only become known to the Greeks in the first century before the Christian era, this reference at least cannot go back to Hellenistic authors such as Menippos; and his growing popularity in the Roman Empire is shown by the fact that he gained respectability at Athens just about the time of Lucian's residence there.[14] As for Lucian's silences, it is hardly very grave that he fails to mention

11. Arist. *Apol.* 9–13 (Geffcken, *Zwei griechische Apologeten* 12–21). With Aristides 9.6–8 (adulteries of Zeus), cf. *Deor. Conc.* 7; with 10.5–6 (death of Asclepios), *Deor. Conc.* 6; with 11.3 (adulteries of Aphrodite), *Deor. Conc.* 8; with 12 (Egyptian gods), *Deor. Conc.* 10. Observe the comment of Helen B. Harris, publishing the first translation of this section of Aristides' work (*The Newly Recovered Apology of Aristides* [1891] iv): "the undue length, detailed descriptions and emphasis of denunciation of this portion . . . indicate that these frightful histories still held sway over men's minds to an extent which it is difficult for us to realize."

12. Nilsson, *Gesch. gr. Rel.* 2² 327–335 (Athens), 372–384 (the period in general): Bompaire's arguments (*Lucien écrivain* 495–497) against Nilsson are little more than affirmations.

13. Nilsson, *Gesch. gr. Rel.* 2² 640–657 (Attis), 658–667 (Sabazios), 624–639 (Egyptian gods); on Corybas, Schwenn, *RE* 11 (1922) 1441–46, esp. 1445–46; on Mithras, below.

14. On Mithras generally, Nilsson, *Gesch. gr. Rel.* 2² 668–679; H. A. Thompson, in an unpublished paper, shows that the evidence for Mithras at Athens goes back at least to the second century (contrast Nilsson, *Gesch. gr. Rel.* 669).

such well-known Egyptian gods as Serapis, since these were not animal-headed like Anubis and therefore less easy targets for ridicule.[15]

Much the same may be said of the mythical or historical mortals whom Momos mentions last: though all had received cult long since, they were enjoying renewed prestige in the religious revival of the Roman Empire. The underground oracle of Trophonios at Lebadea was visited by Apollonios of Tyana in the previous century, and Pausanias gives it a long and reverential account.[16] "Amphilochos, who though the son of a polluted matricide gives oracles in Cilicia," is a particular target of Lucian: he is represented as the chief inspiration for the swindler Alexander of Abonuteichos, and the credulous Eucrates in the *Lovers of Lies* talks of the oracle as "most manifest and true." Once again Pausanias provides the foil, calling it "the most reliable oracle of my time," and there is ample evidence of its popularity in the great oracular vogue of the high Roman Empire.[17] In his account of Olympia, where both Polydamas and Theagenes were victors in the pancration, Pausanias dwells on Polydamas' miraculous feats of strength and even more on the curious traditions associated with Theagenes. He reports that Theagenes was worshiped as a god by the Thasians (a statement now confirmed by an inscription of the second or third century), and knows of his statues curing illnesses among both Greeks and barbarians.[18] Philostratos similarly corroborates Lucian when he devotes the *Heroicos* to the cults of the Trojan heroes; though he is mainly interested in Protesilaos, he also mentions Hector.[19]

It is true that Lucian omits certain gods who might be thought to have deserved a place in his work. Hadrian promoted the cult of his favorite Antinoos in Bithynia, Egypt, and elsewhere, and this act is often noted by Christian writers as an offense against morals. Lucian's

15. *Contra,* Helm, *Lucian* 164. Serapis is also omitted by the Christian Aristides.

16. Philostr. *VA* 4.24, 8.19; Paus. 9.39.5–14.

17. Luc. *Alex.* 19, cf. 29 (Alexander), *Philops.* 38 (Eucrates), Paus. 1.34.3. On this shrine, located at Mallos, Latte, *RE* 18 (1939) 862; for the legend of the hero's birth alluded to by Lucian, Bouché-Leclercq, *Histoire de la divination* 3.341.

18. Paus. 6.5.4–9 (Polydamas), 11.2–9 (Theagenes); for the inscription, Dunant and Pouilloux, *Thasos* 2.157–158 no. 322. On curative statues see further below, Ch. 5.

19. For Hector, Philostr. *Her.* 19.3–9.

silence might be due to tact, but also to the feeling that Antinoos was too artificial a divinity to be worth satirizing.[20] The omission of the deified emperors has often been thought grave.[21] Here there is more reason to invoke considerations of diplomacy, but like Antinoos the emperors hardly answered Lucian's satirical purpose. His aim is to question the credentials of certain gods who received cult equal to that of the long established Olympians: the emperors for all their trappings of divinity were not generally felt as gods who answered prayers or gave oracles and cures.[22] Seneca could more safely ridicule the admission of Claudius to Olympos, but even he does not treat an emperor like Augustus as more than a junior god.

A recent theory, if correct, would suggest that the *Assembly of the Gods* was closely linked with the emperors in another way and would give it a sharp relevance. The reign of Marcus Aurelius, which roughly coincided with Lucian's residence in Athens, was a period of political turbulence there, marked particularly by attacks on the aging Herodes Atticus. Marcus and Lucius tried in 165 to reform the Areopagus and to purge intrusive elements, and events of the subsequent years, above all the devastation of the great plague, moved Marcus to issue a long decision in which he tried both to exclude the unworthy from positions of prestige and to assure the political life of the city. It has been proposed that Lucian's satire is covertly aimed at the commotions that preceded the reforms of the two emperors in 165.[23] There is no doubt that he casts the debate in terms of Greek civic life, nor that many imperial writers equate the ruling emperor with Zeus. He might therefore be thinking of contemporary issues at Athens and expecting the most knowledgeable of his readers to notice the allusion, but he cannot have meant these events to be the key to the enjoyment of

20. For Lucian's omission, Helm, *Lucian* 163–164; on cults of Antinoos, Robert, *Asie Mineure* 132–138; Parsons on *POxy.* 50.3537; Lambert, *Beloved and God* 177–197; for Christian attacks, Chadwick on Or. *Cels.* 3.36.

21. Thus Wilamowitz, *Die gr. und lat. Litt. und Sprache*[3] 248, "vor allem Hadrian und die anderen Kaiser hütet er sich wohl anzugreifen": for a reasoned protest, Misch, *Gesch. der Autobiographie* 1[3] 402. On second-century Greek writers and the imperial cult, Bowersock in *Culte des Souverains* 179–206 (on Lucian, 201–202).

22. Nock, *JRS* 47 (1957) 115–123 (*Essays* 2.833–846).

23. Oliver, *AJPh* 101 (1980) 304–313 (*Civic Tradition* 76–84); on the date of Marcus' and Lucius' joint letter, Oliver, *AJPh* 101 (1980) 308–311 (*Civic Tradition* 80–82); for Marcus' famous letter to the Athenians, Follet, *RPh* 53 (1979) 29–43; *SEG* 29.127; Ameling, *Herodes Atticus* 2.182–205.

his work, since such disputes were endemic to Greek cities of the empire, including Athens.[24]

The *Tragic Zeus* is closely related to the *Assembly of the Gods,* though much longer and more elaborate. The action begins and ends in heaven, but it is an event on earth that provides the impetus and the culmination: the dispute between the Epicurean Damis, whom Lucian chooses to depict as an outright atheist, and the Stoic Timocles, the issue being providence and the existence of the gods. The dialogue begins as the two philosophers are preparing to continue their debate, which they started the day before. Zeus, whose tragic language gives the work its name, is so alarmed by the prospect that he calls an emergency meeting of the divine assembly.[25] Here the chief speaker is again Momos, who blames the gods for their neglect of human affairs and makes fun of Apollo's attempt to predict the outcome by an oracle.[26] The gods eventually resolve to listen to the debate, in which both Damis and Timocles are given a selection of stock arguments in favor of their positions. It is implied that Damis has the edge, for in the farcical close Timocles resorts to abuse and violence, and Hermes advises Zeus not to worry: only a few men share Damis' convictions, and "those who think the opposite are far more numerous, the great majority of the Greeks and all the barbarians."

Though the treatment is comic, the final effect is quietly critical. The anthropomorphism of the gods does not merely lend the work charm and liveliness, it also indirectly satirizes conventional conceptions of them. When Lucian represents them as lazy hedonists concerned only for their sacrifices and other perquisites, the effect is to make them much like the conventional idea of the Epicureans.[27] Cer-

---

24. Contrast Oliver, *AJPh* 101 (1980) 307 (*Civic Tradition* 78), "the main target is surely the complete enfranchisement of unworthy elements in a noble city of ancient prestige." For disputes about citizenship in Augustan Athens, Robert, *REG* 94 (1981) 339–340.

25. On the opening lines, in which "a philosopher's color" cleverly anticipates the theme of the whole work, Coenen, *Lukian: Zeus Tragodos* 40.

26. Momos in this work sometimes recalls Wagner's Loge: cf. the last sentence of his long speech, "there is no great danger to Momos if he goes dishonored, for he was not among the honored before, when you were still prosperous and enjoying sacrifices" (22), with Loge's words (*Das Rheingold,* scene 2), "Mich kümmert's minder; / an mir ja kargte / Freia von je / knausernd das köstliche Frucht: / denn halb so echt nur / bin ich wie, Selige, ihr!" On the oracular scene, see below.

27. *I. trag.* 4, 6, 13, 15, 18, 22.

tainly Lucian is not offering an Epicurean tract. He represents Damis as an atheist, when he presumably knew that most Epicureans rejected atheism.[28] For his purpose it was enough that they were often accused of it,[29] and the stratagem sharpened the contrast between Damis and Timocles. Similarly he does not bother to make his philosophical arguments particularly original or cogent. Momos' observation that the good suffer while the wicked prosper had already been advanced against the idea of providence by Cotta in Cicero.[30] When Lucian contends that oracles have often led the pious to their destruction, or at least given them no help, his point is much more devastatingly made by the Cynic Oenomaos of Gadara, who probably wrote his *Exposure of Frauds* in the same epoch.[31] The reply of Damis to Timocles' arguments in favor of providence and the existence of the gods again recalls Cotta, and also Lucian's approximate contemporary Sextus Empiricus.[32] The fact that Lucian's coevals made the same points more forcefully, however, does not show that he is carelessly adapting some written source, Menippos, Oenomaos, or another.[33] Like any educated man who had strolled past the Painted Stoa,[34] he knew the disputes that rival philosophers conducted and the basic issues. To enter into detail would only have made him join the arguments which he ridicules.

A similar conclusion can be drawn from the *Zeus Refuted*. Here Zeus is cross-questioned by a certain Cyniscos ("Cynikin") about the gods' relation to the Fates, Destiny, and Providence, all of which Lucian treats as practically identical. His interest is to show the incompatibility of notions of fate, however named, with a belief in divine intervention. Once again his arguments coincide with ones found in Cicero, Oenomaos of Gadara, and others, and again he has been seen as dependent on literary sources like Menippos.[35] He is

28. For Diogenes of Oenoanda's sharp rejection of atheism, Smith, *AS* 29 (1979) 86–87.

29. Cf. *Alex.* 25, and perhaps *Symp.* 9.

30. Cic. *Nat. D.* 3.79–85. Cf. Momos' joke about the bearded Asclepios being the son of Apollo, *I. trag.* 26, with *Nat. D.* 3.83.

31. Luc. *I. trag.* 20; Oenom. *apud* Euseb. *PE.* 5.20–22. On Oenomaos see des Places, *Eusèbe: La préparation evangélique Livres V, 18–26, VI, 7–16.*

32. Bruns, *RhM* 44 (1889) 390–395; Helm, *Lucian* 142–147.

33. For Menippos, Helm, *Lucian* 148–150; for Oenomaos, Bruns, *RhM* 44 (1889) 395–396.

34. Cf. Zeus listening to Damis and Timocles in the Painted Stoa, *I. trag.* 16.

35. Bruns, *RhM* 44 (1889) 375–389; Helm, *Lucian* 120–130.

clearly influenced by philosophic debates, whether spoken or written, and above all by attacks on Stoic views of providence. The fact, however, that his arguments once again lean in the direction of Epicureanism suggests that he expresses convictions of his own and not of sources chosen at random. His use of a Cynic as Zeus' inquisitor does not make the work itself Cynic, since this sect was traditionally associated both with Zeus and with the outspoken questioning of received opinions, and shared with Epicureanism a distrust of oracles and arguments from providence.

It might not have been expected that a sympathizer with Epicureans and Cynics should describe a holy site with the reverence of a Pausanias, and yet there is one work in which Lucian comes close to doing so, the essay *On the Syrian Goddess*. Here he imitates Herodotos in language and manner, though without pretending to speak in another person than his own, and describes the famous sanctuary of Atargatis at Syrian Hierapolis both from his own observation and from information supplied by the priests. For a long time the work was considered spurious, since it seemed inconsistent with Lucian's religious views and with his supposed tendency to neglect what was not classical.[36] In recent decades opinion has turned in its favor, and Galen's mention of a Lucian who imitated another Ionian writer, Heracleitos, may be considered decisive.[37]

Whatever this conclusion implies about Lucian's religious beliefs, it is a triumph for his powers of observation and his independence of classical forebears. It had long been observed that some of his details were confirmed by other literary witnesses such as the Elder Pliny and Aelian, but the evidence of archaeology has added much more.[38] The "standard" (*semeion*) which he mentions standing between the images of "Hera" and "Zeus" is now known from several representations.[39] His description of the high priest's gorgeous robe and golden tiara is confirmed by a relief from Hierapolis itself.[40] When he narrates how he cut his hair and dedicated it in a vase of precious

36. Thus among others Caster, *Pensée* 360–364.
37. *Contra* for instance Helm, *RE* 13 (1927) 1761; in favor, Bompaire, *Lucien écrivain* 646–653; Hall, *Lucian's Satire* 374–381. Galen: above, Ch. 2 at n. 72.
38. Oden, *Studies* 43–46.
39. *Syr. D.* 33; Seyrig, *Syria* 37 (1960) 233–241 (*Antiquités Syriennes* 6.79–86); Oden, *Studies* 109–115.
40. *Syr. D.* 42; Stucky, *Syria* 53 (1976) 124–140.

metal, he appears to describe the same ritual as that whereby a man of Cition in Cypros some thousand years before cut his hair and dedicated it in a clay vessel to Astarte.[41]

There remains the apparent problem of Lucian's inconsistency in questions of religion. An easy recourse is to invoke irony, and to see his solemnity as open or covert mockery.[42] Humor is certainly present, and though it seems principally directed at mannerisms of Herodotos, it also touches the sanctuary, or rather the narrator who takes such things seriously: the effect is entirely different when Arrian adopts the Herodotean style to describe the sights and geography of India.[43] That both authors, however, and also some of the historians ridiculed in the essay *On Writing History* should imitate Herodotos suggests that mockery is not Lucian's primary motive. As an educated "Assyrian," proud of his native city and ethnic origin, he contrives both to bathe the greatest sanctuary of northern Syria in a Herodotean aura and to bring it, as Herodotos brought the shrines of Egypt, within the pale of Hellenism and antiquity. The archaizing movement of the second and third centuries was much concerned with cults, and learned men investigated the legends of cities of the Greek diaspora, such as Aegaeae in Cilicia.[44] Lucian does not pretend that the sanctuary of Atargatis is other than barbarian in origin, but by explaining its antiquities in the manner of Herodotos he comes close to doing so. Another work of which the authenticity has also been contested is comparable, the treatise *On the Dance*. Lucian expatiates on the myths represented in pantomime without any trace of mockery or skepticism, and here too he gives the stamp of antiquity to an entertainment whose Hellenic credentials were suspect.[45] Neither work implies a great departure from the humorous agnosticism implied by a satire like the *Assembly of the Gods*. Lucian confines his accounts

41. *Syr. D.* 60; Dupont-Sommer, *Proc. Tenth Intern. Congr. of Class. Arch.* 287–292. On Lucian's account (59) of the sacred tattoo marks (*stigmata*) employed by the Syrians, Wilcken on *UPZ* no. 121 ll. 8–9.

42. Thus Burckhardt, *Zeit Constantin's des Grossen²* 159, "nirgends hat er den Hohn so weit getrieben als hier"; Oden, *Studies* 14–24.

43. Viz in the *Indike:* cf. Allinson, *AJPh* 7 (1886) 205–206; Stadter, *Arrian* 116–117.

44. On this phenomenon, Robert, *BCH* 101 (1977) 128–129; *Asie Mineure* 412. Cf. *Syr. D.* 16.

45. Ch. 7 at n. 30–32. Cf. also the two treatises on Pantheia of Smyrna, Ch. 7 at n. 37.

mainly to myths, objects, and cultic practices, and the minor miracles to which he gives credence in the *Syrian Goddess,* sweating statues, levitation, and the like, are only a slight concession to popular beliefs.[46]

Lucian's treatment of oracles, though involved with his treatment of the gods, has a different aim and character. Usually his skepticism about the gods is muted, and his humor at their expense friendly. But the existence of oracles, as of magic, he ascribes to human weaknesses, knavery working on credulity. His dislike of oracles is fundamental to one of his masterpieces, the attack on Alexander of Abonuteichos, but it is also present in several other works.

Lucian's attacks on oracular gods are in effect aimed at those humans who participated or believed in oracles. The passage of the *Tragic Zeus* in which Apollo is called upon to predict the issue of the dispute between the two philosophers is a small anthology of stock jokes against prophecy, but it is directed less against the god than the tricks of his prophets, their paraphernalia and hocus-pocus.[47] Of the two oracular sites Lucian mentions in this work, Delphi and Colophon, the first had recovered much of its classical glory after a long decline, thanks to the efforts of devoted spokesmen like Plutarch and of emperors such as Hadrian, and it continued to be influential for at least another century.[48] Colophon, or rather its dependent site of Claros, was at the zenith of its prestige, and again the great impulse had been given by Hadrian.[49] In other passages as well, Lucian links these two sites, often adding the other great shrine of Apollo in Asia, Didyma: these juxtapositions reflect the way in which Asia, in its oracular shrines as in much else, had overtaken Greece.[50] Lucian sometimes includes in these clusters two other sites. One is Delos, which appears not to have had an oracle for centuries and receives mention only in tribute to classical literature. The other is Patara, which

---

46. *Syr. D.* 10, 32, 36–37.

47. *I. trag.* 30–31.

48. Jones, *Plutarch* 26, 28, 31–32; Flacelière, *CRAI* 1971, 168–185. On Delphi in the third century see *Bull.* 1982.450, pp. 420–422.

49. Robert, *Fouilles de Claros;* id. in Delvoye and Roux, *Civilisation grecque* 1.305–312.

50. *Alex.* 8, 29, 43, *Bis acc.* 1, *D. Deor.* 18 (where Lucian pretends that Apollo has set up shop both in Claros and in Colophon). For the other sites mentioned in some of these passages (Delos, Xanthos), see below.

he names after its port of Xanthos, and this is known to have been revived in his lifetime.[51]

Lucian mentions several other oracular sites, and on these points too his observations coincide with what is known of his epoch. Although the shrine of Zeus at Dodona was originally the most important of all, and in classical times second only to Delphi, the ravages of time and the remoteness of its site had reduced it to a shell, and Lucian only notes its decline.[52] By contrast, the healing god Asclepios had long since extended his power so as to predict the future and to give religious advice in the manner of Delphi, and the anti-Christian Celsus claims that the god foretold the future to whole cities. Lucian is therefore not merely fantasizing when Momos proposes in the *Assembly of the Gods* that Asclepios be barred from giving oracles.[53] So also when Lucian mocks the shrines of Trophonios at Lebadeia and Amphilochos at Mallos his testimony is confirmed by the contrasting admiration of Pausanias. The one site whose oracles he does not ridicule is that of Atargatis at Hierapolis, but again these professions of belief are in place in a gentle pastiche of Herodotos.[54]

Just as Lucian's selection of oracular sites reflects the situation of his day, so his criticisms are echoed by his contemporaries. Pressed to foretell the outcome between Damis and Timocles, Apollo attempts to cover his ignorance in allusive, polysyllabic hexameters, and Momos interprets the oracle to mean that Apollo is a fraud (*goes*) and the other gods asses for believing him. Oenomaos of Gadara in his *Exposure of Frauds* recounted how he consulted Clarian Apollo, received an oracle which seemed to promise a life of repose, and then found that the same answer had already been issued to a merchant of Pontos, who took it as an injunction to further activity.[55] Elsewhere Oenomaos and Lucian use the same example of Croesos to show the malicious ambiguity of oracles.[56] Just as Lucian mocks the petty fees

51. Delos: *Alex.* 8, *Bis acc.* 1, cf. Robert, *Asie Mineure* 402. Xanthos: *Bis acc.* 1, cf. Robert, *Asie Mineure* 402 n. 38.

52. *Icar.* 24; cf. Str. 7.7.9, 327 C., Paus. 1.17.5, with Frazer's commentary, *Pausanias* 2.159. For the later history and the remains of the shrine, Parke, *Oracles of Zeus* ch. 6.

53. *Deor. Conc.* 16, with the discussion of E. Edelstein and L. Edelstein, *Asclepius* 2.104–105, esp. 105 n. 17. Celsus: Orig. *Cels.* 3.3. For an oracle of Asclepios at Pergamon under Severus, Habicht, *Asklepieion* no. 34.

54. *Syr. D.* 36.

55. Luc. *I. trag.* 30–31; Eus. *PE* 5.22.1–2.

56. Luc. *I. conf.* 14; Eus. *PE* 5.21.

that oracular gods were supposed to charge for their predictions, so a papyrus of the second century, containing a text not much older, describes how the barbarian Daulis attacked Delphi, threatened to kill the priest, and denounced Apollo: "let not the god prophesy for men's pay, but stop practicing the trade of a starving fraud."[57] The charge that Apollo's powers were belied by the myths is another one common to Lucian and his contemporaries. As he mocks Apollo for not foreseeing the death of Hyacinthos and the transformation of Daphne, so Tatian uses the same two instances to prove the god an ignorant demon.[58]

Lucian criticizes oracles in a different way from gods, and yet the underlying attitudes are the same. The faintly Epicurean skepticism about general conceptions of the gods is extended to beliefs about one of their most important functions, the issuing of advice; it is ridiculous to think of them either behaving like mortals or bothering with mortal affairs.[59] The importance of these subjects in his works is due not to his desire to find an easy target, but to an interest in them which he shared with many others. And while the "great majority" did not share his views, there were vocal minorities that did, Epicureans, Cynics, and on some points Christians. Lucian lived in an age when old beliefs flourished along with new. His religious satire, central not only to the works so far considered but also to the *Peregrinos* and the *Alexander,* is one of the strongest links between him and his time.

57. Luc. *Alex.* 19, *D. Deor.* 18, *I. trag.* 30. *P. Berol.* 11517, with the discussion of Eitrem, ΔΡΑΓΜΑ *Nilsson* 170–180, esp. 178–179.

58. Luc. *D. Deor.* 18, cf. 16, Tat. *Orat.* 8.4–5.

59. Jebb, *Essays* 173: "His device consists merely in pushing bare anthropomorphism to its extreme logical result; much as Swift, in *Gulliver's Travels,* deduces all the marvels, with logical precision, from the relative scales and properties of certain given creatures."

5 Credulity and Fiction

ASKED BY PHILOSOPHY to state his profession, Parrhesiades in the *Fisherman* claims to be a "hater of boasters, hater of frauds, hater of liars and hater of humbugs." Parrhesiades is not Lucian, but nevertheless his claim corresponds to what can be inferred from the author's attacks on his contemporaries.[1] It is natural that an enemy of falsehood should often turn to the subject of true and false belief, and in two works this theme is particularly prominent: the *Lovers of Lies* and the *True Histories*. Aimed simultaneously at the deceivers and the deceived, much of their humor derives from the author's own entry into the game and his ability to surpass the fantasies of others. The *Menippos* is mainly about another very Lucianic theme, that of the underworld and the final unmasking of life's illusions, but one passage, describing Menippos' descent, resembles the *Lovers of Lies* and the *True Histories* in its parody of conventional narratives. Although a very different work, the *Toxaris*, illustrates the subject of friendship by a series of tales allegedly drawn from the recent past, both subject and treatment recall the Greek romance, and it becomes difficult to tell whether Lucian is making fun of contemporary fiction, or paying it the compliment of imitation.[2]

The form of the *Lovers of Lies,* as often in Lucian, is borrowed from Plato. His spokesman, Tychiades ("Son of Chance"),[3] relates to a

1. *Pisc.* 20. So Macleod, *Philologus* 123 (1979) 326–328.
2. Lucian can hardly be the author of the *Asinus* preserved among his works, nor does he seem likely to have written the lost *Metamorphoses* on which it is based: Appendix C. I use the title *Philops.,* adopting Rothstein's emendation to Φιλοψευδεῖς.
3. For the possible significance of the name, below, at n. 28.

sympathetic friend, Philocles, his recent visit to the house of a wealthy invalid, the "great" Eucrates.[4] He had found Eucrates, just recovering from a disease of the foot (apparently gout or rheumatism), in the company of his doctor Antigonos and three philosophers: the Peripatetic Cleodemos, the Stoic Deinomachos, and the Platonist Ion, whom Tychiades praises with ironic fulsomeness. Lucian sets the theme by making Tychiades interrupt the company in a discussion of amulets suitable for Eucrates' case; his mockery of them and his pleas for rational medicine launch the series of seven stories that forms the body of the work.

Already in this introductory discussion Lucian shows his exact knowledge of his material. Thus Cleodemos recommends an amulet made from the tooth of a shrew-mouse *(mugale)* gathered with the right hand and wrapped in a pouch of lion's skin. Deinomachos recommends rather the skin of a deer as a faster animal, "though the lion is brave, and its fat, right paw, and the straight tufts from its beard are very effective if you know how to use them with the spell appropriate to each."[5] The Elder Pliny devotes several books of the *Natural History* to the remedies derived from animals; teeth often appear, the magical power of mice is noted, and lions are recommended precisely for their fat and for the tufts beneath the muzzle; for gout Pliny advises an amulet made from the paw of a hare.[6] This knowledge is not surprising, since the use of amulets was ancient and widespread. Galen too rejected all such magical practices in medicine, echoing the rationalism of Lucian and providing yet another link between the two contemporaries.[7]

There follows a sequence of tales in which Eucrates and his friends try to persuade Tychiades to believe in the supernatural. Lucian artfully links one tale to another, leading the reader on until most of the well-known superstitions have been exposed. Thus the first, con-

4. Εὐκράτης ὁ πάνυ, *Philops.* 5; for Lucian's ironic use of ὁ πάνυ, below, Ch. 9 at n. 26.

5. *Philops.* 7–8.

6. Plin. *Nat.* 28.257–258, 30.21–22, 25 (teeth); 29.59 (mice: for shrew-mice, Keller, *Ant. Tierwelt* 1.16–17 and *P. Mag.* 4.2455); 28.89–90 (lions); 28.220 (hare's paw).

7. In general, Eckstein and Waszink, *RAC* 1 (1950) 397–411; Bonner, *Studies in Magical Amulets.* Galen: 11.792–793 Kühn, cf. Edelstein, *Ancient Medicine* 232–233.

cerning a man bitten on the foot by a snake, follows naturally from Eucrates' illness.[8] The first three speakers invoke notable magicians from Babylonia, the Hyperboreans, Palestine, and Arabia respectively.[9] The Palestinian, an exorciser of spirits *(daimones)*, leads naturally to the stories that follow, which in turn involve walking statues, visions of the underworld, and ghosts.[10] The second ghost story is told by the Pythagorean Arignotos, whom in accordance with Platonic tradition Lucian introduces as a late arrival. The effect of this device is both to add variety and also, because Arignotos immediately belies his august reputation and appearance, to make him the paradigm of philosophic credulity. Arignotos also provides the link to the last and most famous story, that of the Sorcerer's Apprentice; for though it is told by Eucrates, the Sorcerer turns out to be Arignotos' own teacher, the Egyptian Pancrates.[11]

As his discussion of amulets demonstrates, Lucian's knowledge of magical beliefs and practices is very exact. Thus in his first story the Babylonian magician rids a farm of reptiles by a spell which causes them to gather in a single place. After "one aged snake had not heard the summons," the magician sent a younger one to fetch it and then by breathing fire destroyed them all. A very similar story, which appears to be independent of Lucian, has been collected in the Tirol.[12] Lucian's magician from Palestine specializes in the exorcism of spirits from lunatics: "when he stands over them and asks how they entered the body, the patient himself stays silent but the demon answers, speaking Greek or a barbarian tongue according to his origins, and says how he entered the person." This passage enraged pious scholiasts, who saw it as yet another of Lucian's blasphemies. They might have spared their wrath, since it closely resembles tales told about other pagan wizards such as Apollonios of Tyana. Furthermore, according to the anti-Christian Celsus, Phoenicia and Palestine teemed with holy men.[13]

8. *Philops.* 11–12.

9. *Philops.* 11–12 (Babylonia), 13–14 (Hyperboreans), 16 (Palestine), 17 (Arabia).

10. *Philops.* 18–21 (statues), 22–25 (underworld), 27, 30–31 (ghosts).

11. *Philops.* 33–36. This story and its successive treatments by Goethe, Paul Dukas, and Walt Disney, are ignored in Robinson, *Lucian.*

12. *Philops.* 12. Cf. Radermacher, *RhM* 60 (1905) 315–316; id., *SAWW* 206, 4 (1927) 7–9; Nilsson, *Gesch. gr. Rel.* 2² 521–522.

13. *Philops.* 16. For the scholiast, presumably Arethas, 163 Rabe. Cf. *Ev. Marc.* 5.1–13; Philostr. *VA* 3.38; Or. *Cels.* 7.9 (with Chadwick's note); Betz, *Lukian u. das Neue Testament* 11–12; Thraede, *RAC* 7 (1966) 55–56.

Another anecdote that shows Lucian's precise knowledge of practices and beliefs concerns a curative statue. Eucrates claims that a bronze statue of the Corinthian general Pellichos has often cured him from fever. He points out the pieces of gold leaf with which he has adorned it in gratitude, and reports that when an African slave tried to steal offerings made to the statue, he had the mark of lashes on his body the next morning and died a few days later.[14] The belief in curative statues flourished as vigorously in the second century as the belief in magic.[15] Lucian elsewhere mentions how the statues of two athletes of the fifth century, Polydamas and Theagenes, cured fevers at Olympia and on Thasos, and his testimony is confirmed by Pausanias.[16] According to his Christian contemporary Athenagoras, statues of Peregrinus in Parion and of a certain Neryllinus in Alexandria Troas had the same power; that of Neryllinus received crowns and offerings of gold leaf, just as the statue of Pellichos did from Eucrates.[17] The punishment of the slave and his swift death are another borrowing from the common stock of folklore, as is shown by a similar tale in Petronius.[18]

As an illustration of Lucian's information the episode of the Sorcerer's Apprentice is of especial interest. The actual story has no exact parallel and may be his invention, but the Sorcerer is a real person. Eucrates, the narrator, describes him as "a man of Memphis, one of the sacred scribes, of marvellous wisdom, who knew all the learning of Egypt"; and Arignotos recognizes him as his own teacher, Pancrates.[19] The great magical papyrus in Paris cites a master of the art called "Pachrates," whose powers so impressed Hadrian that the emperor "ordered the prophet to receive a double allowance." In an Egyptian context "allowance" should denote the salary regularly paid to members of the Alexandrian Museum. It therefore seems clear that the magician of the papyrus is the "Pancrates" who so pleased Hadrian by a poem written in honor of Antinoos that the emperor enrolled him in this institution. The same person ought to be the Pancrates of Lucian, except that the satirist has altered the features

14. *Philops.* 18–20.

15. Nilsson, *Gesch. gr. Rel.* 2² 524–525.

16. *Deor. Conc.* 12; cf. Ch. 4 at n. 18.

17. Athenag. *Leg.* 26.3–4 (on which Jones, *CPh* 80 [1985] 40–45).

18. Petr. 63, esp. 7 (whip-marks), 10 (death). Cf. Schuster, *WS* 48 (1930) 168–171.

19. *Philops.* 34.

of the real Pancrates for his own purpose. The original can hardly have "spoken Greek unclearly," for instance, for the fragments of his poetry suggest a monotonous but accomplished composer. Pancrates thus becomes a privileged case of Lucian's methods: a real person of the previous generation, whom the author has maliciously cast as the leading character in his tallest tale.[20]

Lucian's information might be good and yet be thought derived from reading rather than observation.[21] Eucrates' story of the ghost of his dead wife is modeled on Herodotos.[22] Arignotos' tale of the ghost that he laid in a house at Corinth resembles down to small details one told by the Younger Pliny about a philosopher at Athens.[23] Eucrates recounts how, wandering in his woods one summer noon, he was met by a colossal figure of Hecate; he turned the iron ring on his finger so that the seal faced inwards, the goddess jumped into a chasm that opened beneath her, and Eucrates was able to see the whole underworld, including his late father. This story draws on the tale of Gyges' ring in Plato, but even more on an often-quoted passage from Heracleides Ponticos. A certain Empedotimos was "hunting with friends and at high noon had been left alone in a deserted spot"; here "he received an epiphany of Pluto and Persephone, was illuminated by the light that played about the gods, and with its aid saw all the truth about the soul from personal observation."[24]

Though some of Lucian's inventions are inspired by literature, allowance must also be made for oral sources—the tales told for small change in the streets and squares by professional storytellers and religious devotees,[25] or related on occasions similar to the one described by Lucian. Nor is it unlikely that such tales were told by

---

20. Papyrus: *P. Mag.* 4.2446–56, esp. διπλᾶ ὀψώνια ἐκέλευσεν αὐτῷ δίδοσθαι. Poet: Athen. 15.677 D = Heitsch, *Gr. Dichterfrag.* 1² 51. Generally, Preisendanz, *RE* 18, 1 (1942) 2071–74; Stoessl, *RE* 18, 2 (1949) 615–619; Heitsch, *Gr. Dichterfrag.* 51–58.

21. This has been supposed, for example, by Radermacher, *ARW* 21 (1922) 234; Bompaire, *Lucien écrivain* 457–458.

22. *Philops.* 27; Hdt. 5.92 η.

23. *Philops.* 30–31; Pliny, *Ep.* 7.27.7–11.

24. *Philops.* 22–24; Pl. *R.* 359D–360A (Gyges); Heraclid. Pont. fr. 93 Wehrli = Procl. *In R.* 2.119 Kroll. For the significance of iron (Gyges' ring is of gold), Mundle, *RAC* 6 (1966) 487.

25. On the former, Pliny, *Ep.* 2.20.1; on the latter (*aretalogoi*), Juv. 15.16; Reitzenstein, *Hellenist. Wundererz.* 8–12.

philosophers. Lucian gives prominence to two philosophers in his company, a Platonist and a Pythagorean: Ion begins the sequence of stories, and Arignotos claims to have laid a ghost and studied with an Egyptian sorcerer. It was in this period that Platonists and Pythagoreans began to import into philosophy the demonology and the oriental lore that were so strongly to color later Greek thought. Lucian's contemporary Numenios of Syrian Apamea is claimed for both schools, and Origen cites his work *On the Incorruptibility of the Soul* to show that serious philosophers among the Greeks, not only those who might be thought mere mythologizers, told tales of miracles.[26] Another Platonist of the same epoch is Apuleius of Madaura, who was accused of using the black arts himself, and whose *Metamorphoses* contain incidents of magic and the supernatural that often recall Lucian.[27] Apuleius leaves his reader uncertain whether to understand his story as fantasy or autobiography, and it is likely that other philosophers were similarly evasive. If Lucian takes malicious license in ascribing such tales to them directly, it was malice to which their own coyness laid them open.

Much of the *Lovers of Lies,* therefore, may be seen as a satire on contemporary philosophers. That it proceeds from Lucian's own interests, and not merely from his reading, is suggested by the similarity of his position here to that taken in other works. The name Tychiades, "Son of Chance," recalls Damis' eloquent description of the world as a pilotless ship in the *Tragic Zeus.*[28] And when at the close Tychiades exalts "truth and right reason in every matter, by the aid of which none of these empty and pointless lies will ever disturb us," that sounds much like Lucian's own tribute to Epicurus in the *Alexander.*[29]

The *Menippos* is a pendant to the *Icaromenippos,* and takes the Cynic philosopher down to the underworld. The basic idea was probably suggested by a work of the real Menippos, but the execution seems Lucian's own. The first part, concerned with Menippos' motives and preparation for his descent, gives Lucian the opportunity to parody

26. Or. *Cels.* 5.57 = fr. 29 des Places. On Numenios, Nilsson, *Gesch. gr. Rel.* 2² 414–415; Dillon, *Middle Platonists* 361–379. The Cronios to whom the *Peregrinus* is dedicated may be his pupil: Ch. 2 at n. 77.

27. Thus *Philops.* 14 and *Met.* 3.17–18 (love-spell); *Philops.* 17 and *Met.* 3.17 (nail from a cross); *Philops.* 34 and *Met.* 2.28 (Egyptian priest).

28. *I. trag.* 47–49; cf. also *Alex.* 36.

29. *Philops.* 40: *Alex.* 47, 61.

several types of narrative. Menippos describes how, seeking to find the right rule of conduct, he went from one philosopher to the next, but finding them at variance with one another, and often with their own principles, he decided to visit Babylon and consult one of the *magi*. Lucian is making fun, as he does elsewhere, of narrators who claim to have traveled far and wide before finding the truth, whether provided by Stoicism, Christianity, or some other creed.[30] The Babylonian magician leads Menippos first to the Euphrates, then to the Tigris, and performs a sacrifice; they sail downriver, the usual chasm appears, and Menippos is conducted below. The motif of Babylonian magic seems to point to the age of Lucian rather than of Menippos. This was the time when the so-called Chaldaean oracles were invented to buttress Greek philosophy with oriental wisdom. Lucian alludes elsewhere, for example when he makes Homer a Babylonian, to the growing preoccupation with the lore, real or invented, of Persia.[31] A work that similarly combines the themes of philosophical search and magical consultation is the curious Christian product called the *Romance of Pseudo-Clement*. Here the narrator describes how he sought to learn the fate of the soul after death, initially by frequenting the schools of the philosophers. Disappointed, he thought of consulting an Egyptian magician, but was led instead to Christianity.[32]

The *True Histories* seems more suited than the *Lovers of Lies* to count as the fantasy of a bookworm.[33] Lucian gives as his purpose to amuse "those concerned with literature" by offering them a change from their usual fare, something that combines the pleasures of wit and charm with that of recognition: "everything in it alludes not without mockery to certain of the ancient poets, historians, and philosophers, who included many monstrous and mythical things in their writings."[34] The only difference between Lucian and his models is that they told falsehoods in the guise of truth, whereas he truthfully

30. *Nec.* 3–6, cf. *Herm.* 15; on this motif, Nock, in *Pisciculi* 172 n. 41 (*Essays* 1.475 n. 41).

31. *Nec.* 6–9. Chaldaean oracles; the edition of des Places (1971); Dillon, *Middle Platonists* 392–396. Homer a Babylonian: *VH* 2.20, cf. below at n. 45.

32. [Clem.] *Rec.* 1.1–5 (ed. Rehm, *GCS* 51 [1965]), esp. 3.1 (philosophers), 5.1 (*magus*). Cf. Boll, *ZNTW* 17 (1916) 139–148, Perry, *Ancient Romances* 291–292.

33. Thus Bompaire, *Lucien écrivain* 672, "rêve de bibliothécaire, à la façon des chartistes d'A. France, qui voient, entre les pages de leurs in-folio, se lever de gracieuses silhouettes de légende . . ."

34. *VH* 1.1–2.

declares his entire tale false.[35] While the work is certainly a literary entertainment, it hardly shows Lucian lost in a world of legend or fantasy. Rather, it reveals his knowledge of the authors and types of literature then in vogue, and, like the *Lovers of Lies,* his gift for parody.

Lucian traces the origin of literary "lying" to Homer's Odysseus as he described his adventures to the Phaeacians; the same episode had also been seized on by Juvenal.[36] The two authors Lucian names as his main targets, however, are Ctesias of Cnidos and Iamboulos. Many other authors criticize Ctesias for his mendacity, but from the frequency of the criticisms it is clear how widely he continued to be read; the one known papyrus is of the second century, and shows his influence on writers of sentimental romance.[37] Iamboulos' fabulous account of his voyages into the Indian Ocean is otherwise only known from Diodoros, writing under Augustus, but though Lucian is the sole witness to his later survival, it would not surprise in this age of fiction.[38] Other authors whom Lucian mentions only in passing were established classics. When he places Herodotos on the Isle of the Damned, being punished with Ctesias as a liar, that recalls a criticism often made of the Father of History, notably by Plutarch.[39] Lucian mocks Plato's *Republic* both directly and through parody, just as he did in the *Lovers of Lies.*[40] By contrast, when as the narrator he sights Cloudcuckooland and salutes Aristophanes as "wise and truthful and wrongly disbelieved," he seems to suggest that he classed Aristophanes with honest fantasists like himself.[41]

An author now lost is sometimes thought to be one of Lucian's chief victims. After giving a long and complicated summary of the book of Antonius Diogenes, *The Wonders beyond Thule,* Photios declares that "it seems the root and source of Lucian's *True Histories* and Lucius' *Metamorphoses,*" the second being the lost Greek original of the *Lucius or the Ass* preserved among the works of Lucian. If

35. *VH* 1.4. This presumably explains the title *True Histories.*
36. *VH* 1.3; Juv. 15.13–26.
37. Jacoby, *FGrHist* 688 T 11 d, e (Plutarch), g (Arrian), F 45 d β (Aelian). Papyrus: *POxy.* 22.2330 = Jacoby, F 8 b.
38. On Iamboulos the most helpful discussion is still Rohde, *Gr. Roman*[3] 241–260; for Diodoros' use of him, D. S. 2.55–60.
39. *VH* 2.31. On Herodotos as a liar, Mayor on Juv. 10.174–175; Schmid-Stählin, *Gesch. gr. Litt.* 1.2.668 n. 3.
40. *VH* 2.17, 29–31; cf. the scholiast on *VH* 1.4, p. 18 Rabe.
41. *VH* 1.29.

Photios is referring to content, his observation can hardly be correct, since the *True Histories* and the lost *Metamorphoses* must have been in this respect entirely different. If he means only that Diogenes inspired the other two authors, then his judgment must be an educated guess. Diogenes, who may have flourished in the first century, continued to be read in later antiquity, and may well have been one of the authors Lucian had in mind, but the *Wonders beyond Thule* can scarcely have been a major source of the *True Histories*.[42]

Besides Diogenes Lucian must have been aware of the fiction being produced in his own time. The chronology of the ancient novel is still far from settled, but like Apuleius in Latin some, at least, of the Greek novelists were active in Lucian's day. The best example is Iamblichos, who claimed to have foretold both the outbreak and the conclusion of Lucius Verus' Parthian War: his *Babyloniaca* was full of the kind of magic derided by Lucian in the *Lovers of Lies*.[43] In general, however, the *True Histories* are aimed rather at romances of travel than of love. Here too Lucian may be thinking of contemporary as well as earlier literature, for the curiosity of the period extended not only to magic and the afterlife but also to the remote and fabulous. Philostratos' *Life of Apollonios of Tyana* has much that recalls the *True Histories,* both in the incidents narrated and in the manner of the narrator: inscriptions set up by gods, meals served by supernatural waiters, and impudent claims to confirm or refute the classics.[44]

Though much of Lucian's humor is literary, the work is not thereby made other-worldly or scholastic. In a society permeated with culture, matters of literature can also be matters of urgent interest. This is most clearly shown by his treatment of Homer and Homeric motifs in the episode of the Blessed Isles. Thus when the narrator asks Homer where he was born, a question "still investigated among us

42. Phot. *Bibl.* cod. 166, 2.140–149 Henry (the comment on Lucian is on p. 148); the scholion on *VH* 2.12 (p. 21 Rabe) need not refer exclusively to Diogenes. A full discussion of the evidence for Diogenes in Rohde, *Gr. Roman*³ 269–309; cf. Anderson, *Studies* 1–7. The papyri attributed to him, *PSI* 10.1177 (Pack² 95) and *POxy.* 42.3012, are of the late second or early third century; he is cited by Porph. *V. Pyth.* 10, 32.

43. For Iamblichos, again there is a full discussion in Rohde, *Gr. Roman*³ 388–409; edition by E. Habrich (Teubner, 1960). For Photios' summary, *Bibl.* cod. 94 (2.34–48 Henry). On the Parthian War: pp. 32–34 Habrich = p. 40 Henry.

44. Inscriptions of Dionysos: *VH* 1.7, Philostr. *VA* 2.9. Waiters: *VH* 2.14, Philostr. *VA* 3.27. Homer or his critics confirmed or refuted: *VH* 1.17, 2.20, 2.32; cf. Philostr. *VA* 2.17 (Nearchos confirmed: *FGrHist* 133 F 12), 3.45 (Ctesias implicitly refuted: *FGrHist* 688 F 45 d).

down to our own day," the poet replies that he is not from Chios, Smyrna, or Colophon, but from Babylon. The subject of Homer's birthplace was not merely a learned controversy, but involved the prestige of many cities. Aelius Aristides, for example, vaunts the claims of Smyrna, which are also represented on its coins. Lucian's choice of Babylon is more than a malicious dig at famous cities of the province of Asia, since the tradition that Homer was Babylonian or Egyptian is found in other late authors and reflects the growing interest in astrology and magic.[45] Lucian's next question concerns the lines athetized by Homer's critics: when the poet claims to have written them all, Lucian ironically mocks "the grammarians of the school of Zenodotos and Aristarchos." Here again, despite the Hellenistic refrences, Lucian is not lost in the past. Epigrammatists of the imperial period still joke about "the puppies of Zenodotos" and "the bookworms of Aristarchos' tribe." The business of interpolating Homer continued to flourish: a typical product is an invocation of the divinities of Egypt spoken by Odysseus in the underworld, and preserved only in one fortunate library.[46] Another incident in the Blessed Isles is the contest regularly held there under the name of *Thanatousia.* Using language borrowed from the accounts of actual contests, Lucian draws his competitors from Homer and from real life. In wrestling, Capros "the second after Heracles" defeats Odysseus: this is a real athlete, victorious at the Olympics in 212 B.C., and the title refers to his double victory in boxing and the pancration. In boxing, there is a draw between the Homeric Epeios and Areios the Egyptian "who is buried in Corinth": this athlete with his typically Egyptian name must also be a real person, probably of the imperial period.[47]

45. *VH* 2.20. On the various birthplaces of Homer, Raddatz, *RE* 8 (1913) 2194–99; for cities disputing the matter in the imperial period, Robert, *Ét. anat.* 262–265; *Monnaies grecques* 125–127; *Asie Mineure* 416–419. For Smyrna's claims, Aristid. *Or.* 17.8, 15, 21.8, 33.29, cf. Luc. *Pro Imag.* 24, and generally Cadoux, *Ancient Smyrna* 209–212; for the coins, besides the catalogs, Heyman in *Studia Paulo Naster oblata* 1.161–174, with the corrections of Klose, *GNS* 34 (1984) 1–3. Homer Babylonian or Egyptian: Raddatz, 2197–98, and also next n.

46. Interpolations: *VH* 2.20. Epigrammatists: Phil. *AP* 11.321, 347 = Gow and Page, *Garland of Philip,* Philip nos. 60, 61. Invocation: *POxy.* 3.412 (Julius Africanus), cf. Robert, *Hellenica* 1.145.

47. *VH* 2.22; see the exposition in Robert, *Asie Mineure* 427–432. It is unlucky that the correction Κάπρος, made by Palmerius and vindicated by Forbes in *AJPh* 60 (1939) 473–474 (Robert, 428), is ignored by Macleod in the Oxford text, who prints Gronovius' Κάρανος.

The *Toxaris* differs completely from the works so far considered. A Greek and a Scythian tell a series of supposedly true stories in order to prove the superiority of their respective races in their conception of friendship. Though the work has been read as a comic fantasy,[48] it seems rather to be a fusion of two literary types, both earnest if not profound. One is illustrated by Plutarch's essay on the virtues of women, a series of tales showing that women can be as courageous as men.[49] The other is the Greek romance, which often employs the theme of male comradeship.

Each of the two speakers, Mnesippos the Athenian and Toxaris the Scythian, tells five tales, all allegedly drawn from the recent past.[50] Those of Mnesippos often recall the sentimental romance of novelists like Chariton, except that they are set in the Roman Empire and suffused in a classical mist. At the end of his first story, a wealthy Ephesian is brought by the "generals" before the "harmost" of Asia, who "sends him up to the great king: and not long after he was sent down to Gyaros, an island of the Cyclades, sentenced to perpetual exile there by the king." Lucian refers to Roman institutions, but in the manner of other Greek authors veils them in classical terminology: though "generals" are still found in Roman Ephesos, the Roman proconsul is assimilated to the governors sent out by classical Sparta, and the emperor to the king of Persia.[51] Mnesippos' last story concerns two young Athenians, Demetrios of Sounion and Antiphilos of Alopeke, who sail together to Egypt, where Demetrios studies Cynicism under "that well known Rhodian sophist," while Antiphilos learns medicine.[52] Although none of these persons need be presumed real, Alexandria was a well-known center both for Cynicism and for medicine.[53]

48. This aspect is emphasized by Bompaire, *Lucien écrivain* 682–687, following Hirzel.

49. Plut. *Mor.* 242E–263C.

50. *Tox.* 10.

51. *Tox.* 12–18. "Generals": Delz, *Lukians Kenntnis* 74; Knibbe, *RE* Suppl. 12 (1970) 274. "Harmosts": LSJ cite App. *BC* 4.7. Persia: Bowie, *P&P* 46 (1970) 33 n. 95 (*Studies in Ancient Society* 201 n. 95); Jones, *Plutarch* 113 n. 22, 114 n. 27.

52. Delz, *Lukians Kenntnis* 11, refers to an actual Demetrios of Sounion in *IG* 2² 2127 ll. 11–12 (father of two ephebes ca. 200); but Demetrios is the commonest of Greek names, and since Lucian's character is a student of Cynicism the name should rather derive from the famous Cynic of the first century.

53. Cynicism in Alexandria: Jones, *Dio Chrysostom* 174 n. 82 (cf. Luc. *Peregr.* 17). Medicine: Robert, *RPh* 13 (1939) 173 n. 3 (*OMS* 2.1326); id., *Hellenica* 2.105 n. 1; Fraser, *Ptolemaic Alexandria* 338–376.

After a series of adventures, which again involve the "harmost" of the province, Demetrios resolves to spend the rest of his life among the Brahmins of India. This last detail sounds fictional, and yet a young student in Alexandria could well have taken advantage of its contacts with India to sail there, and the career of Peregrinus shows the interest of Cynics in Indian wisdom.[54]

Of the five tales told by the Scythian Toxaris the first three move Mnesippos to amused incredulity. The world they depict seems vague and fabulous, and the third of them names two Bosporan kings, Leucanor and Eubiotos, who never existed.[55] It is all the more striking that a fragmentary Greek novel is apparently set in Scythia and has a barbarian chieftain again called "Eubiotos."[56] Toxaris' fourth story is different: he claims to have been a participant, and it is set in the Greek world, at the city of Amastris, which Lucian visited in about 165.[57] Here Toxaris and his friend Sisinnes are robbed of all they have, and Sisinnes enrolls as a gladiator. Challenged to fight for a reward of ten thousand drachmas, he wins and saves them both from destitution. Here, as in the stories of Mnesippos, there is a fusion of the romantic and the realistic. Fantasies of devoted friendship and of desperate combat mingle with the actual conduct of gladiatorial shows in the Greek east. Amastris is a plausible setting for two visitors from northern Pontos, and a Scythian might have had the probably Iranian name "Sisinnes."[58]

The *Toxaris* remains an oddity among Lucian's works. It might be regarded as parody or pastiche in the manner of the *True Histories,* but the tone does not favor this easy solution. It is better to accept the oddity, and to admit that Lucian is sometimes untypical and ex-

54. Cf. the similar story of a student in Alexandria who visited India, *Alex.* 44; note also Plutarch's friend Cleombrotos who sailed "far into the Red Sea" to satisfy his scholarly curiosity, *De Def. Orac.* 410 A–B.

55. *Tox.* 39–55, esp. 44, 54. On the historical setting, Rostovtzeff, *Skythien u. der Bosporus* 96–99; Gajdukevic, *Bosporanische Reich* 84–85.

56. *PSI* 8.981 (Pack[2] 2628). Rostovtzeff, *Skythien u. der Bosporus* 98–99, supposed the connection between the papyrus and this tale in Lucian very close, but see Zimmerman, *PhW* 1935, 1211–16.

57. *Tox.* 57–60; for Lucian's visit, *Alex.* 57.

58. For real and unreal elements in Lucian's references to gladiatorial practice, Robert, *Gladiateurs* 24, 188, 287, 320–321. For contacts between Amastris and northern Pontos, Robert, *Asie Mineure* 417 n. 125 (cf. Luc. *Alex.* 57). Sisinnes: Zgusta, *Kleinasiatische Personennamen* 467–469; for Iranian names in southern Pontos, Zgusta, *Personennamen gr. Städte der nordl. Schwarzmeerküste,* esp. 20–24.

perimental. Even so, the *Toxaris* does not expose its author to the charge of inconsistency. The mildly humorous tone with which Mnesippos listens to Toxaris shows that Lucian does not expect to be read in the spirit of an Iamblichos. Still less does he tell tales of the supernatural kind mocked in the *Lovers of Lies* and the *True Histories*. Lucian disliked "lies" but not elegant or beguiling fiction.

6 The Writing of History

LUCIAN'S ESSAY *On Writing History* is the only work explicitly devoted to the subject to have survived from antiquity, and it enjoyed high prestige in the revival of learning. Though partly eclipsed by the decline of his reputation in the late nineteenth century, it has awakened recent interest as a source for ancient historiography and even, so scanty are the materials, for the events of Lucius Verus' Parthian War.[1] Yet this work like others, so it may be argued, has been injured by a tendency to underrate Lucian's preciseness of observation and report.

The usual title, which is perhaps not the author's, is misleading. Though he discusses general principles of historiography, he is concerned with one event in particular, the Parthian War of Marcus and Lucius, which began soon after their accession and ended in 166. He begins with an anecdote that comments ironically on the large number of historians created by "the present circumstances, the war with the barbarians, the loss in Armenia, and the continuous victories." All his instances of modern historiography are taken from historians of the same war; and when he gives positive advice, it is again the Parthian War that he has in mind. The addressee, Philo, is perhaps a prospective historian of the same conflict.[2]

---

1. Apart from shorter or partial studies, there are Avenarius, *Lukians Schrift zur Geschichtschreibung,* and the much less satisfactory commentary of Homeyer, *Lukian: Geschichte.*

2. Anecdote: *Hist. conscr.* 2. Positive advice: ibid. 49. Philo: note the remark, ibid. 5, "You know yourself, my friend, how this [history] is not something easily managed or such as to be composed without labor." There seems no reason to suppose that the work is aimed, in praise or blame, at Arrian (as Vidal-Naquet, *Flavius Arrien* 368–369, following others).

The work can be dated precisely. At the time of writing, the legate Avidius Cassius had carried the offensive across the Tigris into Media, a maneuver that ended the war and took place in 166. Since Lucian refers to the triumph which was to occur in October of the same year as an event still in the future, he must have written the essay in the middle of 166, perhaps in some haste.[3] He had already heard historians reciting their accounts of the war in Ionia and more recently at Corinth, where it is possible that he wrote or at least recited his own work. Visits to Corinth and Ionia in 165 and 166 cohere with what is known of Lucian's movements in these years and may be significant for the interpretation of his essay.[4]

It has been supposed that the date suggested by the text is fictitious and that the work was really written after the close of the war, between about 166 and 168,[5] but Lucian's credit can stand. He mentions a great plague in Nisibis which "had had the goodness" to remain in the territory of Parthia. The plague which was to devastate the Roman Empire in the second half of the decade is said to have been first contracted by the Romans further south at Seleuceia, and then carried westward by the returning troops of Lucius Verus. Even if Lucian is referring to a different outbreak, he could hardly have written in this tone when the plague was at its height; his adoptive city of Athens was so devastated that in three of the five years between 167 and 172 it had no eponymous archon.[6] Elsewhere in the essay he claims that every nation had been subjugated and none would now dare to make war on Rome: in late 166 or early 167 there began a series of conflicts on the Danube which were to prove graver even than the war with Parthia.[7]

Just as Lucian's ostensible date has been suspected, so also have

3. Avidius Cassius: *Hist. conscr.* 30, 31 (cf. Birley, *Marcus Aurelius* 195; Alföldy, *Senatorenstand* 181–182; Astarita, *Avidio Cassio* 43–52). Triumph: *Hist. conscr.* 31 (cf. Birley, 199 n. 1). Thus Stein in *Strena Buliciana* 264–265.

4. Ionia ἔναγκος: *Hist. conscr.* 14. Corinth or Achaea πρῴην: *Hist. conscr.* 14, 17, cf. 29. See further Appendix A.

5. Thus Homeyer, *Lukian: Geschichte* 11–12, invoking "fingierte Aktualität."

6. Plague: *Hist. conscr.* 15 (most of the geographical details are of course borrowed from Thuc. 2.48.1). On the chronology and the severity of the plague, Gilliam, *AJPh* 82 (1961) 225–251, esp. 229–230; Birley, *Marcus Aurelius* 202–205. Athens: Rotroff, *Hesperia* 44 (1975) 408; Ameling, *Herodes Atticus* 2.195 (discussing *SEG* 29.127 l. 61).

7. *Hist. conscr.* 5. For the outbreak of the Danubian Wars, Birley, *Marcus Aurelius* 201–202, 205, 211–216.

his depictions of contemporary historians, the accusation being that their errors or absurdities are so gross that they seem more like caricatures than real people.[8] Lucian claims to take his examples from recitations which he had attended personally and solemnly assures the reader of his veracity.[9] But though he avoids invention, he is free to choose the most grotesque targets that he could find, while modern readers are used to works that have survived the sifting of ancient and medieval critics. In some instances, moreover, history helps to verify his claim to truth.

Lucian mocks the first of his historians for beginning with an invocation to the Muses and then comparing Lucius Verus to Achilles and the king of Parthia with Thersites.[10] This conforms with the general worship of Homer, of which Lucian himself is a conspicuous example, but is illustrated even further by the surviving literature of the Parthian War. Polyaenos wrote, or rather compiled, his *Stratagems* to benefit Marcus and Lucius at the outset of the war by giving them a large stock of ancient exemplars. He begins his first book by showing that Homer too had included stratagems in his poems.[11] Fronto's *Principles of History,* largely written to praise Lucius' conduct of the war, compares Lucius to Achilles and invokes the example of Homer.[12]

Lucian's second victim has a different disease: the excessive or servile imitation of classic exemplars. This one lifted whole sentences from Thucydides and another mentioned later did so from Herodotos.[13] It is not easy to find analogies to such open plagiarism in the extant literature of the epoch, but it can often be surmised. In the previous generation a certain Cephalio wrote a history in Ionic and named each of his nine books after the Muses.[14] The fad for Herod-

8. Thus Hall talks of "parodic descriptions" and "amusing caricatures" (*Lucian's Satire* 314, 316, cf. 320).

9. *Hist. conscr.* 14. Homeyer ad loc. compares *VH* 1.4: but there Lucian is affirming the falsity of his account.

10. *Hist. conscr.* 14.

11. Polyaen. 1. praef. 2–13. For Polyaenos' date and works, Schmid-Stählin, *Gesch. gr. Litt.* 2.2.754–755; on his methods, Stadter, *Plutarch's Historical Methods* 13–29.

12. Fronto, *Princ. Hist.* 1. There is of course no reason to think that Lucian has Fronto in mind: rightly, Cova, *I principia historiae* 103–110, Hall, *Lucian's Satire* 319–321.

13. Thucydides: *Hist. conscr.* 15 (cf. 19, 24, 26). Herodotos: ibid. 18.

14. *FGrHist* 93: the chief evidence is the *Suda* (K 1449 = T 1), ἔγραψε παντοδαπὰς ἱστορίας ἐν βιβλίοις θ', ἅτινα ἐπιγράφει Μούσας, Ἰάδι διαλέκτῳ. Cf. Bowie, *P&P* 46 (1970) 12–13 (*Studies in Ancient Society* 177).

otos in Lucian's day is illustrated by his own pastiche in the essay *On the Syrian Goddess*. Arrian shows how far even moderate imitation could go. He models his *Discourses of Epictetos* and *Anabasis* on works of Xenophon, and even uses the name "Xenophon" for himself, clearly in tribute to his exemplar rather than by birthright.[15] This appropriation of names has a parallel in a Roman who may have been a historian of the Parthian War. Lucius Verus sent a copy of his war dispatches to Fronto by means of "our Sallust, at present Fulvianus": it looks as if this man, not known outside the pages of Fronto, was preparing to model a history of the war on the Roman Thucydides, Sallust, and like Arrian to borrow his author's name as well as his methods.[16]

When, therefore, Lucian mocks the imitativeness of contemporary historians, he need not be supposed to exaggerate, even if he has picked on extremes, and the same may be said of other mannerisms. One historian digressed at length to tell about a Moorish cavalryman in the war who, while wandering among mountains, had met with two Syrians, of whom one had visited Mauretania when his brother was serving there as a soldier. The historical basis for this account is provided by the many inscriptions of Syrian auxiliaries stationed in Mauretania in the second century, so that the romantic superstructure can reasonably be ascribed to the anonymous historian and not to Lucian.[17] Another historian whom he derides had written about the future; "he has already founded a city in Mesopotamia, of the greatest size and beauty, but is still hesitating and debating whether to call it Nicaea from the victory (*nike*) or Homonoia (Concord) or Eirenias (Peace City)." The phrase "of the greatest size and beauty," is borrowed from the customary praises of imperial cities, whose love of titles Lucian is probably mocking. The first of the three names has its analogue in the various Nicopoleis founded by Roman generals and emperors, and the third in the Eirenopolis founded by Nero in

15. See Stadter, *Arrian*, esp. 27–28, 37, 54. Stadter's argument that "Xenophon" was a given name, *GRBS* 8 (1967) 155–161 and *Arrian* 2, is not convincing.

16. Fronto (L. Verus), *Ad Verum* 2.3.1. Thus Stein, *RE* 7 (1910) 228, who conjectures that he was *ab epistulis*. The "Thucydides" who restored the Armenian king Sohaemos, perhaps in 172, may be a Greek historian of the Parthian War: Cass. Dio 71.3 (*Suda* μ 232), cf. Stein, *RE* 6 A (1936) 627 no. 5.

17. *Hist. conscr.* 28, where Homeyer compares Arrian's account (*Ind.* 33) of the sailors of Nearchos who wandered away from the fleet. For Lucian's story and its historical context, Euzennat, *AntAfr* 5 (1971) 177–178, Robert, *Asie Mineure* 422.

level Cilicia. Cilicia, close to Lucian's own Commagene, also provides the key to the name Concord. The official propaganda of the Parthian War stresses the concord of the imperial brothers in their defense of the empire, and following the lead of the imperial mint several cities of Cilicia issued coins showing the two emperors clasping hands and with the legend *Concord of the Augusti (Homonoia Sebaston)*.[18] The anticipation of future events can also be understood in a society where writers used every means possible to capture the attention of the ruling house. Under Tiberius, for example, a poet unwisely mourned the death of the emperor's son Drusus two years before it occurred, hoping for all the greater reward if the event proved him right.[19]

One feature of Lucian's account has often aroused suspicion. He leaves most of his historians anonymous, and discussing one "wise man" deliberately withholds his name.[20] He identifies four, however, not gratuitously but in citing their opening words. The first is one of the slavish imitators of Thucydides, Crepereius Calpurnianus of Pompeiopolis; this person allegedly lifted his opening sentence from his model, substituting only his own grotesque nomenclature for that of Thucydides and "Parthians and Romans" for "Lacedaemonians and Athenians." The Pompeiopolis in question is almost always taken to be the city of Paphlagonia, and yet there is another city of the name in Cilicia, which received a visit from Lucius Verus on his way to the Parthian war front in 163 and is one of the several cities of the region to proclaim on its coinage the concord of Marcus and Lucius. Crepereius, it may be inferred, is a real person, whose history reflected the attachment of his city to the emperor and the general rejoicing in his victory.[21]

The next historian named by Lucian is a "Callimorphos, doctor of the *ala* (squadron) of javelin-bearers." This person in his preface justified the link between medicine and history with arguments drawn from mythology, and though he began in Ionic soon lapsed into Attic except for a few words like *ietrike* ("medicine").[22] It has been supposed, even by those who defend his existence, that the name Callimorphos ("Fair-figure") is unattested, but it is not, even though

18. *Hist. conscr.* 31. For this explanation of the chapter, Robert, *Asie Mineure* 423–426.

19. Tac. *Ann.* 3.49.

20. *Hist. conscr.* 17.

21. *Hist. conscr.* 15. For this argument, Appendix A.

22. *Hist. conscr.* 16 (*FGrHist* 210), with Cichorius' palmary emendation of ἕκτης to εἴλης, *RE* 1 (1893) 1239–40: ignored by all subsequent editors.

Lucian evidently cites it for malice.²³ Callimorphos' unit is presumably the *ala prima Ulpia contariorum,* which was usually stationed in upper Moesia and must have been called to the Parthian front.²⁴ Other doctors also wrote military history. Trajan's Dacian Wars were described by his doctor Statilius Crito, and two centuries later Oribasios, who held the same position with Julian, wrote a memoir with many details about the fateful Persian expedition.²⁵ Even Lucian's jibe about Callimorphos' uncertain Ionic rings true, since contemporary inscriptions of Greek doctors, many of them like Callimorphos attached to Roman units, show a similar striving for the dialect of Hippocrates.²⁶

Lucian's third historian has a name that is again included for amusement and misleading for modern readers, "Antiochianos the son of Apollo, sacred victor." "Antiochianos" is banal, but "Apollo" as a personal name is a curiosity that begins to be found in the imperial period, while his title, attested in scores of documents, indicates that he had won in one of the international contests officially recognized as "sacred." Whether Antiochianos had really won a long-distance race in the boys' category, as Lucian claims, or whether this is a dry allusion to his prolixity cannot now be judged.²⁷

The last of Lucian's named historians is a "Demetrios of Sagalassos": although his name is not remarkable, his city included among its titles "friend and ally of the Romans," and one of its sons might well have written a history of Lucius' Parthian victories.²⁸

23. For the name, Pape-Benseler cite *CIG* 2.2810, 2848 (Aphrodisias), 3.5726 (Catania): add Robert, *Gladiateurs* 152 no. 119, 301 (Laodiceia on the Lycos).

24. On this *ala,* Cichorius (n. 22): for doctors with auxiliary units, Cheesman, *Roman Auxilia* 43–44.

25. For Crito, references in Jones, *Dio Chrysostom* 111, 116, 123: he is adduced in this context by Baldwin, *Studies* 83. Oribasios: Bowersock, *Julian,* esp. 8, 115–117.

26. Robert, *RPh* 13 (1939) 166–172 (*OMS* 2.1319–25); *Bull.* 1970.667. The lapses from Ionic in the extracts from Cephalio given by Syncellos (*FGrHist* 93 F 1) may not go back to the author.

27. *Hist. conscr.* 30 (*FGrHist* 207). For "Apollo" as a personal name, e.g., *IG* 2² no. 1817 1. 30 (Athens); *MAMA* 5.141 (Dorylaion); Moretti, *IGUR* 2.371 (Rome); for Rome, also Solin, *Gr. Personennamen in Rom* 1.282. In the text of Lucian, τοῦ Ἀπόλλωνος is usually taken together with the following ἱερονίκου, "A., sacred victor of Apollo": but this phrase seems to lack all parallel.

28. *Hist. conscr.* 32 (*FGrHist* 209). For the title in an inscription of Antoninus Pius, Lanckoroński, *Städte Pamphyliens* 2 no. 188 (*IGR* 3.348); it does not appear on coins until the third century.

Consideration of the historical circumstances therefore tends to vindicate Lucian's credit, but it also supplies a context for his essay. Lucius' Parthian victories, though the record of them is now scanty, had great public resonance. The emperors took the titles of *Armeniacus, Parthicus,* and *Medicus,* and coins, inscriptions, and monuments express the general rejoicing.[29] Among the monuments the most conspicuous that survives is one from a city that Lucian knew well, Ephesos. This is the great Parthian monument of Lucius, perhaps begun not long after the war but completed only after his death. Unlike the coins celebrating the concord of Marcus and Lucius, here all attention is on the latter. In the carved reliefs he is shown as a child being adopted by Antoninus Pius; as emperor he overcomes the Parthians in furious battle; and finally he is escorted to heaven to sit among the immortals.[30]

Literature was bound to be enrolled in the campaign of glorification. The same had happened with Trajan's Dacian War sixty years before, when the emperor led the way with his own *Commentarii.*[31] In the first half of 166, Lucius wrote to Fronto pressing him to compose a worthy history of the war, perhaps taking Thucydides as his model. The emperor's former tutor was plied with copies of dispatches and with summary accounts written by the chief generals, to which Lucius promised to add his own.[32] Fronto quickly wrote a prospectus, the *Principles of History,* but seems never to have produced the desired work. It has been suggested that the *Principles* constitutes a subtle refusal of the task, the best Fronto wished or was able to contribute to the literary festival.[33] Polyaenos' *Stratagems,* written some years before, betray a similar attitude. Polyaenos does not "wish to miss his dues on the present occasion," and undertakes when the right time comes to praise the emperors' successes at length. This promise, like similar ones made by other imperial authors, seems never to have

29. For a survey, Stein, *RE* 3 (1899) 1849.

30. For recent discussion, establishing beyond doubt a date in the reign of Marcus, Alföldi-Rosenbaum, *Phoenix* 25 (1971) 182–185; Oberleitner in *Funde aus Ephesos* 66–94, esp. 92–93. For an inscription referring to the purchase of land for this monument, *Bull.* 1977.417 no. 2 (*I. Ephesos* 3.721).

31. Jones, *Dio Chrysostom* 123.

32. Fronto (L. Verus), *Ad Verum* 2.3.1–2. On the date, Champlin, *JRS* 64 (1974) 148.

33. Cogently argued by Cova, *I principia historiae* 57–61.

been fulfilled, and Polyaenos perhaps intended like Fronto to limit his offering to what lay within his powers.[34]

In writing to Fronto, Lucius urged him to linger on the causes of the war and the Roman losses sustained before his own arrival, since that would give the reader a better estimation of the emperor's achievement. The *Principles of History* are an indirect encomium of Lucius. Fronto compares his Parthian successes favorably with those of Trajan. The one major disaster, the defeat of Sedatius Severianus at Elegeia, he claims, occurred when Lucius had not left Rome, whereas Trajan suffered a similar setback at the front; and Trajan's famous dictum about bread and circuses justified Lucius' summoning pantomimes *(histriones)* from Rome to Antioch.[35] Lucian's own work dwells on the defeat of Severianus, and also mentions with proper brevity the successes achieved by the generals fighting under Lucius, the capture of Artaxata by Statius Priscus, the successful siege of Dura-Europos, the defeat of the Parthian general Chosroes, and in particular the final advance of Avidius Cassius.[36] Just as Fronto prefers the medium of an encomiastic letter to the actual task of historiography,[37] so Lucian chose a vehicle in which he could both exalt the emperor's successes in elegant style and indulge his own taste for satire.

The work may also be seen in the context of the author's life and writings. Visiting Achaea and Ionia in 165 and 166, he can hardly have failed to encounter part of the returning troops and probably their commander. Much less is known of Lucius' homeward route than of his outward one, but he seems likely to have revisited Ephesos and if so Achaea as well. Ephesos is known to have received several visits from the emperor in these years; part of the returning army passed through it; and the city celebrated the victory lavishly, both by holding victory contests *(epineikia)* and erecting the great altar.[38]

34. Polyaen. 1 pref. 1, οὐκ ἀσύμβολος . . . γενέσθαι βούλομαι (cf. Luc. *Hist. conscr.* 4, ὡς μὴ μόνος ἄφωνος εἴην), 6 pref. (projected history). For such promises in imperial writers, Ogilvie and Richmond on Tac. *Agr.* 3.3.

35. Fronto (L. Verus), *Ad Verum* 2.3.2 *(circa causas et initia belli diu commoraberis, et etiam ea quae nobis absentibus male gesta sunt)*; *Princ. Hist.* 3, 4, 7, 16 (Trajan), 17 (Severianus), 18 *(histriones)*.

36. *Hist. conscr.* 2, 15, 25–26 (Severianus), 20 (Priscus), 24, 28 (Dura-Europos), 19 ("Osrhoes"), 31 (Cassius).

37. Cf. the Younger Pliny's letter to an aspiring poet of Trajan's Dacian Wars, *Ep.* 8.4.

38. Appendix A.

Ephesos in 165 and 166 must have been the scene of recitations exactly like those which Lucian claims to have heard in Ionia.[39] It is also possible that he published his essay in Corinth while the emperor was visiting the city on his way home.[40]

Lucian's treatises entitled *Portraits* and *On the Dance*, so it may be supposed, celebrate two of Lucius Verus' avocations, his mistress Pantheia and the art of pantomime, and were written during the emperor's stay in Antioch.[41] The essay *On Writing History* belongs in the company of these artful and indirect flatteries. In this work, however, Lucian's motive was not merely the desire to draw attention and favor. His ancestral city was from its situation involved in the course and outcome of the war. With amused indignation he mentions how one historian had located it in Mesopotamia, and the outcome must have created the same feelings of joyful security there as in the cities of Cilicia further from the front.[42] The treatise *On Writing History*, which might rather be called *On Writing a Worthy History of the Recent Parthian War*, joins several threads in its author's career: his origins in Commagene, his rhetorical training,[43] his satire of contemporary foibles, and his association with Lucius Verus.

39. Note the patriotic vanity of a historian from Miletos, *Hist. conscr.* 14.
40. Appendix A.
41. Below, Ch. 7.
42. *Hist. conscr.* 24; thus Robert, *Asie Mineure* 426.
43. This aspect is emphasized by Avenarius, *Lukians Schrift zur Geschichtschreibung* 165–178.

7 The Court of Lucius Verus

IN 163 Lucius Verus arrived in Syrian Antioch, and was to spend most of the next three years there as the commander-in-chief of the Parthian War. The ancient sources tend to ascribe his military successes to his generals, whose emperor frittered away his time in the pursuit of pleasure. For exercise he hunted or trained in gladiatorial armor, for amusement he dined, played at dice, or went to the theater to watch his beloved "pantomimes" and to display the beauty of Pantheia, his mistress from Smyrna. These traditions are no doubt amplified to heighten the contrast between the frivolous Lucius and the austere Marcus, but even the panegyrist Fronto was compelled to justify Lucius' summoning of pantomimes to the war front, and it was not for nothing that the emperor died of apoplexy at forty.[1]

Three of Lucian's works are usually connected with Lucius' sojourn in Antioch, and if that is right, they must be dated either in 163, when the emperor arrived there, or in 164, when Lucian appears to have left it. The longest and most significant of these works is his defense of pantomime, the treatise *On the Dance* of which one passage seems to envisage an Antiochene audience.[2] Two slight but elegant pieces form a balanced pair and praise the beauty of Pantheia, the *Portraits* and the *Defense of the Portraits*. All three reveal a Lucian apparently unlike the one often encountered in his works: discreet,

1. Lucius' pursuits in Antioch: HA *Marcus* 8.12, *Lucius* 4.4–6, 7.1, 7.10, 8.10–11. Cf. Stein, *RE* 3 (1899) 1855–57; Downey, *History of Antioch* 226–227; Barnes, *JRS* 57 (1967) 71. Fronto: *Princ. Hist.* 18: Lucius' death: HA *Lucius* 9.11, cf. Stein, *RE* 3 (1899) 1834.

2. *Salt.* 76, cf. Robertson, *Essays Ridgeway* 184; Robert, *Hermes* 65 (1930) 121–122 (*OMS* 1.669–670).

courteous, and learned. The *Dance* has fallen under particular suspicion, since its author is not blindly attached to the classics and opposed to novelty, but as with other works athetized because they did not fit prior assumptions about Lucian, vindication has come from the social and historical context.[3]

"Dance" is the polite term for an art whose executants were more vulgarly known as "pantomimes" or in Latin "actors" *(histriones)*. It went back to the classical age but reached its full development only under the Roman emperors. A chief performer, usually male, would mime familiar stories, most of which were drawn from classical tragedy. He wore a special mask with closed mouth (a different one with each role), and ostentatious clothes of which the most expressive was his cloak. Though he brought the whole body into play, the arms and hands were of conspicuous importance. A mixed chorus supplied the words, while the music came from an orchestra with wind- and string-instruments, percussion, and a rhythm section in which the players *(podarii, scabillarii)* wore special shoes fitted with clappers *(kroupezia)*. For the ancients this art represented a fusion of dance and drama; modern eyes and ears might variously have been reminded of mime, ballet, or disco-dancing.[4]

Though a form of pantomime was already known to Xenophon, it began to flourish in the Hellenistic period, when it became established in the two great capitals of the Greek east, Antioch and Alexandria. The decisive steps of making the chief dancer mute and of introducing a full orchestra were taken in Augustan Rome with the blessing of the ruler himself.[5] Rome now became the third capital of the art, and many of the emperors were enthusiastic connoisseurs.

3. Against authenticity, Bompaire, *Lucien écrivain* 356–357; the decisive arguments in favor were made by Robertson, *Essays Ridgeway* 180–185, cf. Robert, *Hermes* 65 (1930) 120–122 (*OMS* 1.668–670); Weinreich, *Epigramm u. Pantomimus* 34 n. 4 ("Die Echtheit der Schrift ist heute allgemein anerkannt"). Bompaire, 356 n. 4, cites Helm, *Lucian* 369–370, as an opponent of authenticity, but overlooks his retraction, *RE* 13 (1927) 1759–60.

4. A good general description, though antiquated, in Friedländer, *Sittengeschichte* 2[10] 125–134; the article of Wüst, *RE* 18, 2 (1949) 833–869, is useful but neglects inscriptions and confuses pantomime with other kinds of dance.

5. Xenophon: *Symp.* 8.9. Antioch and Alexandria: *HA Verus* 10.11, *quorum Syria et Alexandria pascitur uoluptate,* cf. Luc. *Apol.* 5, *Salt.* 37, 76, Weinreich, *Epigramm u. Pantomimus* 34. Augustus: Suet. *Aug.* 43.1, 45.3, 74, Macrob. *Sat.* 2.7.12–19, cf. *PIR*[1] P 811, *PIR*[2] B 91, Wüst, *RE* 18, 2 (1949) 864.

None was more so than Lucius Verus, and his residence in Antioch served to raise pantomime and its practitioners to new heights. One of those he brought back to Rome was a certain Paris, over whom the great sophist Hadrian of Tyre was later appointed to give the funeral oration.[6] About this time the doctor Galen denounced the practice of honoring dancers with statues, and of the dozens of bases that survive most come from the second century; two of the most honored artists, both bearing the professional name Apolaustos, were freedmen of Lucius.[7]

Just as imperial favor changed the form of the dance, so also it contributed to its prestige. Greek conservatism had for centuries excluded it from the great contests, such as the Pythia of Delphi, while admitting traditional arts such as tragedy and comedy. In the second century it gained entry into the great contest of the Capitolia at Rome, equal in renown to the traditional ones of Greece. Thereafter, but before Lucian wrote his treatise, the Hellenized city of Naples admitted dance to its Sebasta, and it first appears in contests of the Greek east in the joint reign of Marcus and Lucius.[8] This advance seems to have sharpened an old debate concerning the morality of the triumphant art. Moralists, especially Stoics and Cynics, had always deplored it, and now it threatened bastions of archaic Hellenism. Aelius Aristides undertook to denounce pantomime in an open letter to the city of Sparta, which was in danger of succumbing.[9] Many another speech or pamphlet was no doubt produced to defend or to attack the art, but all those of the second century are lost with one exception, and Aristides' essay is known only from the reply by Libanios. The exception is Lucian's *On the Dance*.

Lucian's essay has rightly been compared to his treatise on history, in which he professes to give general guidance for historians while covertly exalting the successes of Lucius Verus. The *Dance* is a dialogue of a known type in which one interlocutor converts the other

6. Lib. *Or.* 64.41, cf. *PIR²* M 392.

7. Gal. *De Praecog.* 1.13, with Nutton's commentary, 154. Apolausti: *ILS* 5187–91; *PIR²* A 148; Barnes, *JRS* 57 (1967) 72, who rightly separates L. Aelius Aurelius Apolaustus from L. Aurelius Apolaustus Memphius. The Ti. Iulius Apolaustus discussed by Robert, *Hermes* 65 (1930) 106–108, 113–114 (*OMS* 1.654–656, 661–662), *REG* 79 (1966) 757–759, is slightly later.

8. Robert, *Hermes* 65 (1930) 118–122 (*OMS* 1.666–670); Wüst, *RE* 18, 2 (1949) 858–859, seems not to have understood Robert's position.

9. For Aristides' essay, Lib. *Or.* 64, cf. Mesk, *WS* 30 (1908) 59–74, Boulanger, *RPh* 47 (1923) 149–151.

from disapproval to approval or from skepticism to belief, and persuasion is disguised as reasoned exposition. (Philostratos' *Heroicos* is an example from the literature of the Second Sophistic.)[10] As the conversation begins, the Cynic philosopher Craton ("Strong-man") has just finished denouncing the dance, and Lycinos undertakes to show that it is the greatest of life's pleasures. Their preliminary dialogue enables Lucian both to state the usual objections against dance and to adumbrate his own defense of it. Craton is presumably meant as a type of the Cynics and Stoics opposed to the art, and yet his character is given just enough flexibility and humaneness to make his later conversion credible.[11] Lucian's exposition occupies almost all the rest of the work and has three distinct sections, the antiquity of dance, the sanction given to it by classical authors, and a description of the virtues and vices of dancers. The first two sections exploit the vagueness of the term "dance," while the third restricts the vices of dancers to a few amusing anecdotes, reminiscent of those told in the treatise on history. At the end Craton eagerly agrees to accompany Lycinos on his next visit to the theater.[12]

It has been supposed that Lucian knew or cared little about his subject. Certainly he refers to handbooks on it, but only to emphasize his own independence.[13] For a student of rhetoric dance was recommended by its resemblances to the art of declamation, since the declaimer too had to act his part and express words by movements.[14] Lucian refers to dancing in works other than the present one,[15] and as a man of culture and pleasure he must have been familiar with it long before his association with Verus. As in his description of the Syrian goddess or of magical practices, he displays a knowledge of his subject that goes beyond mere book learning to precise observation.

When Lucian traces the history of the dance back to creation and the gods, he is not wholly serious, but even here has exact information: thus he can invoke the dances performed for Brietos, a Bithynian

10. Cf. Hirzel, *Dialog* 2.283–284.
11. *Salt.* 1–6; for Craton as a Cynic, 4.
12. *Salt.* 7–23 (antiquity), 23–32 (poets), 33–79 (virtues), 80–84 (vices), 85 (conclusion).
13. Anderson, *GRBS* 18 (1977) 286, "[Lucian is] writing for an occasion with neither knowledge nor interest in his subject." Handbooks: *Salt.* 33–34.
14. Cf. Luc. *Salt.* 65. For "acting" applied to sophists, e.g., Philostr. *VS* 33.9, 52.12, 101.1.
15. *Apol.* 5, *Pseudol.* 19, *Rh. pr.* 17, *Sat.* 18.

war god otherwise mentioned in literature only by Arrian of Nicomedeia.[16] He dates the real beginnings of the art back to the time of
Socrates, and this may be exactly right, since Xenophon describes
what appears to be an early form of dance at the end of his *Symposium*.[17] Although Lucian has nothing explicit to say about its Hellenistic phase, his catalog of suitable subjects includes the tale of Stratonice,
the beautiful young wife of Seleucos I, and ends with the famous
Cleopatra.[18] He places about the time of Augustus the dance's development into the form still prevailing, and here too agrees with the
other sources, since they show that the great Pylades under Augustus
did not invent the dance, but rather modified it in a crucial way.[19] Of
the several emperors who favored dance down to his own time Lucian
mentions, apart from Augustus, only Nero, in whose reign there
flourished an artist of unusual skill whom the author does not name,
perhaps the Paris whom the emperor eventually put to death.[20] Lucian
does, however, allude to the recent development whereby dance had
begun to be accepted at Hellenic festivals. At the opening of the
work Craton distinguishes mere dancers from serious performers such
as pipers accompanied by a chorus *(kuklioi auletai)* and citharodes,
tragic and comic actors, "all of whom have been thought worthy to
participate in contests." Lycinos replies that "a city in Italy, the best
of the Chalcidic clan, has added this to its contest as a sort of adorn-
ment," a palpable reference to Naples and its Sebasta.[21] It has rightly
been inferred that one of Lucian's principal motives for writing the
treatise was to support the acceptance of the dance among the canonical arts of the Greeks.

He devotes most of his description of dance to the main perform-

---

16. *Salt.* 21, where the mss. give Πρίαπον (retained by Macleod). See, with earlier
bibliography, Robert, *AE* 1979, 231–236; for Arrian, *FGrHist* 155 F 23.

17. Socrates: Luc. *Salt.* 25. Xenophon: *Symp.* 8.9. For this early dating of dance,
Robert, *Hermes* 65 (1930) 109–110 (*OMS* 1.657–658); Weinreich, *Epigramm u. Pantomimus* 11–41; Wüst, *RE* 18, 2 (1949) 834–842.

18. Stratonice: *Salt.* 58 (the text is not in order). Cleopatra: *Salt.* 37.

19. *Salt.* 34. For Pylades' reforms, see esp. Macrob. *Sat.* 2.7.18, unreasonably
rejected by Wüst, *RE* 18, 2 (1949) 847.

20. *Salt.* 63–64. Cf. Dessau on *ILS* 5181a, *PIR²* D 156 with the *addenda*.

21. Craton: *Salt.* 2; on the meaning of *kuklios auletes*, Robert, *RPh* 4 (1930) 54–
55 (*OMS* 2.1154–55). Lycinos' reply: *Salt.* 32. For the identification of this city as
Naples, Robert, *Hermes* 65 (1930) 119–120 (*OMS* 1.667–668), following Sommer-
brodt.

ers, and here too almost every detail can be corroborated. He does not say much about the dancer's physique and movements, probably avoiding a subject which inflamed the critics. Nevertheless, like other authors he singles out the "twisting" motion *(lugizesthai)* of the dancer, though the repertoire was in fact more extensive and included the "splits" and much else.[22] Lucian also dwells on a feature that helped to support his case, the dancer's expressive use of his hands, which had moved the Cynic Demetrios and in the author's own day the renowned Stoic Timocrates to admiration, and this skill is mentioned by many other sources, both literary and epigraphic.[23] Of the dancer's "props" Lucian says most about the mask, noting that it differed from tragic and comic masks by its closed mouth. So also Tatian describes the dancer as "raving in a clay face," and terracotta masks of the kind have survived.[24] With the mask Lucian joins the dancer's "silken clothing," the most conspicuous item being the brocaded cloak which he could use to suggest different objects according to his role.[25] Lucian's enumeration of the various stories that the dancer had to learn is by far the fullest that survives but is again corroborated by contemporary evidence. A monument from Tibur honors one of Lucius Verus' freedmen, the dancer Apolaustos Memphios, and names six of his successful roles, five from well-known plays of Euripides and the sixth the obscure *Tympanistai* of Sophocles, and of this catalog Lucian omits only the last.[26]

Lucian also gives details elsewhere unknown about the other contributors to the performance. He is the only source to mention a

---

22. *Salt.* 77, cf. Tat. *Or.* 22.1, Lib. *Or.* 64.60. Other tricks: Gal. *De San. tuenda* 2.11.40, 6.155 Kühn = *CMG* 5, 4, 2, 68–69, cited by Robert, *JS* 1981, 39 n. 18.

23. *Salt.* 63, 69. This Timocrates is presumably the famous philosopher of Pontic Heraclea, on whom see below, Ch. 9 at n. 20. His pupil Lesbonax of Mitylene should be the second-century sophist, on whom Aulitzky, *RE* 12 (1925) 2104–6 (the notices in *PIR*[1] T 161, *PIR*[2] L 160 are defective). For the many references to the dancers' hands (including Luc. *Rh. Pr.* 17), Robert, *JS* 1981, 38 n. 16.

24. *Salt.* 29, 63, 66; Tat. *Or.* 22.1, διὰ πηλίνης ὄψεως δαιμονῶντα (not "with clay make-up," as translated by Whittaker). For excavated examples, e.g., Grandjouan, *The Athenian Agora VI: Terracottas* 22 and pl. 12.

25. *Salt.* 63; cf. Fronto, *De orat.* 5, Lib. *Or.* 64.52.

26. For this altar, *Inscr. Ital.* 4, 1, 254, Kannicht-Snell, *TrGF* 2.327, DID B 14 a. The titles by Euripides, with the references in Lucian, are *Heracles* (41), *Orestes* (46), *Troades* (46), *Bacchae* (41), *Hippolytos* (40). Wüst, *RE* 18, 2 (1949) 847–850, unfortunately overlooks both this inscription and *ILS* 5195.

subsidiary player, the "actor," who seems to have served as prologue and also performed when a second part was indispensable.[27] His references to the accompanying chorus and musicians vividly convey their raucous effect.[28] Presumably it is again out of tact that he only glances at the frenzy often induced in the spectators, who might sing and shout and, like certain modern audiences, throw items of clothing onto the stage.[29]

The chief purpose of the *Dance*, however, is not to give a history or a description, but to justify the art in terms acceptable to cultured society. Craton's opening speech serves to define the issues: the dance is modern, effeminate, frivolous, and to admire it is inconsistent with "culture and philosophy." Lucian's rebuttal aims to counter all these positions, and like his observations of detail finds a ready echo in contemporary literature and inscriptions. An important theme of the work consists in the dancer's mental and spiritual qualities. Far from being inimical to philosophy, dancing is notable for its wisdom. It could be said to illustrate Plato's division of the soul and Aristotle's doctrine of beauty, and Lucian has even heard the muteness of the chief dancer explained as Pythagorean. Writing about Apolaustos Memphios, Athenaeus calls him "the philosophic dancer of our time," and avers that his silent art explains the Pythagorean system better than any words.[30] An epigram found near Rome similarly praises a pantomime for "displaying histories and expressing all with his hands, skilled in the wise and holy dancing of Bromios."[31] Just as Lucian holds that the dancer must be "perfect *(apekribesthai)* in every respect, so that the general effect is rhythmical, well-formed, well-proportioned, consistent, irreproachable, unobjectionable, deficient in nothing," so also several inscriptions of a dancer of the same period note his "artistic precision *(akribeia)* and the proper conduct of his life."[32]

The similarities between Lucian and contemporary inscriptions point

27. *Salt.* 68, 83, cf. Wüst, *RE* 18, 2 (1949) 2850 and below, Ch. 10 at n. 51.

28. *Salt.* 2, 26, 63, 68, 83.

29. *Salt.* 83–84 (I take this to be the implication of ἀνερρίπτουν). Cf. Dio Chrysostom on the Alexandrians, *Or.* 32.89. For riots in the theater, Cameron, *Circus Factions* 223–226.

30. *Salt.* 69–70; Ath. 1.20C–D.

31. Weinreich, *Epigramm u. Pantomimus* 73–77 (Peek, *GVI* 742).

32. *Salt.* 81. Inscriptions for Ti. Iulius Apolaustus (above, n. 7): Robert, *Hermes* 65 (1930) 113 (*OMS* 1.661), *REG* 79 (1966) 758 and n. 3 there.

to the theoretical controversy that existed in the second century about the dance. What can be inferred from Libanios of Aristides' attack shows that it used several points adumbrated by Lucian's Craton. One was nationalistic: dance was a pest that had begun in Egypt, been carried further by Syrians, and now threatened to infect Sparta, the last refuge of Greek manliness and archaism.[33] Another argument was drawn from morality. Aristides fulminated against the depraved characters of the dancers, their long hair and effeminate dress and movements, and proposed that the noisy players with their specially fitted shoes should have their feet cut off, shoes and all.[34] Libanios in his reply makes many of the same points as Lucian, and both authors, for example, find dance in the natural order and enlist Homer, Hesiod, and Socrates in its support.[35] It is idle to speculate whether Lucian was provoked by Aristides or vice versa, or whether Libanios knew Lucian as well as Aristides, since the literature on the subject must have been voluminous. Even if Libanios did use Lucian, it does not follow that his speech is a mere exercise. The difference between the two authors is that in Libanios' day Christian preachers had succeeded Greek philosophers as the chief enemies of the theater.[36]

The two essays on Pantheia, although more openly encomiastic than the *Dance,* rank with Lucian's most polished and artistic works. Pantheia was from Smyrna, and Lucian's praise of her musical talents and his comparison of her with the Milesian Aspasia show that she was a professional courtesan of the kind for which Ionia was noted.[37] Though Lucius may have met her in Ionia, Antioch was the scene of their liaison, at least until Marcus contrived to marry his own daughter Lucilla to him. Pantheia may have remained as a concubine, however, for years later Marcus remembered her sitting disconsolately beside Lucius' tomb until she too was gone.[38]

33. Lib. *Or.* 64.80 (Egypt), 9 (Syria), 6 (Sparta).

34. Lib. *Or.* 64.31, 37, 50, 58 (dancers), 95–98 (shoes).

35. Lib. *Or.* 64.12 (creation), 15 (Homer), 12 (Hesiod), 18 (Socrates); the parallels with Lucian are given by Förster.

36. For a selection of references, Castorina on Tert. *De spect.* 17.1; generally, Müller, *NJA* 23 (1909) 36–55.

37. Sources in *PIR*[1] P 69 and Stein, *RE* 18, 2 (1949) 697; add the anonymous reference in *HA* Verus 7.10 (cf. Barnes, *JRS* 57 [1967] 72). Luc. *Im.* 13–14 (music), 17 (Aspasia). For Ionian *hetairai,* Hor. *Carm.* 3.6.21, Plut. *Crassus* 32.6.

38. Marriage of Lucius and Lucilla: *HA* Marcus 9.4, Verus 7.7. Pantheia's mourning and death: M. Ant. *Medit.* 8.37.

Both essays are dialogues and use the form to cunning effect. In the first Lycinos converses with a friend Polystratos, and is supposed to have seen Pantheia at the theater without knowing her identity. This enables him to give a physical description in which he compares various of her features to masterpieces of classical art, for example, her head to that of Praxiteles' Cnidian Aphrodite. Only when this inventory is complete does Polystratos recognize the lady, whom he names not directly but by reference to Xenophon's heroine in the *Cyropaideia,*[39] and as one of her acquaintances he is able to describe her spiritual qualities with examples drawn from classical literature. The work thus forms a diptych in which Lucian contrives to praise the physical and mental endowments of Pantheia in turn, adducing first the plastic and then the literary arts. These references to the classics serve more than one purpose. Immediately they characterize Pantheia as a person of culture: her name recalls a well-known heroine of romantic fiction, her city is the birthplace of Homer (for in this work Lucian evinces no doubt about his origin) and a colony of Athens, and when Lycinos first sees her, she is carrying a book and conversing with her attendants.[40] A less obvious effect is to flatter the other readers at whom the work is aimed, in the first place the emperor Lucius. In exalting such masterpieces as Praxiteles' Cnidia and Pheidias' Lemnia, Lucian could count on the sympathy of his cultured readership, and it is no coincidence that Hadrian had built at Tivoli a reproduction of the temple of Aphrodite at Cnidos or that Pausanias should praise the Lemnia as "a work of Pheidias especially worth seeing."[41] There is a clear affinity with the *Dance.* As Lucian there gave an antique pedigree to a pastime of Verus, and praised the dancer as much for his knowledge as for his physique, so here he makes Pantheia into a collage of ancient masterpieces, and praises her wisdom and understanding.

In the *Defense of the Portraits,* a dialogue between the same two speakers, Polystratos reports to Lycinos the bashful protest of Pantheia against the praises contained in the other work, whereupon

39. *Im.* 10; a similar periphrasis for the pantomime Paris in Lib. *Or.* 64.41. It may be suspected that "Pantheia" was a professional name.

40. *Im.* 15 (Homer and Athens: cf. *Pro Im.* 24), 9 (book).

41. Hadrian's villa: Aurigemma, *Villa Adriana* 44–45, with Love, *AJA* 74 (1970) 154, 76 (1972) 70–72. Pheidias' Lemnia: Paus. 1.28.2; on this statue, and Lucian's testimony, Hartswick, *AJA* 87 (1983) 335–346.

Lycinos answers the imputations of exaggeration and flattery. This work too forms a diptych with the order of the speakers reversed, and it may be assumed that these works belong together. The second gives Lucian an opportunity to praise Pantheia's modesty, and thus to reinforce his earlier claims for her wisdom. In addition, his speech of self-defense, which recalls such elegant essays as the *Apology for a Slip in Salutation,* enables him once again to display his classical learning.

Dialogue as a vehicle of encomium seems to have had its origin among the Socratics, and Lucian's immediate model may well have been the *Aspasia* of Aeschines Socraticus, in which (as in Lucian) Aspasia was talked of in her absence and specimens of her wisdom were cited.[42] Among works of the imperial period, the closest is perhaps the second *Melancomas* of Dio Chrysostom. This too is one of a pair of works written to honor an imperial favorite, the deceased athlete Melancomas loved by Titus, and like Lucian, Dio manages to represent Melancomas as a paragon of spiritual as well as physical beauty.[43] It is not surprising that with the revival of learning Lucian's essays on Pantheia inspired courtly writers of Renaissance Italy.[44]

These two essays, and the *Dance* as well, seem to consort ill with the claims to blunt and honest speech that Lucian makes elsewhere; his rebuttal of the charge of flattery in the *Defense* may be addressed to his critics as much as Pantheia. It does not follow, however, that the three must be regarded as atypical or aberrant. Certainly particular circumstances may have evoked particular works, just as Dio Chrysostom's two pieces on Melancomas reflect a short and ill-represented phase of his career. With Lucian, it may be held, the desire to provoke laughter was controlled, and perhaps even surpassed, by the desire to be seen as a man of culture.

42. Lucian refers to Aeschines' dialogue in *Im.* 17; cf. the long citation in Cic. *Inv.* 1.51–52. Generally, Ehlers, *Der Dialog Aspasia* 65–66, 98–99.
43. D. Chr. 29, esp. 6, 12; cf. Jones, *Dio Chrysostom* 15.
44. Hirdt, *Gian Giorgio Trissinos Porträt.*

8 Rome

ROME, its citizens and its institutions, are constantly present in Lucian. Two works, the *Hirelings in Great Houses* and the *Nigrinus,* constitute a cruel portrait of the capital. The workings of the Roman Empire provide the articulation for narratives like that of the *Peregrinus* and the *Alexander.* Individual Romans of high station often appear as characters, for example, in those two works and in the *Demonax.*

Rome has often seemed a useful measure of Lucian's place in his society. The *Hirelings* in particular has been interpreted as a protest of the Greek intellectual against the prevailing coarseness of Roman taste, the attack of oppressed poverty on exploitative capitalism. Yet it so happens that the same work is one of those which seem to offer hope of recovering some of Lucian's written sources, since the parallels with Juvenal are often striking, and hence the same work has also been used to argue Lucian's abstraction from the real world and his reliance on earlier literature. It is not easy to find a middle way, and to see the author as both well read and observant, interested but not partisan, and here again culture may offer the guiding thread.

Whether a work of borrowed learning or of direct experience, the *Hirelings* is for Lucian unusually polished and elaborate. It purports to be addressed to a certain Timocles, a young man aspiring to be a salaried philosopher in a Roman household. This Timocles ("honorfamed") may be suspected to be either a pseudonym or a fiction, like the Stoic Thesmopolis whose misadventures are used for illustration.[1]

---

1. *Merc. cond.* 2–3 (Timocles), 33–35 (Thesmopolis). Cf. the Hetoimocles of *Symp.* 22–27 and the Thesmopolis of *Gall.* 10–11, both philosophic parasites.

In form the work has three parts. In the introduction Lucian sets out his own reasons for writing and the various excuses given by those who hire themselves out. The central section is a kind of "Hireling's Progress," which treats the dependent's career from his first entrance into the great man's house to his ignominious ejection. In the conclusion Lucian draws a verbal picture of the Hireling's life borrowed from the *Picture of Cebes*.[2] The whole work is marked by its graphic vividness. The introduction has three extended similes, that of the shipwrecked sailor, the hooked fish, and the frustrated lover, while the main section conveys the tribulations of the Hireling with mordant particularity, especially in the episode of Thesmopolis.

Lucian claims to direct his work not at all Greeks who enter the service of rich Romans, but only at an educated minority. Timocles is represented as a philosopher, and the long-suffering Thesmopolis as a Stoic; but Lucian also includes "teachers of literature *(grammatistai)*, rhetors, musicians," by whom he must mean teachers or theorists rather than players, "and generally those who expect to be paid as teachers of cultured subjects *(paideiai)*."[3] Throughout the work Lucian depicts his Hireling as an educated man, supposedly able to profit his employers by his lessons in morality, and equipped with the usual long beard and shabby cloak.[4] Though his position recalls that of the domestic chaplain of recent centuries, there is the important difference that Lucian's Greek does not live in the house but elsewhere, like the traditional client of Roman satire, and like that unfortunate he is obliged to get up early, run to the great man's house for the morning levée, follow him about the city, and then after taking a public bath attend on him for dinner. When, however, the client is requested to travel with the household, he is presumably put up on the patron's property.[5]

From such educated dependents Lucian distinguishes "the other

2. *Merc. cond.* 1–9, 10–41, 42.

3. *Merc. cond.* 4, cf. 24, 25. Note that Athenaeus' imaginary banquet has among the guests philosophers, teachers of literature *(grammatikoi)*, rhetors, doctors, and a *mousikos*, who seems to be a historian of music: Athen. 1.1C–F, 4.174B–185A (cf. Bowersock, *Sophists* 14–15).

4. *Merc. cond.* 16, 17, 19, 24, 25, 36.

5. For the client living apart from his patron, see esp. *Merc. cond.* 24–26, 31. The "bell" of 24, 31, is probably not a house bell but a public one signifying the start of the day, cf. Wilhelm, *Neue Beiträge* 5.46 = *Akademieschriften* 1.288, Robert, *Ét. anat.* 290. Travel: *Merc. cond.* 3, 33–35.

mob, gymnastic trainers, flatterers and the like, laymen with small minds, debased by their very nature."[6] He implies a similar distinction when he ironically contrasts the mistreatment of the educated Greek with the attention lavished on entertainers of a lower kind: the "pansy" (*kinaidos*), who in this context is an effeminate joker or dancer;[7] the "dancing master," probably the owner of a troupe of dancing girls;[8] "or some fellow from Alexandria spouting Ionic"—this is an *Ionikologos* who specialized in obscene poetry of the kind associated with the Hellenistic Sotades.[9] There was, however, one questionable profession to which Lucian's educated Greeks could descend, that of magician. Many Greeks, so he alleges, for lack of any other skill set up as prophets and wizards, offering "love-spells and incantations against enemies," an expression which he also uses of the "fraud" who became the lover and teacher of Alexander of Abonouteichos.[10] The growing interest of philosophers in the occult, to which the *Lovers of Lies* gives vivid witness, could well have caused certain of those hired as teachers to slip into the role of magician.

Lucian claims to draw his information about the Hireling's life from actual victims, some of whom were still in service while others had escaped.[11] There is nothing intrinsically improbable in such a claim, since he had visited Rome, and Greeks who had consorted with Romans, like the sophist attacked in the *Mistaken Critic,* were to be found in cities other than the capital.[12] Lucian would also not have neglected satirical literature on the subject, if such there were in Greek. Whether he also knew the equivalent literature in Latin, especially the satires of Juvenal which often recall his own, is less clear. In the third of these Juvenal makes the character Umbricius describe

6. *Merc. cond.* 4. By *gymnastai* Lucian probably refers to consultants, as much medical as gymnastic, like the *aliptes* mentioned in a similar context by Juvenal (3.76): cf. Robert, *Hellenica* 13 (1965) 167–170, Sherwin-White on Pliny, *Ep.* 10.5.1.

7. *Merc. cond.* 27. *Kinaidos* is used both of effeminate dancers (Parsons on *POxy.* 31.2575 ll. 3–4, *OLD* cinaedus 1) and of a type of joker (Mart. 1.41.13, with Howell's commentary; Pliny, *Ep.* 9.17.1, with Sherwin-White's): the *kinaidos* Chelidonion (for the significance of the name, Housman on Juv. 6.371 [O 6]) in *Merc. cond.* 34 seems to combine the two, as no doubt happened in actuality.

8. Cf. Mart. 1.41.12, *de Gadibus improbus magister,* with Howell's commentary.

9. Ath. 14.620E–621B.

10. *Merc. cond.* 40, cf. *Alex.* 5.

11. *Merc. cond.* 1, cf. 33.

12. *Pseudol.* 21.

the tribulations of the poor man at Rome, among them the indignities of the client forced to compete with artful Greeks. The fifth also resembles Lucian in that the author gives advice to a client, Trebius, but whereas Lucian's Timocles has not yet entered service, Trebius cannot tear himself away, and the emphasis is almost entirely on the miserable food and drink which he receives. At some points the two authors come very close. Umbricius claims that the "hungry Greekling" knows all the arts, "teacher of literature, rhetor, geometer, painter, gymnastic trainer, seer, tightrope-walker, doctor, magician"; so also Lucian observes that, when the elderly Greek is dropped by one patron, he is thought by others to be an adulterer or a poisoner, "since you are a Greek of easy morals and ready to perform any injury."[13] Lucian's complaint that the Greek Hireling and the more honored guests receive different food and wine occurs in Juvenal's advice to Trebius.[14] The abuses to which both authors refer, however, such as the serving of different wines to different guests, were so inveterate that mere community of subject matter can prove little, and to establish Lucian's knowledge of Juvenal requires close coincidence in language or expression. Such coincidences have been alleged, but the question seems incapable of objective solution. Furthermore, even if Lucian did know Juvenal, from his own reading or in translation, nothing would be proved about his other sources of knowledge.[15]

A second problem raised by Lucian's essay, perhaps less difficult to answer, is that of its status as a document of social or even political criticism. The view that it is an attack on "Roman capitalists," or that the client Greeks are "proletarian intellectuals," goes back to the fountainhead of modern socialism.[16] Certainly the attacks on the Roman

13. Juv. 3.75–78; Luc. *Merc. cond.* 40. Lucian makes similar inferences about the Mistaken Critic's expulsion, *Pseudol.* 21.

14. Luc. *Merc. cond.* 26, Juv. 5.24–155. On this practice, Pliny, *Ep.* 2.6, with Sherwin-White's commentary.

15. The view that Lucian used Juvenal as a "source" was argued at length by Mesk, *WS* 34 (1912) 372–382, 35 (1913) 1–33; cf. Bompaire, *Lucien écrivain* 504–508; most recently, Courtney in his edition of Juvenal, 624–629. The passage on which Courtney lays most weight is *Peregr.* 45, on the laughter of Democritos: but this theme is so common in Lucian (Ch. 11 at n. 8) that he could have devised the expression without help from Juv. 10.32.

16. Marx and Engels, *Collected Works* 5 (1976) 143, "a detailed description of how the people regarded [philosophers] as public buffoons, and how the Roman capitalists,

rich are outspoken and harsh, and the last paragraph of the central section compares all Roman patrons to sumptuous tomes, purple and gold without, tales of infanticide or incest within.[17] The argument to which Lucian returns most often to dissuade Timocles is that the educated Greek is "independent" *(eleutherios)*, whereas the client's life is servitude.[18] It does not follow, however, that in Lucian's view all Greeks are oppressed, still less that his cultivated Greek is a proletarian. The servitude which Lucian deplores is a voluntary one; his independence is not political liberty but, as often in Greek thought, deliverance from the false valuation of externals. Thus it is that Lucian does not bother to address those Greeks of the lower kind, gymnastic trainers and the like, who had no ideas higher than that of making money. When he urges that a meal of thyme and salt eaten in freedom tastes better than the rich man's banquet, he is not exalting the life-style of the lower classes. Rather, he (like another half-Epicurean, Horace) is decrying pleasures which later lead to pain.[19] Similarly when he dismisses Roman patrons as hypocrites, dabblers in Greek culture, or sumptuous exteriors concealing unspeakable vice, he refers to a type of man whom Roman satirists often attacked as well: the "king" *(rex)* fawned upon by needy parasites. Horace's Nasidienus, Petronius' Trimalchio, and Juvenal's Vibius all belong to this class. Lucian surpasses the three Latin authors, even Juvenal, in the ferocity of his contempt, but it is directed at the patron's character, not at his nationality. Earnest and respectable men like Lucian's acquaintance Rutilianus, a man ill with piety and superstition, would have read the *Hirelings* without a blush of self-consciousness.[20]

As he often does, Galen resembles Lucian both in tone and in description. Inveighing against the quack doctors who gain advance-

---

proconsuls, etc., hired them as court jesters for their entertainment"; Peretti, *Luciano* esp. 129. For the contrary view, Momigliano, *RSI* 60 (1948) 430–432 = *Quarto Contributo* 641–644; Palm, *Rom, Römertum und Imperium* 52; and most recently, Balsdon, *Romans and Aliens* 185–187; Hall, *Lucian's Satire* 221–251; Vidal-Naquet, *Flavius Arrien* 325.

17. *Merc. cond.* 41, cf. 25.

18. *Merc. cond.* 1, 4, 5, 7, 8, etc.

19. *Merc. cond.* 19, 24: cf. Hor. *Carm.* 1.31, 15–16 with the comments of Nisbet and Hubbard.

20. Cf. Palm, *Rom, Römertum und Imperium* 52, "Kein gebildeter Römer dürfte an dieser Schrift Anstoss genommen haben."

ment while the genuine are neglected, Galen blames "this great and populous city," in which such charlatans can conceal their vices, and contrasts it with the small ones of the Greek world, in which everyone knows all about his neighbor's culture, possessions, and character. The wealthy of Rome honor the learned only to the extent that they can use them; unable to bear true experts or real philosophers, they are flattered by "poor and uncultured" impostors who in turn are enticed by the prospect of large profits.[21] Far from being an intellectual opposed to Rome, Galen concludes this very work with a proud account of the intimacy he enjoyed with the imperial family and his success in treating its health.[22] Just as Galen for all his professional jealousy was aiming his barbs at real rivals, so also Lucian may have had particular persons in mind when he uses a Stoic to typify the Greek Hireling, for other writers attest the ambitions which Marcus Aurelius' interest in philosophy awakened in the unscrupulous.[23]

The *Hirelings in Great Houses* is thus a satire mainly on a type of rich Roman, though also on the Greeks and especially the Greek philosophers who became their willing slaves. The contrast of poverty and wealth serves a philosophical and moral purpose rather than an ideological one, since Rome is attacked as a center not of power but of wealth, the city which contained the greatest population, the largest number of millionaires, and probably the starkest social contrasts of any. It thus provided the perfect target for the philosophical satirist who had chosen as his twin themes the ignorant rich and the misguided man of culture.

At some time (which need not have been very long) after publishing the *Hirelings* Lucian produced a related work, the *Self-Defense.*[24] Late in life he had accepted a post in Egypt for which he received a salary from the emperor, and the *Self-Defense* is designed to explain away the apparent inconsistency with the *Hirelings.* Sabinus, the addressee, "a good and philosophic man," may be a Platonist of Athenian extraction.[25]

The chief interest of Lucian's self-defense is to show how the earlier

21. Gal. *De Praecog.* 1.13–15, 4.9, 4.14 (charlatans), 4.17 (Rome).
22. Gal. *De Praecog.* 9–12.
23. Above, Ch. 3 at n. 29.
24. *Apol.* 6, μετὰ μικρόν, seems to imply a short interval since the *Hirelings:* πάλαι in 3 need only mean "previously," "before," cf. Ch. 2 at n. 64.
25. Ch. 2 at n. 79.

work appeared to his contemporaries. Lucian mentions two effects, the laughter it raised and its usefulness for educated men. There is no suggestion that it was taken as an attack on Rome, or that his receiving pay from the emperor was thought incompatible with Hellenism.[26] The *Self-Defense* suggests instead an author at ease with the institutions of Roman rule and ready to turn them to his own advantage.[27]

One of Lucian's arguments is also made by a contemporary, whose friendship to Rome cannot be doubted. Even the emperor, Lucian maintains, receives pay not merely in the material form of yearly taxes and tribute, but in "praises, general good repute, obeisance *(proskyneisthai)* for his benefactions; and the images, temples and sanctuaries which he receives from his subjects, these too are wages for the care and forethought which he employs in seeing to the state and improving it." The same convention, whereby a structure designed to evoke loyalty and to reward it with social advantage is represented as a spontaneous expression of gratitude, recurs in Aelius Aristides. Giving the inaugural speech for the temple of Hadrian at Cyzicos, he represents it as a "thank-offering" *(charisterion)* on behalf of the reigning emperors, Marcus and Lucius, made in gratitude for their guardianship and benefactions.[28] Lucian's reference to the obeisance directed to emperors is similarly echoed in a work ascribed to Aristides, the disputed oration *To the King,* where the author describes litigants leaving the emperor's court of justice "with affection and obeisance." It has sometimes been thought that such language dates the oration to the third century or later, but the parallel in Lucian defends its ascription.[29]

The *Nigrinus* resembles the *Hirelings* in several ways, although it is a more complex work in which Rome is only one item in a series of opposite pairs: Rome and Athens, wealth and poverty, vice and virtue.[30] The narrator, whom it is convenient to call Lucian, is a person who resides in Athens but has come to "the city" to be cured of eye

---

26. *Apol.* 1 (laughter), 3, 12 (educated men). Thus, rightly, Balsdon, *Romans and Aliens* 187.

27. Ch. 2 at n. 76.

28. Luc. *Apol.* 13; Aristid. 27.22, 24, 39. Cf. Bowersock in *Le culte des Souverains* 196–198 (Aristides), 201–202 (Lucian).

29. Aristid. 35.19; on this word as a criterion for dating the speech, Jones, *JRS* 62 (1972) 144–145, where I regretfully overlooked the present passage.

30. Ch. 3 at n. 6.

trouble. His visit to the famous Platonist Nigrinus corrects his spiritual vision when he learns not to admire wealth, reputation, and the like,[31] and Lucian thus plays a role similar to that of the addressee Timocles in the *Hirelings*. Nigrinus is a Roman by birth,[32] who lives physically in the city but in spirit has withdrawn to a height from which he watches its turmoil "as in a teeming theater."[33] When Lucian visits him from Athens, Nigrinus is led to recall his own stay there and the impression of his first return from Athens to Rome.[34] Rome is therefore the foil for Nigrinus' virtue, while Athens serves to emphasize the Attic qualities of his character: moderation, generosity, and plainspokenness.

At the center of the work is a speech of Nigrinus reported by the narrator. In essence this contrasts the attitudes to wealth and material goods of the Athenians and the Romans, though the emphasis is on the latter. Like Lucian's own discourse in the *Hirelings*, Nigrinus' discourse on Rome is directed both at the wealthy and at those who pursue them, and here also every detail can be illustrated from other sources. Nigrinus begins his condemnation with a general summary of the city's vices. The chief of these is the love of pleasure, which he represents as leading a band of other ones, "adultery, love of money, perjury." A very similar denunciation of modern vice, though not specifically aimed at Rome, is made by the author of the essay *On the Sublime*, writing in the first or perhaps the second century.[35] Nigrinus' tirade is no doubt meant to recall the fulminations of many a philosopher, but it does not follow that his observations are either dated or indirect, and still less can they be construed as an attack on Rome as an institution of power and government. Other of Nigrinus' criticisms recall Roman satire, and the reason is again less likely to be Lucian's dependence on outdated sources than the prevalence of habits which Romans no less than Greeks enjoyed satirizing. Thus

31. *Nigr.* 4, 35–37. For Rome referred to simply as ἡ πόλις like the Latin *urbs*, *Nigr.* 2, 16, 29, 34, *Merc. cond.* 26.

32. Palm, *Rom, Römertum und Imperium* 50, following Solanus in the edition of Hemsterhuys and Reitz. On his identity, Ch. 3 at n. 7.

33. *Nigr.* 18.

34. *Nigr.* 12, 17.

35. *Nigr.* 15–16; [Longin.] 44.7–12, with which Russell, p. 187, compares Philo, *Quod omnis probus* 62–74. Note that both "Longinus" and Lucian mention *captatio* as a vice of the age ([Longin.] 44.9, Luc. *Nigr.* 17).

Nigrinus taxes the rich for the absurd dispositions they make in their wills, "some ordering expensive clothes they had in life to be burned with them, others that certain slaves should remain by the tomb, some that their tombstones should be crowned with flowers." And he adds that the same people show equal lack of taste in the perverse delicacy of their dinners. So also Petronius' Trimalchio serves his guests a bizarre series of dishes and, growing maudlin, announces various arrangements for his burial and funerary monument, among them that a freedman watch at his tomb and that his corpse be buried in the finest clothes. Trimalchio does not mention arrangements for crowning his monument (though such dispositions are attested elsewhere), but requests that his tomb be surrounded by orchards and vineyards, "since it is ridiculous to adorn the houses we live in and not those in which we have to spend more time."[36] Elsewhere Nigrinus mocks the practice whereby rich men's slaves precede them and tell them to watch their step if they are about to cross an obstacle or a pothole, and similarly one of Trimalchio's slaves is posted at the door of his dining room to ensure that the guests enter right foot forward.[37]

Nigrinus' scorn is directed not only against the rich, but also against their flatterers and clients. Among these he singles out "those who pretend to be philosophers," and even more those philosophers who receive pay, "since a man who preaches contempt of wealth should show himself more than anyone superior to gain." As in the *Hirelings* this is a detail that seems particularly characteristic of the second century, and it happens that the same observation about philosophers is made by Antoninus Pius.[38]

One charge, not aimed against any particular class, may concern a very recent phenomenon. Nigrinus deplores "the circus, the statues of charioteers, the names of horses, the conversation about these things in the streets, for horse-madness is quite ubiquitous and has seized many worthy-seeming people nowadays." Lucian's "nowadays" suggests a current craze, and though horseracing had long been a passion at Rome, it seems to have been unusually strong in the mid-second century, perhaps under the social influence of Lucius Verus. Lucius made such a pet of his horse Volucer as to build a tomb for

36. Luc. *Nigr.* 30–31, Petr. 71.8 (freedman), 77.7 (*uitalia*), 71.7 (trees). For Lucian's similar remarks on burial practices in the *De Luctu,* Ch. 3 at n. 17.

37. Petr. 30.5–6.

38. *Nigr.* 24–25. Pius: *Dig.* 27.1.6.7, cf. Bowersock, *Sophists* 34.

him on the Vatican Hill; and one of Galen's complaints about contemporary Romans, perhaps exaggerated, is that they set up statues of charioteers and pantomimes in the temples of the gods.[39]

Another work, or series of works, is connected with Rome and has likewise been scrutinized for political implications: the *Saturnalia*.[40] Lucian must have been referring to the Roman festival of the name, but if he had any particular setting in mind it was not necessarily Rome.[41] In the first of the three separate but connected parts, the priest of Cronos questions the god much as the Cynic questions Zeus in the *Zeus Refuted,* asking mainly about the myths connected with him and the customs of his festival. This section of the work derives its humor from Lucian's characteristic pose of ironic credulity and affords little scope to political interpretation.[42] In the second part the priest, here named "Cronosolon," lays down laws for the conduct of the festival. Lucian refers to the mock rules of feasting known in many societies, and similar "laws" have survived in Latin.[43] Cronosolon has been appointed legislator after complaining to Cronos that "damnable wretches are laden with wealth while I myself and many others of the cultured live in poverty and indigence." His rules are directed alike at the behavior of the host and the guests, the rich and the poor. Many of them recall the vices attributed to the rich in the *Hirelings* and the *Nigrinus,* for example, the serving of different wines to host and guests, but the tone is different. The "damnable wretches" in the end receive nothing worse than good-natured banter, and the rules presuppose a friendly relationship between them and the "cultured": a modern author might similarly chaff a publisher or patron in a message written on a Christmas card.

The third section is the longest, and its tone is much sharper. It consists of two pairs of letters, the first written by "Me to Cronos" and "Cronos to Honorable Me," the second by "Cronos to the Rich"

39. *Nigr.* 29. On the mania for horseracing generally, Cameron, *Circus Factions* ch. 3, esp. 54 on Verus. Volucer: HA *Verus* 6.1–6, cf. Barnes, *JRS* 67 (1967) 70. Galen: *De Praecog.* 1.13.

40. For political interpretation of the *Saturnalia,* Baldwin, *CQ* 11 (1961) 202–203; for trenchant disagreement, Bompaire, *Lucien écrivain* 512–513.

41. A date in winter is implied by 9, 11, 31: thus Bompaire, *Lucien écrivain* 318 (who assumes that the scene is Athens). For the Saturnalia celebrated by Roman expatriates, A. Gell. 18.2.1, 18.13.1, HA *Verus* 7.5.

42. *Sat.* 1–9.

43. *Sat.* 10–18. Cf. Bücheler, *Petronii Saturae*[6] 344–345.

and their reply. The first letter contains, besides the usual charges of selfishness, gluttony, and the like, complaints against inequality and a plea for "a more democratic way" and "wealth in common." Similarly, Cronos in his letter to the rich uses the classic slogan of "redistribution" *(anadasmos)*.[44] Because the setting is again the Roman Saturnalia, this part of the work at least might seem a manifesto aimed at the wealthy of Rome. That interpretation, however, overlooks the context in which the political allusions occur. The language is a joking tribute to the myth of Saturn, and the general air of fantasy recalls a work like the *True Histories*.[45] In a passage of especial brilliance Lucian envisages a comic punishment of the rich whereby their meals are ruined and "their pretty long-haired slaves, whom they call Hyacinth, Achilles or Narcissos, suddenly become bald at the moment of offering the cup and grow a prickly beard."[46] Far from a covert attack on Rome, the *Saturnalia* could have been written for the amusement of a Roman patron. Lucius Verus is supposed to have celebrated the Saturnalia with riotous fervor in Antioch.[47]

A short work shows even more clearly the affinity between Lucian and the upper class at Rome. This is the *Apology for a Slip in Salutation,* in which he justifies his greeting the addressee at his morning levée with the salutation "farewell" *(hygiaine)*. It seems implied that Lucian addressed the man in Greek, so that he is either an educated westerner or more probably some eastern senator domiciled in Rome. Lucian mainly intends the work to be a literary tour de force, but in one passage he shows a striking knowledge of a Roman institution, the instructions *(entolai)* given by the emperor to provincial officials. When he alleges that these began by requesting the recipient to look after his health, he seems to be corroborated by the letters in which Pliny assures Trajan of his safe arrival in Bithynia.[48] Another work addressed to a highly placed benefactor, who seems to be a Roman citizen, is the *Harmonides,* and here too the tone is one of friendly deference.[49]

44. Inequality: *Sat.* 19–39, esp. 19, 22, 24, 25, 31, 36. *Anadasmos: Sat.* 31, cf. 36.
45. So, rightly, Bompaire, *Lucien écrivain* 513.
46. *Sat.* 24. Note Herodes Atticus' foster son Achilles, Philostr. *VS* 66.21.
47. *HA* Verus 7.5, *uernas in triclinium Saturnalibus et diebus festis semper admisit* (in the context of the Parthian War).
48. *Laps.* 13; cf. Pliny, *Ep.* 10.15–18. I owe this point to Fergus Millar.
49. *Harm.* 3.

In real life Lucian appears to take Rome and its institutions for granted. A friend of several notable Romans, he can even refer to Arrian of Nicomedeia as "a man among the first at Rome."[50] He visited the capital, claims a knowledge of Latin, and can allude, though very rarely, to Roman myth and history.[51] He counts Peregrinus' opposition to Rome as a sign of his eccentricity, and not the least of Alexander's vices is that "he filled practically the whole Roman Empire with his robberies."[52] Though Lucian is the first Greek to refer to all the inhabitants of the empire as "us,"[53] he does so without any sign of making a conscious gesture. In this casual acceptance of Roman power, he, as so often, recalls the realistic Galen, who both complains about the vices of Rome and yet boasts of his success there.

Although the attitudes that a writer takes in everyday life are not necessarily reproduced in his work, there is no audible dissonance in Lucian's treatment of Rome. When he writes about contemporary persons or things, he assumes the normal institutions of Roman wealth and power, proconsuls, armies, jurisdiction, patronage. If there is any conclusion to be drawn from his calling the inhabitants of the empire "us," it is perhaps that, as an entity above and apart from cultured Greeks, Rome was beginning to cease to exist.

50. *Alex.* 2.

51. Latin: *Salt.* 67, *Laps.* 13. Myth and history: *Salt.* 20, 46, *D. Mort.* 25, *Pseudol.* 8, *Zeux.* 3.

52. *Peregr.* 19, *Alex.* 2.

53. *Alex.* 48, *Hist. conscr.* 5, 17, 29, 31: first noticed by Palm, *Rom, Römertum und Imperium* 54.

9 Demonax and Sostratos

LUCIAN'S DIVERSITY has often confused his critics and led them to dismiss as spurious works which seemed not to conform to accepted ideas of him.[1] The same is true of his *Demonax*. Most of his essays on individuals are hostile, and even the *Nigrinus* is more a satire of Rome than a portrait of the Platonist who is the ostensible subject. Like the *Nigrinus,* the *Demonax* portrays a philosopher against the background of a city, but here the city is Lucian's favorite, Athens. His connection with Athens also helps to explain a lost work to which he refers in the *Demonax,* his essay on Sostratos.

He begins the *Demonax* with a personal declaration unusual for this evasive author: "Our generation was destined after all not to be totally devoid of men worthy of consideration and record, but even to display extraordinary excellence of body and thoroughly philosophic dispositions. I speak with reference to the Boeotian Sostratos, whom the Greeks called and believed to be Heracles, and especially to Demonax the philosopher. I saw them both and did so with admiration, but with the latter, Demonax, I associated for a very long time."[2] It once seemed unlikely that Lucian, the enemy of Cynics and of superstition, should have exalted Demonax and a new Heracles, but an excellent examination has vindicated the work beyond reasonable doubt.[3] That conclusion is of major importance for Lucian's own biography, since the *Demonax* alludes to a large number of his

1. Cf. Ch. 4 at n. 36 on the *Syr. D.*, Ch. 7 at n. 3 on the *Salt.*
2. *Demon.* 1.
3. Against authenticity: Bernays, *Lucian* 104–105, followed by von Arnim, *RE* 5 (1903) 143. Bernays was presumably influenced by his notion of Lucian's relations with the Cynics, in which he could not accommodate the *Demonax*. The examination referred to is that of Funk, *Untersuchungen,* esp. 566–614.

[90]

contemporaries and is the first of his works to be cited by title, in Eunapios' *Lives of the Philosophers*.[4] Though lost, the treatment of Sostratos can also be seen to bear directly on the author's own life.

The *Demonax* is one of Lucian's latest works and has a very simple structure.[5] After the preface, Lucian describes the philosopher's birth and upbringing, characterizes his philosophy, and then relates an incident at the beginning of his stay in Athens. This establishes Athens as the setting of whole work, just as it was the setting for Lucian's acquaintance with Demonax.[6] The second and longest part is a series of Demonax' sayings, mostly jokes, each set in its context by a brief preface: the ancient term was *chreia* or *apophthegma*.[7] The impression of disorder given by this section is delusive. Lucian contrives at once to juxtapose related or contrasted subjects and to maintain a tone that suggests the informal and spontaneous nature of his hero.[8] The anecdotal style is also a bow to tradition, having its origins in Xenophon's recollections of Socrates and later associated with lives of the Cynics. (Diogenes Laertios casts his accounts of Diogenes and Crates in very similar form.)[9] In the closing section Lucian describes Demonax' last years, his suicide by starvation, and his death and burial.

Lucian's biography is not the only source of knowledge about Demonax. About thirty quotations of him, some certainly spurious, survive in John Stobaeos and other Byzantine collections.[10] A few of these sayings belong to the same class of "apophthegms" as those in Lucian, but others may well be extracted from written works.[11] Though

---

4. Ch. 2 at n. 89.

5. Funk, *Untersuchungen* 614–617, and now Follet, *REG* 90 (1977) 50–51. A firm *terminus post* is given by the death of Herodes' favorite Polydeuces (*Demon*. 24, 33), shown by Follet to have occurred in or about 174; an even later one is suggested by Lucian's attitude towards Herodes Atticus, who died in 177 (Follet, 51).

6. *Demon*. 3–11.

7. *Demon*. 12–62. On *chreia, apophthegma* and related terms, von Fritz, *RE* Suppl. 6 (1935) 87–89.

8. Thus in *Demon*. 12–18 he passes from the "eunuch" sophist Favorinus (12–13) to another sophist (14), effeminacy (15–18), the exaggerated manliness of a Cynic (19), the definition of happiness (20), and so on: it is true that toward the end of this section the thread is less easy to follow.

9. D.L. 6.20–81 (Diogenes), 85–93 (Crates). Thus Funk, *Untersuchungen* 632–635.

10. For a thorough analysis, Funk, *Untersuchungen* 659–668, whose numbering will be adopted in what follows. These other *testimonia* are often overlooked, thus by von Arnim, *RE* 5 (1903) 143, and Dudley, *Cynicism* 158.

11. Curiously Funk, *Untersuchungen* 630, talks of Demonax' "schriftstellerische Tätigkeit," which he then subsequently denies, 667–668.

many Cynics followed the example of Socrates and shunned writing, the exceptions included Diogenes, Crates, and in Demonax' day Peregrinus Proteus and Oenomaos of Gadara. Demonax may even have written plays, as Diogenes and Crates were supposed to have done, for two of the quotations are in iambic trimeters, and Lucian comments on his liking for poetry. [12] These quotations show that Demonax did not owe his importance to Lucian, though they corroborate the biography only rarely. [13]

Lucian's reliability must therefore be judged from his own evidence. He seems to have toned down Demonax' Cynicism, claiming instead that he was an eclectic: though he appeared to imitate Diogenes, he really resembled Socrates, and also admired Aristippos, the founder of hedonism. [14] Whereas eclecticism and moderate hedonism make Demonax sound like a projection of Lucian, one trait, Demonax' attachment to his friends, is confirmed by the medieval quotations. [15]

With these reservations something of the historical Demonax can be recovered. He was from Cyprus, and born into a wealthy family, though he made the customary renunciation of wealth on taking up philosophy. If his age at death was really not much less than a hundred, as Lucian claims, he was born between about 70 and 80. [16] His masters are all well known, and to study with them he must have had the means that Lucian ascribes to him. Two were famous Cynics, Agathoboulos of Alexandria, who also taught Peregrinus, [17] and Demetrios, who is best known for his activities in Rome. [18] A third was Epictetos, whose Stoicism had a strong Cynic tinge. [19] Lucian lays particular emphasis on a fourth teacher, Timocrates of Heraclea, "a

12. Fr. 1 and 2 (Nauck, *TGF* 826–827). Plays of Diogenes: D.L. 6.73, 80. Of Crates: D.L. 6.98. Demonax' liking for poetry: Luc. *Demon.* 4.

13. Compare, however, fr. 16 (encounter with a sophist), with Luc. *Demon.* 12, 14.

14. *Demon.* 5, 11, 21, 50, 61, 62 (Cynicism), 5 (eclectic), 5, 62 (Socrates, Diogenes, Aristippos).

15. *Demon.* 10, 63; fr. 8, 18–21.

16. Origin: *Demon.* 5 (note the Demonax at Salamis, Peek, *GVI* 1833). Wealth and renunciation: *Demon.* 3. Age at death: *Demon.* 63, cf. n. 5 above.

17. Agathoboulos: *Peregr.* 17, Jerome-Eusebius on Ol. 124, 3 (p. 198 Helm), Dudley, *Cynicism* 175, 184 n. 3.

18. *PIR*[2] D 39; Billerbeck, *Demetrios;* in Lucian, note *Ind.* 19 and *Salt.* 63.

19. Dudley, *Cynicism* 190–198, Billerbeck, *Epictet: Vom Kynismus* 1–3.

wise man highly endowed with eloquence and understanding." This remarkable person is mentioned with similar praise in other works of Lucian and also by Philostratos. He is a characteristic product of the age, since after beginning as a student of medicine he became a philosopher of moderate Stoic beliefs and a witty teacher of several famous sophists.[20]

Of Demonax' years before his residence in Athens Lucian relates only that he traveled from city to city giving personal and political advice. This is the kind of learned vagrancy best known from Philostratos' *Life of Apollonios* and from Dio Chrysostom.[21] The beginning of his stay in Athens was inauspicious, since he refused to sacrifice to the gods and to be initiated at Eleusis, and saved himelf from stoning only by a speech which artfully combined truculence and deprecation.[22] The story testifies to the anxious piety of Roman Athens and to the continuing popularity of the Eleusinian mysteries, while Demonax' refusal to be initiated seems to show his "imitation" of Cynic models: Socrates, who was believed not to recognize the established gods, and Diogenes, who similarly refused initiation.[23] After this anecdote Lucian suspends his chronological account, which he resumes only at the end of his biography to narrate Demonax' last years, death, and burial. The central section of the work is almost entirely set in Athens, as if Lucian were writing in the city's honor as much as in that of Demonax.

The fifty or so apophthegms which make up this central section, together with some details from the two outer ones, form the fullest picture that exists in literature of second-century Athens: the pendant, much more solemn and less vivid, is the *Attic Nights* of Aulus Gellius.[24] Persons of culture are Demonax' most frequent interlocutors, and particular prominence is given to two giants of the Second Sophistic. The older, who is also the subject of Lucian's first two anec-

20. The most important source is Philostr. *VS* 46.24–47.15 K.; in Lucian, *Alex.* 57 and probably also *Salt.* 69. Cf. also *PIR*[1] T 161; Capelle, *RE* 6 A (1936) 1270–71; Bowersock, *Sophists* 67, 91.

21. *Demon.* 9.

22. *Demon.* 11. ἐν ἀρχῇ in line 24 evidently means "at the beginning," not "in office" as translated by Harmon in the Loeb and understood by Dudley, *Cynicism* 159.

23. On Athenian piety in this period, Nilsson, *Gesch. gr. Rel.* 2² 327–331; on the Eleusinian mysteries, Nilsson 345–352. Refusal of Diogenes: D.L. 6.39.

24. It is true that only a few sections of the *Attic Nights* are presented dramatically, and some of these are set in Rome.

dotes, is the celebrated "eunuch" from Arelate (Arles) in southern Gaul, Favorinus. For Lucian here and elsewhere Favorinus is good merely as a target of personal jokes, whereas Gellius treats him with great respect and with no mention of his physical peculiarities.[25] The other sophist was the king of contemporary Athens, Herodes Atticus. Lucian calls him "the great" *(ho panu)*, an expression which he always uses with a tinge of irony.[26] Once again Gellius forms a contrast, for though mentioning criticisms of Herodes he never speaks of him without awe.[27] All three of Demonax' epigrams are aimed at a feature of Herodes which is well known both from literature and archaeology: his extravagant mourning for members of his family. The sophist seems to have been most afflicted by the deaths of three "foster-sons" *(trophimoi)*, all carried off within a few months in the early 170's, probably by the plague.[28] His favorite among these was his young relative Polydeuces, also known by the affectionate or "hypocoristic" name of Polydeucion.[29] Polydeuces is the only one of the three mentioned by Lucian, who makes Demonax mock the infatuated Herodes for having horses, carriages, or dinners prepared for the lost favorite. A memorial recently discovered at the rustic sanctuary of Artemis at Brauron in eastern Attica exactly illustrates Lucian's anecdote, since the "hero" Polydeuces is shown reclining on a banqueting couch while a horse stands nearby.[30] Gellius describes how a Stoic philosopher rebuked Herodes for mourning a favorite youth to excess, and the youth may well be Polydeuces, though the philosopher can hardly be Demonax.[31] Lucian pays less attention to Herodes' grief for an un-

---

25. *Demon.* 12–13. On Favorinus, see especially *PIR²* F 123; Barigazzi, *Favorino;* Bowersock, *Sophists.*

26. *Demon.* 24, cf. *Alex.* 5, *Apol.* 5, *Herm.* 11, *Icar.* 2, *Navig.* 22, *Philops.* 5.

27. A. Gell, 1.2, 9.2, 18.10, 19.12.

28. On these three, Graindor, *Hérode Atticus* 114–118; Follet, *REG* 90 (1977) 47–54; Robert, *AJPh* 100 (1979) 160–165; Ameling, *Herodes Atticus* 1.113–117. The precise implication of the term τρόφιμοι is unclear, since Polydeuces at least was a relative of Herodes, while Memnon was black.

29. On Polydeuces see previous note; the inscriptions are assembled by Ameling, *Herodes Atticus* 2.166–175. On the many portraits, Datsuli-Stavridis, *AAA* 10 (1977) 126–148, 11 (1978) 228–230.

30. *Demon.* 24, cf. 33. The relief: *BCH* 87 (1963) 710, and Datsouli-Stavridis, *AAA* 10 (1977) 143; for this interpretation, Robert, *AJPh* 100 (1979) 162–163.

31. A. Gell. 19.12, with the discussion of Follet, *REG* 90 (1977) 51–52, who proposes to identify the Stoic with Demonax: but Demonax was a Cynic, and Herodes must have had many critics among Athenian philosophers.

named son and for his wife Regilla, though Regilla's death like Polydeuces' has left many traces in both literature and stone.[32] Thus Philostratos describes a philosopher called Lucius who criticized Herodes for his absurdity and inconsistency in terms very similar to those used by Demonax.[33]

Most of Demonax' interlocutors are philosophers, a tendency which reflects both his own vocation and the preeminence that Athens still enjoyed in this field when the crown of rhetoric, despite Herodes Atticus and others, had passed to Smyrna and Ephesos. Some of these philosophers are well known: Demonax' teacher Epictetos; the Cynic Peregrinus, whom Gellius also heard in Athens; Apollonios the Stoic, mocked both by Demonax and by the emperor Pius for his greed; and Herminos, the eminent Peripatetic.[34] Others appear only in the *Demonax:* two Peripatetics, the vain Agathocles and the lame Rufinus of Cyprus; a Cynic named Honoratus, who dressed in a bearskin, and another who carried a cudgel instead of the usual stick.[35] One of Demonax' targets is a "Sidonian sophist" who in the fashion of the age claimed an affinity with all the leading schools of philosophy. This person seems more likely to be a philosopher than a rhetor, but he cannot be identified.[36] Demonax also makes fun of two philosophers "debating a vexed question with complete lack of education," a scene which recalls one sardonically described by Galen.[37]

The other great branch of contemporary culture, the demonstrative rhetoric associated with the Second Sophistic, is represented apart from Favorinus and Herodes only by Demonax' jibes against a rhetor's bad declamations and the fad for excessive Atticism.[38] Two other

---

32. *Demon.* 25 (son), 33 (Regilla). For Herodes' mourning of an infant son, probably an earlier one, Fronto, *Ad M. Caes.* 1.6.8. On his mourning of Regilla (*PIR²* A 720), Graindor, *Hérode Atticus* 92–100, Ameling, *Herodes Atticus* 1.100–102.

33. Philostr. 64.20–65.12 K.

34. Epictetos: *Demon.* 55. Peregrinus: *Demon.* 21, cf. A. Gell. 8.3, 12.11. Apollonios: *Demon.* 31, cf. *HA* Pius 10.4, Marcus 2.7 (*PIR²* A 929; von Arnim, *RE* 5 [1903] 144, followed by Dudley, *Cynicism* 159 n. 1, absurdly takes this to be Apollonios of Tyana). Herminos: *Demon.* 56, cf. Nutton, *Galen: De Praecog.* 189.

35. *Demon.* 29 (Agathocles), 54 (Rufinus), 19 (Honoratus), 48 (Cynic): another Cynic in 50. Compare Herodes Atticus' rebuke of a philosopher who begged, A. Gell. 9.2.

36. *Demon.* 14.

37. *Demon.* 28; Gal. *Anim. Pass.* 2.7 (*Scr. min.* 1.77–80).

38. *Demon.* 36 (rhetor), 26 (Atticism): cf. A. Gell. 1.10 (Favorinus rebuking a young man for using *voces nimis priscas et ignotas*).

professions much in evidence in the society of the time were those of poetry and law, and one of Demonax' interlocutors is a bad poet called Admetos, another a man "expert in laws."[39]

It is a comment on the age that after men of culture, those who most frequently appear in the *Demonax* are wealthy Romans and Greeks. Only one of the Romans is named: "Cethegus the consular," who drew ridicule as he passed through Athens on his way to the province of Asia.[40] A proconsul of Achaea forgives an insolent Cynic out of deference to Demonax and is taxed for his effeminacy, while another Roman "entrusted with armies and the largest province," presumably Syria, asks Demonax for his advice on government. These consultations recall his master Epictetos receiving Roman visitors in Nicopolis.[41] Like these Roman magnates, rich Greeks came to Athens as tourists or to study with local philosophers. A "certain Pytho, a handsome youth of high birth from Macedonia," probably belongs to a great house of Beroea, one of whose members had been a bene-factor of his city at the beginning of the century.[42] One Polybios, "a completely uneducated and ill-spoken man *(soloikos)*," proclaimed in Romanized Greek: "The emperor has honored me with the Roman citizenship." This person might be the Polybios of Sardis who proudly erected a bust of Cicero there and in turn has been identified as the author of a work *On Solecism*.[43] Athletes also could enjoy a prestige equal to that of the wealthiest members of the upper class and, in fact, were sometimes drawn from it. Demonax mocks an Olympic victor for wearing effeminate clothes and, observing pancratiasts (ath-

39. Poet: *Demon.* 44; on certain of the society poets of the day, notably Paion of Side, Robert in *Stele Kontoleon* 10–20. Lawyer: *Demon.* 59; for lawyers and terms such as ἐμπειρία νόμων, Robert, *Hellenica* 5 (1948) 29–34.

40. *Demon.* 30, referring to M. Cornelius Cethegus. The date is probably 164–65, but Lucian calls him "consular" because of his consulship in 170, cf. Groag in *PIR²* G 98, 114; he is honored in an inscription of Ephesos, *I. Ephesos* 6.2068 (*OGIS* 512).

41. *Demon.* 50, 51: another Roman in 38. Cf. for example Arr. *Diss. Epict.* 3.4, 3.7.

42. *Demon.* 15. For Q. Popillius Python of Beroea, Cormack, *JRS* 30 (1940) 51–52; for other Popillii there, Dimitsas, *Makedonia* 63 nos. 50, 51, 70 no. 60, 84 no. 101. For Lucian in Beroea, Ch. 2 at n. 25.

43. *Demon.* 40; the word order of Polybios' boast, Ὁ βασιλεύς με τῇ Ῥωμαίων πολιτείᾳ τετίμηκεν, seems to be Latin. Polybios of Sardis: *I. Sardis* no. 49, with the commentary of Buckler and Robinson.

letes comparable to modern "all-in" wrestlers) who broke the rules
by biting, he remarks that they deserve the name given them by their
admirers: "lion." Philostratos attests that a certain type of muscular
athlete was called "lionlike."[44]

The city of Athens and its institutions only appear in the background of the *Demonax,* but these glimpses are vivid. Several incidents
of the biography involve the civic assembly. Demonax first appeared
before it to answer the charge of impiety, and was nearly stoned. A
very similar story is told about the sophist Lollianus in the same
period.[45] On another occasion Demonax intervened to dissuade the
Athenians from instituting gladiatorial games in emulation of Corinth,
and again very similar stories are told about other philosophers.[46] In
his extreme old age he quelled a riot *(stasis)* merely by appearing; it
is known that Athenian politics of the 160's were exceptionally tur-
bulent.[47] After his death the city voted him a public burial, and his
bier was borne by the local philosophers, two honors which are often
attested in literature and inscriptions.[48]

Demonax' first appearance before the Athenian assembly also illustrates the intensity of belief in Roman Athens, a trait that appears
in several other details. One of Demonax' companions proposes that
they go together to the sanctuary of Asclepios and pray for the man's
son, which suggests the great ascendancy that Asclepios enjoyed in
this era: his sanctuary on the south slope of the Acropolis had lost
none of its glory.[49] The *Demonax* also preserves traces of popular
belief independent of the official cults. When Demonax laughs off a
question about a dark patch on his leg (perhaps a varicose vein) by
saying "Charon bit me," he reflects a view of Charon as the god of
death, and not merely the ferryman of the underworld.[50] In his last

44. *Demon.* 16, 49; Philostr. *Gymn.* 37. Cf. Robert in *L'épigramme grecque* 271.

45. *Demon.* 11; Philostr. *VS* 39.2–8 K.

46. *Demon.* 57, cf. Dio Chr. 31.122, Philostr. *VA* 4.22.

47. *Demon.* 64. For the disturbances connected with Herodes Atticus, Philostr.
VS 67.10–21 K., Ameling, *Herodes Atticus* 1.136–151. This anecdote also has an
analogue in Philostratos, *VA* 1.15.

48. *Demon.* 67. For a man's bier carried by his colleagues or friends, Robert, *AC*
37 (1968) 413–416.

49. *Demon.* 27, cf. Edelstein, *Asclepius* 2.182. On the Asclepieion on the Acropolis,
testimonia in Edelstein, 1.374–380, Travlos, *Pictorial Dictionary* 127–128, Walker,
ABSA 74 (1979) 256–257.

50. *Demon.* 45. Cf. Nilsson, *Gesch. gr. Rel.* 2² 547–548.

years, "he used to go uninvited into any house at random and sleep and dine there, and the inhabitants thought it the manifestation of some god and that some good spirit [*agathos daimon*] had entered the house; and as he went past the women selling bread, each would tug him towards her begging him to take her bread, and whoever gave him some thought it her own good luck." The Greek belief in demons is very old, and a story similar to this is told about Crates. Yet these stories also suggest the world of spirits and holy men familiar from later centuries.[51] Athens shared the general obsession with magic and divination, as is shown by the large number of magical tablets from the Roman period,[52] and Demonax could well have mocked a seer *(mantis)* who gave predictions for a fee and a magician *(magos)* who claimed great potency for his spells.[53]

Despite the jokes and repartee, Lucian seems to have a personal involvement in the *Demonax* which gives it an unusual resonance. In part the work forms a graceful compliment to Athens, the adopted city of both author and subject. Moreover, there is a great similarity between Demonax and the picture that Lucian elsewhere paints of himself: educated but not doctrinaire, puncturing vanity and yet putting a high value on friendship, self-sufficient but no enemy of pleasure. The *Demonax* thus becomes a kind of indirect autobiography, all the more persuasive because the author is not posing as he is in the *Dream* or the *Double Indictment*.[54]

The *Sostratos* is known only from the introduction to the *Demonax,* and in many ways must have been even more unusual. The subject seems to be identical with a person described at length by Philostratos, who in turn uses and perhaps embroiders the account given by Herodes Atticus in a letter.[55] Philostratos does not give his true name,

51. *Demon.* 63. Crates: Apul. *Flor.* 22, Jul. *Or.* 6, 201B–C, cf. Funk, *Untersuchungen* 619–620. On demonology in later Greek religion, Nilsson, *Gesch. gr. Rel.* 2² 539–543.

52. Note Elderkin, *Hesperia* 5 (1936) 43–49, esp. 43, "Obviously the Athenians of the Roman period believed in the potency of the cryptic curse and used it extensively."

53. *Demon.* 37 *(mantis),* 23 *(magos).* This second passage is not in order: perhaps read αὐτόν for αὐτῷ in line 12, "so that with them he could persuade and dispose everybody in any way he wished."

54. Funk, *Untersuchungen* 672, "ein Stück Autobiographie des Schriftstellers selbst."

55. Philostr. *VS* 60.29–63.6 K. For detailed treatments see now Kindstrand, *Ann. Soc. Litt. Hum. Reg. Upsal.* 1979–1980, 50–79; Ameling, *Herodes Atticus* 1.115–160.

but says only that he was called "Herodes' Heracles" by many people and "Agathion" by the inhabitants of Boeotia and Marathon. The letter of Herodes appears to have described an encounter at or near the beginning of their acquaintance, and to have suggested a half-human and half-heroic being. Their relationship must later have been more intimate, since the appellation of "Herodes' Heracles" recalls the language used for the favorites of Hellenistic monarchs and for Polydeuces, and Lucian's claim to have seen and admired Sostratos implies that the youth had accompanied Herodes in Athens.[56]

From Lucian's summary account, and the fabulous one preserved by Philostratos, a clear picture of Sostratos is hard to form. He was born in Boeotian Delion, a place suitably remote and yet conveniently near to Herodes' estate at Marathon.[57] Whereas Philostratos emphasizes exalted characteristics such as his meatless diet, purity of language, and keenness of perception, Lucian seems rather to have stressed his activity, "his open-air life on Parnassos, uncomfortable places of sleep, food gathered on mountains, deeds corresponding to his name which he performed by killing brigands, laying roads in impassable places and bridging difficult streams."[58] From the juxtaposition with Demonax, it may also be inferred that Lucian treated Sostratos as a kind of self-taught philosopher, perhaps reporting his sayings as Herodes did in his letter. Unlike the *Demonax,* however, the *Sostratos* must have given its hero some of the features of romance, and Lucian's hardy giant roaming the mountains of Boeotia recalls the pretended

---

Kindstrand rightly identifies the Heracles surnamed Agathion of Philostratos with the Sostratos "whom the Greeks thought to be Heracles" of Lucian, but also argues that he is the "Sosastros" of Plut. *Quaest. conviv.* 660 E, though this person was dead in Plutarch's time (thus, rightly, Ameling, 157). Ameling, 157–158, is unduly skeptical about identifying the persons mentioned by Philostratos and Lucian.

56. Kindstrand, *Ann. Soc. Litt. Hum. Reg. Upsal.* 1979–1980, 59, argues that in the phrase τὸν Ἡρώδου Ἡρακλέα (Philostr. *VS* 60.29 K.), the name of Herodes is interpolated: but note the favorite of Antiochus II of Syria called Ἀντιόχου βασιλέως Ἡρακλῆς, Athen. 7.289F–290A = *FGrHist* 80 F 1 (Weinreich, *Menekrates Zeus* 97), and the inscription of Polydeuces at Delphi, τὸν Ἡρώδου ἥρωα (*FDelphes* 3, 3, 74: Ameling, *Herodes Atticus* 2.172).

57. Philostr. *VS* 61.15 K., where the manuscripts are divided between Δηλίῳ and δήμῳ: the correct reading is adopted by J. Schmidt, *RE* Suppl. 8 (1956) 782, but is usually ignored.

58. *Demon.* 1: cf. Funk, *Untersuchungen* 645.

robber Haemus of Apuleius' *Metamorphoses*.[59] Though it is curious that he should mention such an essay in his biography of an eminent Cynic, he may have been inspired by the great Arrian, who composed the *Discourses of Epictetos* and also a life of the Mysian bandit Tillo-robos.[60]

Lucian's motives for writing the *Sostratos* are mostly beyond recovery, as they are not for the *Demonax*. In some way they must be connected with the controversial arbiter of Athenian culture, Herodes Atticus. Lucian only refers to Herodes in two works: the coolness of the *Demonax*, which appears to follow Herodes' death, contrasts with the flattery of the *Peregrinus*, which precedes it.[61] Herodes seems to be in his mind elsewhere, and the *Lexiphanes*, if the target is correctly identified as Philagros of Cilicia, pillories one of the few sophists who dared to quarrel with him.[62] The *Sostratos* may have been, like Lucian's writings associated with Lucius Verus, flattery disguised as exposition.

59. Apul. *Met.* 7.4–5. Funk, *Untersuchungen* 646, rightly talks of "Räuberromantik."

60. Luc. *Alex.* 2. On this work see Ch. 12 at n. 3.

61. *Peregr.* 19. Herodes is not named, and so seems to have been still alive: cf. Ch. 10 at n. 7.

62. Other works: e.g., *Icar.* 18, on those who own estates at Marathon; Husson on *Nav.* 13.3. Philagros: Ch. 10 at n. 18.

10 Concealed Victims

MANY OF LUCIAN'S WORKS satirize certain types or classes, for example credulous philosophers or hirelings in great houses, but in six he attacks individuals. Two of these works, the *Peregrinus* and the *Alexander,* are exceptional in the detail with which they discuss named and contemporary persons. The other four, the *Lexiphanes,* the *Teacher of Rhetoric,* the *Uncultured Man* and the *Mistaken Critic,* resemble one another in that the victim is given either no name or one patently fictitious, and the description is sometimes so vague or general as to raise doubts of the person's existence. Another property shared by these four works is the author's concern with culture. All the victims seem to claim a literary profession, rhetor, sophist, or historian, and in attacking all four Lucian assumes the vantage point of the "cultured."[1]

Whether Lucian intended any of his targets to be taken for an actually living person does not allow a simple answer. In ancient invective the rules of truth were very lax, and there is no clear line between what the speaker intends his reader or listener to believe and what is thrown out for sheer malice or entertainment.[2] Especially when the accuser is a satirist, he will be inclined to comprehend the faults of whole classes in his depiction of an individual: the Teacher of Rhetoric, for example, seems to be conceived as the embodiment

---

1. Professions: *Ind.* 20 ("philosopher, rhetor, historian" or perhaps "author"), *Lex.* 23 (sophist), *Pseudol.* 5, 8 (sophist), *Rh. Pr.* 13, 14, 24 (rhetor). Culture: *Ind.* 4, 5, 7, etc., *Lex.* 17, 23, 24, *Pseudol.* 2, 3, 9, *Rh. Pr.* 17 (implicitly).

2. A good discussion in Nisbet, *Cicero: In Pisonem* 192–197, esp. 196–197, "Such inventions were meant to cause pain or hilarity, not to be believed."

of a group.[3] Nor need the quota of actuality be the same in all four works, or even in all parts of a single work: Lucian says almost nothing of Lexiphanes as a person, but he gives a full biography of the Mistaken Critic.

The question of the actuality of Lucian's attacks, moreover, is separate from that of their contemporaneity. Even if the Teacher of Rhetoric is deemed to be so vaguely described as to defy identification with any actual rhetor, the work can still be shown to embody precise observation of the rhetors of Lucian's day. Nor does the fact that his accusations had been made before prove that they are tralatician or outmoded. If he tells a story about the critic's pilfering which resembles one told by the elder Seneca,[4] that may mean only that the practice in question had persisted to his own time.

A further problem that affects all four of these works jointly is that of names. Lucian gives no name to two of his figures, the Uncultured Man and the Mistaken Critic:[5] Lexiphanes ("word-displaying") is an obvious fabrication devised to suit the subject. The Teacher of Rhetoric claims to be "a namesake of the sons of Zeus and Leda," a phrase which suggests that Lucian intended a particular name but did not care to supply it,[6] and this use of concealment suggests that the victim, rather than being indefinite or fictional, is still alive. This conforms with Lucian's treatment of the living elsewhere. The only historians whom he names in the treatise on writing history are those who name themselves in passages he selects for quotation. It is likely that when he alludes to Herodes Atticus in the *Peregrinus* as a "man outstanding in culture and reputation," the sophist was still alive but had died by the time Lucian named him in the *Demonax*.[7] Even Pantheia, for all Lucian's flattery of her, is named not directly but by a periphrasis similar to that in the *Teacher of Rhetoric*, "a namesake of the famous and beautiful wife of Abradates."[8] Lucian's reluctance to

3. Note the second person plurals, *Rh. Pr.* 26 (though Lucian may be thinking of his unnamed addressee as much as of the Teacher).

4. Below, n. 58.

5. The notion that the Critic was called "Timarchos," already found in the later manuscripts, is a mistaken inference from *Pseudol.* 27: cf. Jones, *GRBS* 13 (1972) 480.

6. *Rh. pr.* 24.

7. *Peregr.* 19, *Dem.* 24, 25, 33.

8. *Im.* 10.

name names is to be expected in attacks on living persons. So also his contemporary Aristides does not specify those who criticized him for not declaiming or who "burlesqued the mysteries" of oratory, even though his observations are often no less pointed than Lucian's.[9]

Of the four works the *Lexiphanes* is the simplest in form and the least varied in subject. Lexiphanes is a sophist with a verbal disease, a passion for obscure or fabricated words, and he also sprinkles his speech with quaint Atticisms comparable to the English "prithee" or "quotha." In the first part of the work Lexiphanes reads to Lycinos his *Symposium,* exhibiting all his faults to the full. In the second Lycinos with the help of the doctor Sopolis cures him by administering an emetic, and then lectures him on the correct training and behavior of a sophist.[10]

Lexiphanes is the only one of the four victims to receive a false name, and this in itself might seem an indication of his unreality. In addition, the charges made against him are very similar to those which Lucian makes against the Teacher of Rhetoric. Both victims use obscure words, either dug up or newly invented. Both overwork the same handful of Atticisms. Both neglect ancient literature in favor of the declamations *(meletai)* of recent sophists.[11] Moreover, these charges resemble ones made by writers before and after Lucian. The Greek epigrammatist Ammianus, writing under Hadrian or Pius, similarly pretends that a few ready Atticisms and the right appearance are enough to make the modern philosopher.[12] A generation after Lucian there occurs in Athenaeus' banquet of sophists a scene in which the Cynic Cynulcos accuses two of the guests, Ulpianus of Tyre and Pompeianus of Philadelphia, of linguistic mannerisms very similar to those attributed by Lucian to Lexiphanes, some even involving the same words. It has been inferred that Lexiphanes might be one of those described by Cynulcos as "Ulpianite sophists," but it seems

9. Aristid. *Or.* 33, 34. Cf. Shackleton Bailey, *Cicero: Ad Atticum* 1.279, "Avoidance of personal names, especially in delicate contexts, is a feature of Cicero's letters, but he has no system—it was mostly a matter of habit or instinct." Cf. also Cameron, *JRS* 56 (1966) 31, on Macrobius' *Saturnalia.*

10. A good discussion of the *Lexiphanes* recently in Hall, *Lucian's Satire* 279–291.

11. Obscure words: e.g., *Lex.* 17, *Rh. Pr.* 17. Atticisms: Hall, *Lucian's Satire* 285 (Lexiphanes), *Rh. Pr.* 16, 18. Declamations: *Lex.* 23, *Rh. Pr.* 17, cf. also *Pseudol.* 6.

12. Ammian. *AP* 11.142, 157; his date is shown by the epigrams aimed at Polemo, *AP* 11.180, 181 (*PIR*² A 862).

more likely that Athenaeus knew the *Lexiphanes* and borrowed some of Lucian's barbs for use against sophists of his own generation, just as Lucian borrowed some of those made by the epigrammatists.[13] None of these authors need be supposed to have invented the foibles or mannerisms which they ascribe to contemporary sophists, for if jokes or unkind stories are repeated from generation to generation, it is usually because they continue to correspond to something in reality.[14] That sophists of Lucian's generation were sometimes disposed to judge a word acceptable by ancient authority rather than by contemporary usage is shown above all by the lexicon of Pollux, a farrago expressly designed for the improvement of Commodus. The *Loves,* a work which survives in the corpus of Lucian, is written in a style which an unkind critic might have parodied very much as Lucian parodies that of Lexiphanes. Rather than being the work of a young or unformed Lucian, it is probably by someone who imitated his matter rather than his language.[15]

Whether Lucian wrote the *Lexiphanes* with a definite person in mind is perhaps beyond certainty.[16] If he did, many of the clues which the first hearers and readers would have had are lost. He claims to be a friend of Lexiphanes, and the setting of the work seems to be Athens.[17] It is worth repeating the suggestion that he throws out a

13. Ath. 3.97D–98C. In favor of making Lexiphanes one of the "Ulpianite sophists," Hall, *Lucian's Satire* 288–289. For Athenaeus' possible use of Lucian, Martin, *Symposion* 279, citing Mengis, *Die schriftstellerische Technik des Athenaios* 97–98. For Athenaeus' dates, Honoré, *Ulpian* 12–13.

14. Note that κάρα, mocked in *Lex.* 5, is plausibly restored in a letter of Sex. Iulius Maior Antoninus Pythodorus, dated to August 163: *IG* 4, 1² 88 1. 11; for this man's connections with authors of Lucian's day, Habicht (to whom I owe this observation) in *Asklepieion* no. 27. τητινός (*Lex.* 1) now turns up in an inscription of the second century B.C. from Chalcis in Euboea, Knoepfler, *BCH* 103 (1979) 175 (*Bull.* 1980.377).

15. Against the authenticity of this work, the excellent study of Bloch, *De Pseudo-Luciani Amoribus,* and briefly Helm, *Lucian* 354, who observes: "es ist, als ob man den 'Lexiphanes' vor sich hätte." On the setting of the work, Jones, *GRBS* 25 (1984) 177–181.

16. For a discussion of the various suggestions, Hall, *Lucian's Satire* 285–289, 543–544. Anderson, *Theme and Variation* 71 n. 40, adds Alexander the Clay Plato (Philostr. *VS* 76–82), arguing from Lycinos' comparison of Lexiphanes to a clay doll (*Lex.* 22): but for this image cf. *Peregr.* 10 and esp. *Prom. es* 1–2.

17. Friend: *Lex.* 1, 18. Lexiphanes' *Symposium* is certainly set in Athens, *Lex.* 2, 10 (on 10, Clinton, *Sacred Officials* 9–10).

hint in Lexiphanes' *Symposium,* when the sophist says of himself, "You know that I am country-fond *(philagros),"* for this could also mean "you know that I am Philagros," and Philagros of Cilicia was a well-known sophist who visited Athens in Lucian's lifetime. According to Philostratos, a young pupil of Herodes taxed Philagros with letting slip an unclassical word, and generally the visitor gave offense because his style was "new-sounding and disjointed in its ideas." If Lucian did intend Lexiphanes to be taken for Philagros, however, he must greatly have exaggerated some of his victim's peculiarities and quite neglected others.[18]

Though the Teacher of Rhetoric has several traits in common with Lexiphanes, Lucian's attack on him is much more pointed and personal. The work is also more artful in form than the *Lexiphanes* and gives the impression of an assault prepared with malicious care. It purports to be an essay of advice, addressed as was usual to a young man beginning his career, though it is soon revealed as a satire of the practices it purports to recommend.[19] The pattern on which the discussion is laid is familiar in such essays, that of the choice between two paths. This metaphor was introduced into Greek literature by Hesiod, whom Lucian quotes, but it received classic form in the famous myth of the Choice of Heracles recounted by Xenophon after the sophist Prodicos.[20] Prodicos refined the idea by making Virtue and Vice the guides on their respective paths, while in later versions the path leads to a personification seated on a throne: this is how Cebes depicts Happiness and Dio Chrysostom Kingship and Tyranny in a speech delivered before Trajan. When, therefore, Lucian represents Rhetoric sitting on a high throne and surrounded by Wealth and other figures he may be suspected of gentle parody.[21]

18. For this suggestion, Jones, *GRBS* 13 (1972) 475–478; against, Hall, *Lucian's Satire* 544 ("there is nothing in Philostratus' account of Philagrus which fits Lexiphanes"). On Philagros in Athens, Philostr. *VS* 83–86. For a possibly similar instance of Lucian's sly fun with names, below at n. 62.

19. A good discussion in Hall, *Lucian's Satire* 252–278. The self-refuting advice recalls Horace, *Sat.* 2.5.

20. Hes. *Op.* 287–292 (cf. *Rh. Pr.* 7), Xen. *Mem.* 2.1.21–33.

21. Ceb. 21; Dio Chr. *Or.* 1.66–82; *Rh. Pr.* 6; note also the remarkable passage cited by Galen from the methodist Julianus of Laodicea, in which the author claimed to reveal Method sitting on "most high thrones": Gal. *Adv. Iul.* 3 (18, 1, 256 K.). Cf. Petr. 118.5, *ceteri enim non uiderunt uiam qua iretur ad carmen, aut uisam timuerunt calcare.*

Lucian begins by extolling his easy path to Rhetoric, but the reader would soon have seen the irony, both from the florid description that he gives of the path and from the fact that it was usually, though not always, the less desirable of the two.[22] The irony becomes more manifest, however, when Lucian, reverting to the example of Xenophon, depicts two contrasted figures as guides along the paths. The guide of the Hard Way is a manly, sunburned figure, whose appearance corresponds to the toil and difficulty of the course he recommends, whereas his counterpart, the guide of the Easy Way, is the Teacher of Rhetoric. Thus the Teacher takes over the role of self-refuting adviser, which at first belonged to Lucian. In a brief epilogue Lucian again speaks in his own voice, undertaking not to block the path of the Teacher and his like, or to compete with them for the favors of Rhetoric.

The form and matter of the *Teacher* recall Lucian's *Dream,* in which he himself was the prize in a contest between Craft and Culture. There Culture promised him fame and riches and took him in her chariot, just as here he represents the young student yearning for fame and wealth and riding in the chariot of Rhetoric. There seems to be no significance in the similarity: Lucian merely follows an artistic pattern, inherited from Aristophanes, Xenophon, and others, combining it with reminiscences of the Judgment of Paris, Plato's *Phaedros,* the *Picture of Cebes,* and much else.

As the final sentences suggest, Lucian treats the Teacher as the representative of a whole class, those who are "rhetors and have acquired that sonorous and honorable name of sophist."[23] More than any of his other satires, this one is aimed broadside at that phenomenon of society under the High Empire which its admirer and historian, Philostratos, called the Second Sophistic.[24] The correspondences between Lucian and Philostratos, or what is known of Philostratos' sophists from other sources, are frequent. Thus Lucian's teacher claims to be "a king of oratory" *(basileus en tois logois):* the same title was given to Herodes by his pupils and remained in use until the fourth

22. This in Hesiod and in Cebes 15; cf. also *Ev. Matt.* 7.13–14, and generally, Becker, *Bild des Weges* 57–59.

23. *Rh. Pr.* 1. For the distinction between rhetor and sophist, see the references in Ch. 2 at n. 31.

24. See Hall, *Lucian's Satire* 267–273. The examples given in the text can be added to hers.

and fifth centuries.[25] The Teacher replies to the acclamations of his followers by asking, "What is the Paianian to me?" By contrast, when acclaimed as "one of the Ten," Herodes more modestly replied, "Well, I am better than Andocides."[26] The Teacher describes "the green palm leaves on my door, worked into crowns," which he uses as bait for unwary clients. So also Aristides accuses his rivals of carrying around palm fronds to advertise their success.[27] Like Lexiphanes, the Teacher seems to have features of several sophists, but the central target may nevertheless be a real person.

That Lucian does intend a real person is suggested by the account that he makes the Teacher give of his life and career. Much of this is from the common stock of invective, but some details seem too innocuous to be fabrication. The Teacher's father was an obscure person of questionable status who had been a slave in the area of Xois and Thmouis, while his mother was a seamstress. Servile origin was a common taunt, as was manual labor: Galen represents the father of the methodist doctor Thessalos as a carder of wool; Celsus makes Jesus the son of a poor country woman who earned her livelihood by spinning.[28] That Lucian makes the Teacher originate from two barbarously named towns of the Nile Delta is also suspicious but at least suggests Egyptian origin.[29] The Teacher began his career as the catamite of "some miserable, stingy lover," and Lucian makes similar charges against the Mistaken Critic and Alexander.[30] His next allegation, that the Teacher had changed his name from "Pothinos" (Adorable) and had "become a namesake of the sons of Zeus and Leda," seems another mixture of the malicious and the harmless. Supposed changes of name were always useful weapons,[31] but Lucian appears to have a definite name in mind. The scholiasts took him to

25. *Rh. Pr.* 11; Philostr. *VS* 90.28, 101.13–14; see the discussion in Robert, *Hellenica* 4.95–96, adducing this passage.

26. *Rh. Pr.* 21; Philostr. *VS* 72.13. Cf. Polemo's dedication of a statue of "Demosthenes, son of Demosthenes, of Paiania": Phryn. *Ecl.* 396 Fischer, Habicht, *Asklepieion* no. 33, with his commentary.

27. *Rh. Pr.* 25; Aristid. *Or.* 33.27, with Keil's note.

28. *Rh. Pr.* 24; Gal. *De Cris.* 2.3, *Meth. med.* 1.4 (9.657, 10.10 K.), Or. *Cels.* 1.28.

29. Cf. Dio Chrysostom on a Phoenician "not from Tyre or Sidon, but from some village on the mainland," *Or.* 31.116; Or. *Cels.* 1.28, Jesus from a "Jewish village."

30. *Rh. Pr.* 24; *Pseudol.* 28; *Alex.* 5. So also the charge that the Teacher had been the lover of an old woman, *Rh. Pr.* 24, cf. *Alex.* 6.

31. The *locus classicus* is Dem. 18.130; cf. Luc. *Gall.* 14, 29.

mean Pollux, the author of the extant *Onomasticon,* and this view is now generally followed. Pollux was a well-known sophist from Naucratis, an ancient Greek settlement on the Nile, and receives a notice from Philostratos. Certain features in Lucian's picture of the Teacher recur in Philostratos' description of Pollux, notably the "honeyed voice" and his disconcerting blend of knowledge and ignorance.[32]

If it is correct that the *Teacher of Rhetoric* envisages a particular sophist, Lucian must have expected his reader to wonder whether he wrote to satisfy some grudge or affront, and the closing paragraph, in which he renounces the attempt to seek the favors of Rhetoric, appears to suggest some kind of disappointment. According to Philostratos, Pollux' "honeyed voice" induced Commodus to grant him the Athenian chair of rhetoric subsidized by the emperors. It was probably on the occasion of this appointment that the Athenians planned to send a delegation to the emperor in favor of the sophist Chrestos. Such an event might well have raised a storm of pamphlets, and Lucian's may have been one.[33] Yet these literary feuds were integral to the Second Sophistic, and Lucian might well have fixed on Pollux as a target without so public a reason.[34] The *Teacher of Rhetoric* varies the perennial refrain that the modern generation thinks only of self-advancement and pays no respect to the classics. It may mark a stage in Lucian's career when he decided, as he claims elsewhere, to renounce the life of rhetoric, but he may have exaggerated the pose of the injured conservative in order to sharpen his satire on modern sophists.[35]

The two other attacks on concealed victims, the *Uncultured Man* and the *Mistaken Critic,* share certain features of inspiration and form. Both appeal to the classic invective of Archilochos, Hipponax, and Aeschines' *Against Timarchos.* Both are addressed directly to their objects, and to preserve the illusion of scarcely controlled fury Lucian

32. Scholiast, pp. 174, 180 Rabe. Cf. Philostr. *VS* 96–98. On the controversy over the identification, and in favor of Pollux, Hall, *Lucian's Satire* 273–278: for dissent, most recently Gil, *Habis* 10–11 (1979–1980) 87–98, who proposes Apuleius.

33. Philostr. *VS* 97 (chair), 95 (Chrestos). On the chronology of the imperial chair, Avotins, *HSCPh* 79 (1975) 313–324, esp. 320–321; Hall, *Lucian's Satire* 396–402.

34. Bowersock, *Sophists* ch. 7, "Professional Quarrels." Note the attack on Pollux by Athenodoros of Ainos, Philostr. *VS* 98.17–22.

35. A similar complaint, merely satirical, in Petr. 1–5. Lucian's abandonment of rhetoric: *Bis acc.* 26–32.

uses such devices as the abrupt beginning, sudden shifts of subject, and at least in the *Uncultured Man* a general looseness of organization. Though in some respects these two works resemble the *Lexiphanes* and *Teacher of Rhetoric,* the truer affinity is with Lucian's two masterpieces of denunciation, the *Peregrinus* and the *Alexander.*

Lucian's main weapon in his attack on the Uncultured Man is his book collecting, an emphasis reflected in the title, probably given by a later editor, *To the Uncultured Man Who Bought Many Books.* The basic charge, however, is the graver one of lack of culture *(apaideusia).* The person does not merely collect books, but by his ignorance of their contents and his ostentation becomes the laughingstock of educated men, among whom Lucian includes himself. Moreover, the latter part of the satire involves other topics: the man's personal vanity, his social ambition, and above all his taste for "youths already past their bloom and hardened."[36]

As usual, some of Lucian's charges recall those of other satirists or his own against other victims. Petronius makes play with Trimalchio's pretentions to literary knowledge, including his two libraries;[37] and a weakness for grown males, as opposed to boys, was a standard charge, preferred by Lucian against the Mistaken Critic.[38] Other items, however, seem too particular to suit a mere lay figure. The Uncultured Man once fancied that he resembled a certain "king," who need not have been a Roman emperor but seems to have lived in the recent past.[39] He is eager to gain the favor of the present emperor by his show of education; this detail, though no doubt applicable to many ambitious men of the age, does not look like a stock item of satire.[40] One detail may be significant precisely for its lack of emphasis. The man's flatterers have allegedly persuaded him that he is a philosopher, rhetor, and historian, and so he buys books to corroborate their praises. Just as Lucian appears to reveal the truth of his quarrel with

36. Culture: 1, 3–5, 7, 19, 24, 26, 28. Vanity: 20–22. Ambition: 22–23. Homosexuality: 23–25, cf. 22.

37. Petr. 48.4, cf. 48.7, 50.5–6.

38. *Pseudol.* 27–28. *Im.* 1, "an extraordinary sight . . . if she even struck Lycinos, despite being a woman," seems to suggest that Lucian admitted to the usual taste for boys.

39. *Ind.* 20–21. The charge that the Man imitated the "walk, appearance and glance" of the "king" suggests that he is a recent one.

40. *Ind.* 22–23. Cf. Ch. 3 at nn. 29–31.

the Mistaken Critic only in passing, so the Uncultured Man may be suspected to be someone well known as a man of literature, though his identity is beyond recovery.[41] His reality is also suggested by Lucian's several references to persons of comparatively modern times: Demetrios the Cynic; "the false Nero in our ancestors' day"; men who had bought the lamp of Epictetos or the staff of Peregrinus Proteus; a rich man in Asia who recently lost both feet from frostbite and wore wooden ones with elegant shoes.[42]

The chief interest of the *Uncultured Man,* however, lies not in its references to persons past or present but in its presuppositions about contemporary culture. As in the *Mistaken Critic,* the situation required Lucian to put his learning on parade. He could not, for instance, have referred his victim to Eupolis' *Baptai* without knowing the work himself, and in fact he slyly alludes to its contents when he swears an oath "by Kotys."[43] So also his comparison of the man to Thersites wearing the arms of Achilles involves not only the book of the *Iliad* which he cites, the second, but two later ones as well.[44] There is no reason to doubt that the Uncultured Man was a collector of books, since bibliomania is well attested in this period, for example by Aulus Gellius.[45] But Lucian's quarrel with his adversary is not that he collects books; rather, Lucian objects to his using the products of culture to conceal his own lack of it.

As an essay in invective the *Mistaken Critic* has no equal in Lucian, at least for those not offended by the cheerful indecency. Being addressed to a living person, it excels in verve even the *Peregrinus* and the *Alexander.*[46] It resembles those works in intention as well,

41. *Ind.* 20 (above, n. 1). A thought might go to Damophilos, a philosopher and rhetor in the reign of Marcus who wrote *On valuable books* (Περὶ ἀξιοκτήτων βιβλίων), *Suda* δ 52, *PIR²* D 4.

42. *Ind.* 19 (Demetrios), 20 (false Nero), 13 (Epictetos), 14 (Peregrinus), 6 (rich man). "Bassos, your famous sophist" (23) seems not to be identifiable, but note Apollonios of Tyana's *bête noire,* Bassus of Corinth: see Penella on Ap. Ty. *Ep.* 36.

43. *Ind.* 27–28.

44. *Ind.* 7, with Macleod's apparatus. Galen compares Thessalos and Julianus to Thersites, *Adv. Iul.* 2, 8 (18, 1, 253, 289 K.).

45. Zetzel, *HSCPh* 77 (1973) 230–233, 240–243.

46. On the *Pseudol.* generally, Hall, *Lucian's Satire* 292–297. Contrast Macleod, *CQ* 6 (1956) 109: "uninspired works such as the *Adversus Indoctum,* the *Eunuchus,* and, in particular, the *Dies Nefastus* [that is, the *Pseudol.*]."

being a denunciation which reviews the public and the private life of its subject. Another purpose is to rebut the Critic's charge that Lucian has used the word "ill-omened" *(apophras)* in a barbarous way, applying this normally feminine adjective to a masculine subject. Because the work is designed to serve for both offense and defense, it is correspondingly intricate in form. After a general prologue Lucian summons the personification of Scrutiny *(Elenchos)* to reveal the immediate causes of the quarrel, a meeting of the two men in Olympia and a more recent one at Ephesos. This use of a fictitious spokesman recalls the unnamed stranger with whom Lucian shares the task of denouncing Peregrinus.[47] Lucian next takes up the subject of the word "ill-omened," and then the Critic's career, which he divides into two parts, the public one of his reputation and advancement, the private one of his sexual habits. To this Lucian appends the man's stylistic faults, his chicanery and his personal appearance, and closes with an epilogue.[48]

Many of these charges are familiar, and Lucian may not have intended them all to be believed. Since the victim claimed to be a sophist, it was to be expected that he should combine a bizarre vocabulary with glaring faults of grammar.[49] Accusations of passive homosexuality were no less predictable, though Lucian dwells on this subject with much more particularity than in the *Uncultured Man.*[50] An allied topic is that of the pantomime, for in his invectives, unlike the essay *On the Dance,* Lucian has no motive to conceal the unsavory reputation that attached to this art. While the Uncultured Man looked "like one of the pansies *(kinaidoi)* who associate with dancers," the Critic allegedly "supported" them as a prologue and claqueur, dressed up in purple robe and golden shoes. It seems to be in the same role of supporting actor that Lucian imagines the Critic playing "now Ninos, now Metiochos, and then a short while later Achilles"; the first two characters both appear in mosaics of Syrian Antioch, which in this city probably recall performances of pantomime. Since Demosthenes

47. *Pseudol.* 1–3 (preface), 4–9 (Scrutiny), cf. *Peregr.* 8–30.
48. *Pseudol.* 11–17 *(apophras),* 18–22 (public career), 23–28 (sexual habits), 29 (language), 30 (deceit), 31 (appearance), 32 (epilogue).
49. *Pseudol.* 5, 8, 25 (sophist: "rhetor and sophist," 19), 29 (vocabulary and grammar). Cf. Hall, *Lucian's Satire* 296–297.
50. Note esp. the stories about the Critic's behavior in Rome, *Pseudol.* 27, cf. 21.

had taunted Aeschines on his acting career, it is possible that Lucian intends only to allude to a classic of invective, but like his allegations of the Critic's homosexuality, it may be that he expected some of this mud to stick.[51]

Although some of Lucian's charges may be traditional, the general impression conveyed by the Mistaken Critic is that he is attacking a real person, for it makes no difference that the person is now difficult to identify.[52] The best evidence is the way Lucian hurries over what seems to have been the Critic's real point: not that *apophras* was a new word, or inappropriate to a reprobate, but that Lucian had used it in an unclassical way.[53] Of the Critic's career Lucian gives an account which, though colored by bias and malice, seems to have a framework of neutral and harmless detail. Born in "the fairest and greatest of all the cities of Phoenicia,"[54] he subsequently spent time in Palestine, Antioch, Alexandria, and Rome, where he lived in the household of a distinguished Roman.[55] Thereafter he resided in Athens, and his quarrel with Lucian perhaps has an undertone of Attic rivalry, each party claiming to be more assimilated than the other.[56] The first salvo was allegedly fired at Olympia, when the Critic gave a declamation on the subject of Pythagoras being excluded from the mysteries as a barbarian. He had suborned a friend from Patrai to suggest the topic, the audience noticed his borrowings from other sophists, and Lucian in particular ruined his performance by laughing at the most pathetic moment. Their latest encounter was in Ephesos on the third day of the year, "when the Romans by ancient custom make certain prayers for the whole year." Lucian refers to the vows for the well-being of

51. *Ind.* 22, *Pseudol.* 19 (prologue), 25 (roles); cf. *Salt.* 2, 54 on Parthenope as a role in pantomime, and 83 on the supporting actor. For the mosaics of Antioch, Levi, *Antioch Mosaic Pavements* 1.117–119, Hägg, *Novel in Antiquity* figs. 4–6. Note also that there were written romances of Ninos and Semiramis, Metiochos and Parthenope: references in Hägg, *Novel in Antiquity* 18, 238. Demosthenes on Aeschines: *De Cor.* 129, 180, 242, *De falsa Leg.* 337.

52. Note, however, Bompaire, *Lucien écrivain* 484, "il est probable que la plupart des tentatives de cette sorte sont vaines."

53. *Pseudol.* 16: thus most commentators, including Bompaire, *Lucien écrivain* 472.

54. *Pseudol.* 19. For the standard praise, "fairest and greatest," Robert, *Asie Mineure* 423.

55. *Pseudol.* 10, 20–22, 27. Palestine is only mentioned in 10 and 27: the order in the two passages differs, but need not be chronological.

56. Athens: *Pseudol.* 27, cf. 11.

the imperial house administered by the governor of each province, though his reference to Numa as their institutor is an obvious anachronism.[57]

There is little here that does not correspond to the known patterns of the sophistic career in the second century, and the charges of plagiarism, the unruly audiences, the quarrels over language all have their equivalents in Philostratos.[58] It is natural to ask whether Lucian refers to a known sophist. "The fairest and greatest of all cities in Phoenicia" should mean Tyre, Sidon, or Berytos. A sophist from Sidon is mentioned in the *Demonax* but is otherwise unknown.[59] Tyre produced two sophists mentioned in the literature of the period. One is the Ulpianos who appears in the banquet of Athenaeus, a fanatic of verbal purism, who was perhaps the father or another relative of his namesake, the jurist.[60] The other is much more famous, a great figure of the Second Sophistic known not only from Philostratos, Galen, and later authors, but also from an inscription of Ephesos. This is Hadrian of Tyre whose career touches the Critic's at several points. Before practicing as a sophist, Hadrian lived at Rome in the household of Flavius Boethus, a consular from Ptolemais in Palestine. He taught for a time in Ephesos, where he was the rival of Aelius Aristides in Smyrna. Toward the end of the reign of Marcus he was appointed to the imperial chair of rhetoric at Athens; he then succeeded to the chair at Rome, where he died at an advanced age.[61]

A detail in Lucian's description of the Critic can perhaps be added

57. Olympia: *Pseudol.* 5–7 (cf. the incident at Olympia in *Peregr.* 4–7). Ephesos: *Pseudol.* 8. On these vows, Sherwin-White on Pliny, *Ep.* 10.35, Herrmann, *Der römische Kaisereid* 73, 110.

58. All three appear in his account of Philagros, *VS* 84–85; for unruly audiences compare also Sen. *Suas.* 7.14, Aristid. 34.47.

59. *Demon.* 14: it is possible that he was a philosopher.

60. On this Ulpianos, the full discussion in Honoré, *Ulpian* 12–15. Hall, *Lucian's Satire* 297, inclines to identify the Critic with Ulpianos.

61. The chief source is Philostr. *VS* 89–94; for the other references, *PIR²* H 4 (the inscription from Ephesos is now *I. Ephesos* 5.1539, and also Page, *Further Greek Epigrams* 566–568, with the obsolete attribution to the emperor Hadrian). Residence with Boethus: Gal. *De Praecog.* 5.11 (for Boethus, *PIR²* F 229, Nutton 164). Ephesos and rivalry with Aristides: Philostr. *VS* 107.24–26. Chairs at Athens and Rome: Philostr. *VS* 92.28–93.18; on the chronology, Avotins, *HSCPh* 79 (1975) 320–321, Hall, *Lucian's Satire* 400–402 (who ignores Avotins but comes to a similar conclusion). In favor of this identification, Jones, *GRBS* 13 (1972) 478–487 (though I would now retract or modify some of my arguments).

to the argument. Discussing his profligacy at Rome, Lucian avers that, "only one man would have believed you if you had denied doing any such thing and would have been your helper *(boethos),* your last employer, a man among the best of the Romans; you will allow me to pass over his name, especially since everyone knows whom I mean." This "helper," it may be suspected, is the Flavius Boethus in whose house Hadrian of Tyre lived. It has already been argued that Lucian makes similar play with the name Philagros in the *Lexiphanes;* there is a more obvious pun later in the *Mistaken Critic,* when he assimilates the name Tisias to the verb *exetise,* "paid." Puns on names occur throughout Greek and Latin literature, and though they are often mischievous, they also appear in contexts surprising to the modern reader.[62]

If the Critic is Hadrian of Tyre certain consequences follow for Lucian's own life and work. Flavius Boethus was a friend both of Hadrian and of Galen, whose demonstrations he attended; it is now generally agreed that the "Lucianos" whom Galen mentions for his tricks at the expense of philosophers and linguists is the satirist.[63] Some of the charges made by Lucian against the Critic would at least rest on a plausible basis, without necessarily being true. The departure from his patron's household need not have had the scabrous reason that Lucian alleges, but it marked a decisive stage in Hadrian's career, in that he went on to become a public teacher.[64] Lucian's allegations of unbridled profligacy may again be fabricated, but there is no doubt that Hadrian attracted attention and hostility to an extent unusual even among the sophists, and that the charge of homosexuality had some color.[65] Even the alleged connection with pantomime may have

62. *Pseudol.* 21 (βοηθός), 30 (Tisias). For plays on names, Macleod, *JRS* 69 (1979) 21 (*Collected Essays* 285); Jones, *HSCPh* 85 (1981) 123.

63. Above, Ch. 2 at n. 72.

64. Note Galen's expression (*De Praecog.* 5.11), οὔπω σοφιστεύων, ἀλλ' ἔτι συνὼν τῷ Βοηθῷ; cf. Bowersock, *Sophists* 13–14, Nutton, *Galen: De Praecog.* 190.

65. Note Philostr. *VS* 90 (a drinking party with pupils of Herodes), 91–92, cf. 94 (his ostentation as public sophist and his intimacy with his pupils), 92 (a murder charge against him). The epigram at Ephesos (n. 61) suggests at least self-satisfaction. Less salient points of contact between the Critic and the historical Hadrian are: his rhythmical, modulated style of "song" (*Pseudol.* 7; *VS* 93.23), and his extravagant clothing (*Pseudol.* 21; *VS* 91.18–19). The Glaucos mentioned at *Pseudol.* 26 might belong to a well-known Athenian family of which Philostratos mentions two members, Callaeschros and Glaucos, *VS* 95.5, 103.17; cf. Follet, *Athènes* 262–267, Jones, *Phoenix* 32 (1978) 231.

had a basis, for Hadrian delivered a notable funeral oration for the pantomime Paris, whom Verus had brought from Antioch to Rome.[66]

The circumstances in which Lucian wrote the *Mistaken Critic* can still only be guessed. It is possible that the meeting of the two enemies in Ephesos is connected with one of Lucius Verus' own visits there in the Parthian War, though it may have been casual, since Hadrian appears to have been established there in the 160's.[67] The main consequence of the identification, if it is correct, is that it brings Lucian into the main stream of the cultural life of the period. He claims to know the Critic's full history, and as an attack on a contemporary sophist his essay has no rival in fierceness or particularity, though in length it is surpassed by the querulous effusions of Aristides. With the *Teacher of Rhetoric* it forms the best illustration of a literature now known only from mentions in Philostratos: the personal invective directed against sophists by colleagues or cultured men in related professions.[68]

Lucian's four attacks on disguised victims are all, it may be argued, directed against real persons. There is a range of approaches, from the mild fantasy of the *Lexiphanes* to the harsh invective of the *Mistaken Critic*. It is idle to speculate whether Lucian first brought these works before the public in spoken or in written form and whether the partial anonymity made them less local as well as more discreet. The debt to earlier literature, Archilochos, Old Comedy, Attic oratory is acknowledged, and there must be other borrowings not now visible. Lucian's similarities to recent or contemporary literature, however, should be explained not by a mere imitation of lost models, but by a community of values and reactions that are the mark of a shared culture. One author whom he recalls but need not have known is the epigrammatist Ammianus. Living in the Smyrna of Hadrian and Antoninus Pius, Ammianus had ample opportunity to mock the Second Sophistic as it reached its zenith. He too mimics Atticisms and sole-

66. Lib. *Or.* 64.41, cf. *PIR*² M 392. Curiously, Philostratos tells how Hadrian used to draw Roman audiences away from attendance on pantomimes, *VS* 93.23–31.

67. For the first hypothesis, Jones, *GRBS* 13 (1972) 484–485, dating the visit to 162; Nutton, *Galen: De Praecog.* 190 n. 2, argues for 164. For Verus' visits to Ephesos, and the proposal of a third in 166, Appendix A.

68. Aristides: *Or.* 28, 33, 34. On sophistic invective generally, Bowersock, *Sophists* 89–93. Philostratos appears only to name one tract, composed by Proclos of Naucratis against all those then teaching at Athens (*VS* 116.18–21): but the many quarrels he mentions must have been conducted in writing as well as in speech, cf. Bowersock, 89.

cisms, plays wittily with a sophist's name, and makes the usual charges of gross indecency.[69]

Closer yet in both time and spirit to Lucian there is Galen. Galen's attacks on the methodist doctor Thessalos and his follower Julianus of Laodicea share with Lucian attitudes as well as details—the comparisons with Thersites, the allegations of lowly origins, the play on names.[70] Thessalos scorned the classic teachers such as Hippocrates; he claimed to be able to train a doctor in six months; Julianus set up as the sole revealer of Method.[71] Literature and learning were not confined to the library, or allowed at the furthest into a common room of refined malice and allusive barbs. They paced the streets and the squares, they frequented the lecture halls and the great festivals, not as wraiths or shadows but with the solidity of real beings.

69. *A.P.* 11.157 (Atticisms, though referring to philosophers), 146 (solecisms), 181 and probably 180 (play on names Antonius and Polemo), 221 (*fellatio* or *cunnilingus*). On Ammianus' circumstances, Robert in *L'épigramme grecque* 282–283, 287; cf. Hall, *Lucian's Satire* 262–263.

70. Thersites: above, n. 44. Birth: above, n. 28. Names: "the herd of Thessalian asses," *Adv. Iul.* 6, cf. 8 (18, 1, 274, cf. 289 K.).

71. *Meth. Med.* 1.1 (10, 7–18 K.: Hippocrates), 1.2 (10, 5 K.: training in six months), *Adv. Iul.* 3 (18, 1, 256–257 K.: Julianus and Method).

11 Peregrinus of Parion

IN 165, shortly after the Olympic Games, the Cynic philosopher Peregrinus committed suicide by throwing himself on a pyre.[1] Lucian's essay *On the Death of Peregrinus* is not the masterpiece of invective that the *Mistaken Critic* is, nor does it have the personal spite of the *Alexander*. Yet it has probably generated more emotion than any other of his works, mainly because of its famous discussion of Christianity. It has many other claims to attention, since the subject was a well-known figure of the time, mentioned by several authors besides Lucian; and the passage on Christianity, though it has distorted judgment of the work, gives an unusual opportunity to contrast Lucian's observations with the abundant testimony of his contemporaries.

The *Peregrinus* is addressed to a certain Cronios, probably identical to a Platonist respectfully mentioned by later members of the school.[2] Lucian treats Cronios as an old friend, able to share a joke about a charlatan whose tricks they could both see through.[3] The effect is to bring Lucian's intended readers into an inner circle of sanity that excludes "pathetic" or "misguided" creatures like Peregrinus, his Cynic followers, and Christians.[4]

The sentence following the address establishes the subject: "the wretch Peregrinus, or as he liked to call himself, 'Proteus,' has undergone the very experience of the Homeric Proteus, for after becoming

1. On the date, below at n. 34.
2. Ch. 2 at n. 77.
3. *Peregr.* 1–3, 34, 37–39, 43–45.
4. Note especially the key word κακοδαίμων, applied to both Peregrinus (*Peregr.* 1, 42) and the Christians (13); also employed by the anti-Christian Celsus, Or. *Cels.* 3.59. Similarly μάταιοι, βλᾶκες (*Peregr.* 37, 39).

everything and turning a thousand tricks for the sake of notoriety, finally he became fire too, so much did he crave attention." The rest of the introduction supplies just enough detail to pique the reader's interest: the pyre built by Peregrinus at "the most popular of the Greek festivals," the speeches spoken by Lucian beside the pyre and before a large audience, his near escape from lynching by the Cynics. Only after this rapid summary, as if Lucian's mirth was at first too great to contain, does he begin a continuous narrative. He had just arrived at Elis when he heard a certain Cynic ranting in the usual way, whose "shouting ended with 'Proteus.' " Lucian allows the Cynic, whose name is later given as Theagenes, to speak in his own voice. "Does someone dare to call Proteus a hunter for notoriety *(kenodoxon)*, O earth and sun and rivers and sea and ancestral Heracles? Proteus, who was imprisoned in Syria, who granted his ancestral city five thousand talents, who was ejected from the city of Rome, who is more conspicuous than the sun, who can vie with the Olympian himself? Because he has determined to take himself from life through fire, will some put this down to love of notoriety? Did not Heracles do the same? Did not Asclepios and Dionysos by means of the thunderbolt? Did not finally Empedocles do it by throwing himself into the craters?"[5] This speech serves several purposes. It suggests a defensiveness among Peregrinus' followers to the charge of thirst for attention, which at the same time it corroborates by the tragic language and grotesque comparisons, and it also sets up the biographical scaffolding which Lucian intends to demolish.

The Lucian who is an actor in the story now turns to a neighbor in the crowd and learns to his surprise that "Proteus" plans to cremate himself.[6] Throughout the work the author is at pains to suggest that he had no more than a casual interest in Peregrinus' doings, but here as elsewhere the artifice is barely concealed, since, as he soon reveals, Peregrinus had announced his plan in a work published after the last Olympics, so that the event cannot have taken Lucian by surprise. This device is immediately followed by another, equally transparent. After Theagenes has been led off sobbing, an anonymous person steps up

5. *Peregr.* 4. The appeal to earth and heaven is an unkind reference to Demosthenes on Aeschines, 18.127; the series of mythological examples also has a poetic ring, cf. for example, Marcellus of Side in his poem for Regilla, the wife of Herodes Atticus: Moretti, *IGUR* 3.1155 A 53–54 (Ameling, *Herodes Atticus* 2.154).

6. *Peregr.* 5.

in his place, "and at first he laughed for a long time, clearly doing so from the heart, and then he began: 'Since the cursed Theagenes made the tears of Heraclitos the end of his worthless speech, I will do the opposite and begin with the laughter of Democritos.' And again he laughed a long time, so as to draw most of us along with him."[7] The unnamed person claims to have observed Peregrinus' intentions from the beginning and to have made inquiries among his fellow citizens, and on this basis he now gives a biography of him that occupies about half the work. This person is a double of Lucian, since this speech must be the one which in the introduction he claims to have given himself, and in addition the laughter of Democritos is characteristic of Lucian or his substtutes in this and other works.[8]

After the anonymous person has finished his speech, the rest of the story takes place no longer in Elis but at Olympia, where the actual games and the accompanying fair *(panegyris)* were held, and also at the desolate site of Harpina some four kilometers to the east.[9] In Olympia Lucian listens indifferently to Proteus accounting for his past life and inviting all men to witness his death.[10] The next stage sets the author another narrative problem, since again he has to combine his pose of indifference with a detailed description of Peregrinus' death, but he solves it by claiming that he was unable to leave Olympia for lack of a carriage, and so was at leisure when one of his friends took him along to the immolation.[11] The closing section serves two main purposes. One is to recall the opening theme of hunger for notoriety and to reinforce it with the charge of hypocrisy: this Lucian does both by direct comment and by adding small details, for example, the cowardice shown by Peregrinus earlier during a rough crossing of the Aegean.[12] The other seems to be aimed at certain manifestations subsequent to Peregrinus' suicide. Lucian pretends that, while returning to Olympia, he made up a tale of Peregrinus' ascent to heaven in the form of a vulture, and that he soon after met an old man who

---

7. *Peregr.* 7.

8. *Peregr.* 45, *Sacr.* 15, *Vit. Auct.* 13. Cf. the anonymous *tertius gaudens* in *Eun.* 10.

9. On the disputed site of Harpina, Bölte, *RE* 7 (1912) 2407–9.

10. *Peregr.* 32–34.

11. *Peregr.* 35–37.

12. *Peregr.* 43. Τρῳάς here is not, as often understood, "the Troad," but the well known port of Alexandria Troas: for this designation see Jones, *CPh* 80 (1985) 42.

claimed to have seen the philosopher walking in the Echo Colonnade. This sounds like another stratagem, as if Lucian knows that a cult of Peregrinus already existed, and hopes to belittle it by claiming to have contributed to its birth.[13]

Thus even when read on its own terms the *Peregrinus* hints at a background of some depth and complexity. This impression is strengthened when the reader tries to recreate the setting in which his ancient counterpart would have met the work. To begin with the date, Lucian strives to give the impression of reacting to an event just past, yet there are signs that he wrote at least some months after the events he describes. There must have been an interval for his prophecy of a posthumous cult of Peregrinus to be fulfilled, though it need not have been very long. Another reason for supposing a delay before the writing of the work might be drawn from the mention of Peregrinus' disciple, Theagenes, since he is known to have died in Rome and Lucian tends not to name the living; but he may well not have been so scrupulous with a person he disliked. The other arguments for supposing a long lapse of time between Peregrinus' death and Lucian's work are based on supposed similarities or signs of development between his works and are largely subjective.[14]

A more difficult question than the dating is that of Peregrinus' history and personality. For most of his career the only witness is Lucian, who is obviously not concerned to give a sober account. Certain of the charges that he makes are so hackneyed that they seem designed to provoke amusement rather than indignation. It is also to be expected that fact and fiction will be variously blended, the proportion of fact being higher when Peregrinus himself is not at issue.

Lucian says little about Peregrinus' origins and boyhood. He was probably born about 100.[15] His name suggests a Roman citizen, and even Lucian concedes the wealth of his family.[16] Though in accordance

13. Thus for example Hall, *Lucian's Satire* 28. For the Echo Colonnade, Paus. 5.21.17 and now Koenigs, *Die Echohalle.*

14. Caster, *Pensée* 238–243, argues at length that the *Fugitivi,* also subsequent to Peregrinus' death, precedes the *Peregrinus.* There are undoubted similarities between the *Peregrinus* and the *Alexander,* but they do not indicate that the two works are close in date; rather, they show merely that Lucian used similar methods on similar victims.

15. Philostr. *VS* 71.19–20 implies that he was a contemporary of Herodes Atticus, who was born ca. 101; the calculations of Bagnani, *Historia* 4 (1955) 112, are variously unlikely.

16. *Peregr.* 14 (30 talents).

with the rules of invective he belittles the worth of Peregrinus' native city, Parion, it was in fact an important port and Roman colony, advantageously situated near the eastern entrance of the Hellespont.[17]

The first incidents of Peregrinus' life which Lucian, or rather his double, narrates, involve adultery in Armenia and corruption of a handsome boy in Asia. Asia was Peregrinus' native province, but Lucian does not explain why he visited Armenia, whether the word designates the kingdom to the east of the Upper Euphrates or the region called Lesser Armenia west of the river. The next incident is one to which he recurs several times in the work: Peregrinus' murder of his old father. Even Lucian, however, does not report it as more than hearsay, and accusations of parricide, as of obscure origins and pederasty, were very lightly made.[18]

The murder allegedly leads to the first of Peregrinus' extended absences from Parion and to the episode which brought centuries of opprobrium on the author. In Palestine Peregrinus "learned the splendid wisdom of the Christians" and soon became a leading member of the community. He gained even further stature by being imprisoned for his beliefs and was called a "new Socrates," but was finally released by the governor of Syria, "a man fond of philosophy," as unworthy of punishment.[19] There is no other evidence for this incident, even in the Christian authors who refer to Peregrinus, but the essentials are above suspicion. Christianity had recently reached the age of intellectual maturity. The behavior of its adherents is noted by several of Lucian's contemporaries, among them, Galen, Aelius Aristides, Fronto, Marcus Aurelius,[20] and correspondingly the new sect had now begun to produce its first great crop of intellectual defenders or "apologists." It was already possible for cultured Greeks to be attracted by the new faith, and both Tatian and the great Justin

17. On Parion, J. Robert and L. Robert, *Hellenica* 9 (1950) 80–94, L. Robert, *Hellenica* 10 (1955) 271–277; Olshausen, *RE* Suppl. 12 (1980) 982–986. For denigration of a man's origin, cf. Ch. 10 at n. 29 and generally Süss, *Ethos* 257.

18. *Peregr.* 10, 14–15, 37. Parricide: Süss, *Ethos* 259. Pederasty: *Alex.* 42 and on sexual slander generally, Süss, 249–250.

19. *Peregr.* 11–14. θαυμαστήν in 11 is of course ironic, cf. *Merc. cond.* 25, *Peregr.* 17. There is no good reason to suppose the philosophic governor of Syria to be Flavius Arrianus (as, for example, Stadter, *Arrian* 198 n. 85): Lucian had an ulterior motive for calling someone who treated Peregrinus with contempt "philosophic," cf. *Peregr.* 18, ἀνὴρ σοφός.

20. A convenient survey in Labriolle, *Réaction* 71–94; on Galen, Walzer, *Galen on Jews and Christians.*

were converts from Greek philosophy. Like these, Peregrinus may have become an apologist, since Lucian ascribes "many books" to him during this period, though they naturally have not survived his apostasy.

Lucian is interested in the Christians mainly as the dupes of Peregrinus, like the citizens of Parion and the Cynics at Olympia, though since they provided yet another example of human absurdity, he gives more detail than was necessary for his main purpose. His knowledge, however it was acquired, is on some points surprisingly exact.[21] He knows of Jesus of Nazareth and his crucifixion, of the Christians' brotherly love, and the importance of their "sacred books." What he says of the help shown by them to their imprisoned brothers, and of the communication between the churches of Asia and Syria, is exactly illustrated by such texts as the *Letters* of Ignatius and the *Acts of the Martyrs of Lyon*.[22] The detail of Peregrinus' title of "new Socrates" is especially striking. Though it has been thought a mere cliché, it is rather to be juxtaposed with those passages in the apologists in which the punishment of Socrates is made to prefigure the persecution of Jesus and his followers.[23] Yet Lucian sees Christianity through Greek eyes, and has various misconceptions: the founder introduced a "novel form of initiation," and Peregrinus is not merely a "prophet" but a "thiasarch and convener," titles which have no place in early Christianity.[24] In this and the *Alexander,* the other work in which he mentions the Christians, he is much less hostile to their creed than certain of his coevals, such as Fronto, and his information is comparatively full, but in the end they are merely another example of human credulity and ignorance.

By Lucian's account, Peregrinus returned to Parion, where he found his estate plundered during his absence and the rumors of his parricide still current. He therefore came before the assembly dressed in the

21. The best discussion is in Betz, *NT* 3 (1959) 229–334. Contrast Bagnani, *Historia* 4 (1955) 111: "Lucian's ignorance of Christianity and Christian doctrine is really monumental."

22. The parallels between Lucian and the *Letters* of Ignatius (ed.[4] Camelot, Sources chrétiennes 10) have even inspired the view that Peregrinus was their author: elaborately refuted by K. von Fritz, *RE* 19 (1937) 662–663.

23. Bompaire, *Lucien écrivain* 479, "cliché étrange." For Christ and Socrates, e.g., Athenag. *Leg.* 31.2; Just. *Apol.* 1.5.3, 1.46.3, 2.10.4–8; compare Betz, *NT* 3 (1959) 231; Döring, *Exemplum Socratis* 146–147.

24. Betz, *NT* 3 (1959) 229–230.

Cynic cloak, publicly gave his entire estate to the people, and "the poor creatures, gaping for distributions, immediately shrieked, 'The one philosopher! The one lover of his city! The one follower of Diogenes and Crates!' "²⁵ Every detail of this narrative has its illustration in the life of the contemporary Greek city: the gift of estates, the distributions that would be made from the income, the acclamations and their wording.²⁶ If Lucian can be believed, Peregrinus' disciple Theagenes set the value of his gift at five thousand talents, while Lucian alleges that the whole city with its five neighbors would not fetch so much, and the true figure was fifteen. This would still represent three or four million Roman sesterces, a very respectable fortune, and it is less surprising than Lucian pretends that Peregrinus' gift should have been so rapturously received.²⁷ One point of Lucian's account is particularly suspect. He represents Peregrinus as already dressed in Cynic garb and making the Cynic renunciation of wealth when his apostasy from Christianity was still in the future, since according to Lucian it occurred during his "second absence" from Parion. More probably, therefore, it occurred either on his first absence or after his return to Parion, and Lucian delays it in order to give an unflattering motive for an incident he plans to relate presently, Peregrinus' quarrel with his city.²⁸

Peregrinus now departs for his "second absence," and it is here that Lucian places his apostasy, ascribing it vaguely to some transgression against the Christians' dietary rules. Deprived of their support, he began to regret the renunciation of his estate and tried to reclaim it by a petition to the emperor: Lucian implies that he had now returned to Parion. The city sent a counter-embassy, and the emperor, who is probably Antoninus Pius, ordered him to be content with his previous decision.²⁹ Although Lucian has tampered with the facts so that the reasons for Peregrinus' petition are now irrecoverable, there

25. *Peregr.* 14–15.

26. For "distributions" from the income brought by public gifts, e.g., Laum, *Stiftungen* 1.103–104; for the language of these acclamations, Robert, *Hellenica* 13 (1965) 215 n. 4.

27. Similarly Dio Chrysostom's estate can be reckoned at about six million sesterces: Jones, *Dio Chrysostom* 6. Like Peregrinus Dio found his property plundered after a long absence: *Or.* 45.10.

28. Thus, following others, Schwartz, *Lucien: Peregr.* 98.

29. *Peregr.* 16.

is nothing implausible in the details of the petition and the counter-embassy. A similar quarrel occurred between Ephesos and the wealthy Vedius Antoninus, again in the reign of Pius. Both parties wrote to the emperor, who curtly rebuked the city for ingratitude towards its benefactor. If he was less sympathetic towards Peregrinus than towards Vedius, that fits with his known concern for the financial health of the cities and his mistrust of Greek philosophers.[30]

Peregrinus' third journey took him to study with the Cynic Agathoboulos in Egypt, also known as the teacher of Demonax.[31] Alexandria was a famous center of Cynicism, but Lucian's comic description of Peregrinus' training in "indifference" looks to be little more than a caricature. His next stage was in Rome, where "immediately after disembarking he began to abuse everybody, especially the emperor, knowing him to be very gentle and mild." Though the emperor paid no attention, the prefect of the city banished him, so that he gained the reputation of a martyr to philosophy, like Musonius, Epictetos, and Dio. The emperor is clearly Pius, to whom ancient observers often ascribe the quality of mildness, and the prefect of the city may be Q. Lollius Urbicus, who also punished Christians.[32] The comparison with three famous victims of imperial displeasure, of whom Musonius had been banished by Nero, and Epictetos and Dio by Domitian, may be Lucian's embroidery, but if not, it is a measure of the public stature that Peregrinus had now acquired.

Henceforth Greece is the only known theater of Peregrinus' activity. Though he appears to have spent most of his time in the area of Athens,[33] the rest of Lucian's account is concentrated on Elis and the Olympic Games. These were the traditional forum for speakers eager to find an audience, and to a Cynic they were recommended by their connection with Zeus and his son Heracles, their reputed founder. The number and dating of Peregrinus' visits are disputed, but Lucian seems to mention four festivals, of which the last was immediately followed by his immolation. Since this is dated by Eu-

30. *I. Ephesos* 5.1491 (*Syll.*³ 850). For Pius' views on benefaction and Greek philosophers, Williams, *JRS* 66 (1976) 74–78.

31. *Peregr.* 17. On Agathoboulos, Ch. 9 at n. 17.

32. *Peregr.* 18. On Pius' reputation for mildness, von Rohden, *RE* 2 (1896) 2509; on Lollius Urbicus, *PIR*² L 327.

33. Luc. *Dem.* 21; A. Gell. 8.3, 12.11; Philostr. *VS* 71.10–22 K.

sebius to 165, the three others should be of 153, 157, and 161.[34]

On the first of these occasions Peregrinus "at one moment abused the Eleans, at another tried to persuade the Greeks to take up arms against the Romans, and at another slandered a man outstanding in education and repute because among his many benefactions to Greece he brought water to Olympia . . . on the ground that he was making the Greeks effeminate." Because of this attack Peregrinus was forced by the angry bystanders to take sanctuary in the temple of Zeus, and at the next Olympics produced a speech or pamphlet extolling the water supply and apologizing for his retreat.[35] Some of this must be tendentious, but Lucian's materials are genuine. The reference to armed rebellion is to be connected with an uprising in Achaea under Pius of which almost nothing is known.[36] The fountain and its donor are by contrast very famous. Lucian refers to Herodes Atticus, whom Philostratos also represents as the target of Peregrinus' abuse.[37] Among Herodes' many benefactions to cities of Greece and other lands was the great Nymphaeum at Olympia of which substantial remains have been discovered. This building raises many problems, but the archaeological evidence accords with completion by the year 153, and thus corroborates Lucian.[38] The periegete Pausanias gives a very full description of Olympia about the year 173 and yet curiously fails to mention the Nymphaeum. It has been suggested that he shared the reservations of contemporaries about the grandiose monument, though in general he speaks of Herodes with guarded respect and (as will emerge) did not care for Peregrinus.[39]

---

34. Euseb. ad. Ol. 236, 1 (p. 204 Helm); Luc. *Peregr.* 19–20. The essential question is whether *Peregr.* 20 refers to four celebrations of the Olympics or three, but the language strongly implies four: τότε μὲν . . . , ἐς δὲ τὴν ἑξῆς Ὀλυμπιάδα . . . , ἀπὸ Ὀλυμπίων τῶν ἔμπροσθεν . . . , καὶ νῦν . . . In favor of three, Settis, *ASNP* 37 (1968) 23–24: but his argument that ἔμπροσθεν means "just mentioned" is not convincing.

35. *Peregr.* 19–20.

36. HA *Pius* 5.5. The inscriptions from Sparta mentioning νεωτερισμοί, which used to be cited in connection with this event, are now known to refer to internal reforms under Marcus: Oliver, *Marcus Aurelius* 78–79.

37. Philostr. *VS* 71.10–22 K.

38. See now the careful discussions of Ameling, *Herodes Atticus* 2.135–138, and Bol, *Das Statuenprogramm des Herodes-Atticus-Nymphäums* 98–100.

39. Date of 173: Paus. 5.1.2. For this suggestion, Gardiner, *Olympia* 173, cf. Habicht, *Pausanias* 134 n. 74.

Peregrinus' self-immolation, first announced at the Olympics of 161, was the act for which his contemporaries most remembered him, and Lucian's essay is built around it. All the satirist's art is employed in reducing the deed to mere buffoonery, and fact and invention are here particularly difficult to separate.

According to Lucian, Peregrinus' stated motive was to teach men "to despise death and be steadfast in misfortunes," and he invoked the Cynics' hero Heracles as his model and guide.[40] This accords with well-known Cynic doctrine, especially the refined version of it given by Epictetos in the generation before,[41] and suicide in old age was sanctioned by such examples as that of Diogenes.[42] Nevertheless, none of the earlier Cynics had carried imitation of Heracles to the lengths of self-cremation at Olympia, and other influences are likely. One, invoked by Peregrinus' chief disciple, Theagenes, was the self-cremation of the Brahmins, of which the most famous example is that of Calanos in the time of Alexander. But under Augustus too an Indian sage had burned himself up at Athens, and since Peregrinus knew the city well the instance may also have had its effect.[43] Lucian reports that just before his death he changed his name of "Proteus" to "Phoenix" in imitation of the "Indian bird," and though this name had several connotations one may have been imitation of Indian wisdom.[44] It is less clear, however, that Peregrinus was also affected by Pythagoreanism or by his knowledge of Christian martyrdom.[45]

There are signs that he also intended something more ambitious, namely, the foundation of a new cult. The name "Proteus," which he may have adopted at the time of the announcement in 161, had several associations. Transformation into fire and the power of prophecy were known to every reader of Homer, but Proteus had also come to be regarded as a god or *daimon*.[46] The name "Phoenix" is also eloquent, since it recalled not only the wisdom of India but also destruction by

40. Motive: *Peregr.* 23. Heracles: *Peregr.* 4, 24, 25, 33, 36.

41. Arr. *Diss. Epict.* 3.22 (Billerbeck, *Epictet: Vom Kynismus*).

42. Hornsby, *Hermathena* 48 (1933) 65; Dudley, *Cynicism* 180.

43. Str. 15.720; Plut. *Alex.* 69.8 (associating him with Calanos); Cass. Dio 54.9.10.

44. *Peregr.* 27, cf. 39; for the phoenix as Indian rather than Arabian, Rusch, *RE* 20 (1941) 415.

45. Pythagoreanism: see the cautious discussion of Hornsby, *Hermathena* 48 (1933) 73–77; Pack, *AJPh* 67 (1946) 334–345, and Hall, *Lucian's Satire* 178–181, are more positive. Christianity: Hornsby 81–82.

46. Herter, *RE* 23 (1957) 971–973. The other sources make Proteus the son of

fire and mystic regeneration. The clearest evidence for his religious ambitions is at first sight suspect. Just before the Olympics of 165, Theagenes made known a Sibylline oracle reported by Lucian, which in best oracular style predicted Peregrinus' ascent to Olympos.[47] It seems natural to suspect this as a forgery of Lucian, with his evident love of pastiche and deep knowledge of Homer, whose language was often imitated in oracles.[48] He counters the Sibylline oracle with one he ascribes to Bakis, a shadowy prophetess already burlesqued by Aristophanes, but this is perhaps an argument against and not for his invention of the other oracle, for the purpose of the second is to emphasize the fraudulence of the first.[49] Theagenes had every motive to forge an oracle of the Sibyl, since oracles in general were traditionally used to certify new heroes or cults, and those of the various Sibyls had been employed since the Hellenistic period as a weapon of religious and political propaganda; the existing collection of Sibylline oracles is largely the work of Jews and Christians, some of it fabricated in this very period.[50] Like the Sibylline oracle circulated by Alexander of Abonuteichos to gain believers for the new god Glycon,[51] the oracle published by Theagenes may be regarded as a genuine forgery, a real specimen of the religious propaganda mounted by Peregrinus and his disciples.

As well as predicting Peregrinus' flight to "broad Olympos," the oracle bade mankind worship him as a "great night-wandering hero, seated with Hephaestos and lord Heracles." That he should be associated with Hephaestos and Heracles was a natural consequence of his fiery death and the ascent of his soul to the ether, but "night-wandering" suggests a more elaborate mythology. Lucian elsewhere predicts that Peregrinus will be alleged to cure fevers as a "night-

---

Poseidon, Herter 943: by making him the son of Zeus (*Peregr.* 28) Lucian may be unconsciously following the propaganda of Peregrinus' followers, as when he calls the phoenix "Indian," above, n. 44.

47. *Peregr.* 29.

48. On Lucian's centos and pastiches of Homer, Bouquiaux-Simon, *Lectures homériques de Lucien* 337–351; on oracles in Lucian, ibid., 9.

49. *Peregr.* 30. On Bakis, Kern, *RE* 2 (1896) 2801–2; Lucian's oracle recalls that of Ar. *Eq.* 197–201.

50. Oracles and new cults: e.g., the celebrated reply of Delphi concerning Cleomedes of Astypalaea, Parke-Wormell, *Delphic Oracle* 2.38–39 no. 88. Sibylline oracles: a useful survey in Nilsson, *Gesch. gr. Rel.* 2² 109–113, 481–483, esp. 481 on Book 8.

51. *Alex.* 11.

guarding *daimon*," and in his description of the immolation emphasizes the late hour and the rising of the moon.[52] Other details suggest the associated symbolism of the nether world. Peregrinus' pyre was built in a pit; in his last utterance, he called on his paternal and maternal *daimones* to "receive" him, a customary invocation of the underworld; and before his death he appointed "messengers of the dead and couriers from below" *(necrangeloi, nerterodromoi)* to convey the news of his departure.[53] This nocturnal and infernal symbolism does not necessarily conflict with the simultaneous claims of heavenly ascent, since *daimones* were often regarded as roaming freely both above and below the earth.

The elaborate rehearsals were not spoiled by a poor performance. At the appointed hour Peregrinus appeared with the usual Cynic baggage of wallet, cloak, and stick, which he then laid aside to stand only in a linen undergarment. He next placed incense on the pyre, an act of which the primary meaning was sacrifice, but he may also have wished to recall the incense with which the phoenix was supposed to immolate its parent. He then prayed in the direction of the south, the quarter of the sun. Such observances are not unusual, since the Greeks had always venerated the sun, but in Peregrinus they cohere with his new name of "Phoenix" and his transformation by fire. After his final prayer, he jumped into the flames.[54]

The creation of myth did not stop with Peregrinus' death, but rather received new fuel. Lucian maliciously claims to have contributed a few items of his own: a "great earthquake accompanied by groaning of the earth"; and a "vulture [which] flew up from the midst of the flames and rose to heaven saying in a loud voice and human speech, 'I have left earth and go to Olympos.' "[55] Earthquakes were a regular concomitant of supernatural events, and especially of divine epiphanies. Lucian adds the same detail to Eucrates' vision of Hecate in the *Lovers of Lies,* and it is probably his embroidery here.[56] The vulture

52. *Peregr.* 35–36, cf. *Fug.* 1. The presence of the moon has been taken to show that Peregrinus had Pythagorean notions about dwelling in a lunar paradise (thus Hall, *Lucian's Satire* 179–180): but it is clear that his soul was to go to Olympos (*Peregr.* 29, 39).

53. Pit: *Peregr.* 35. Daimones: *Peregr.* 36, cf. Nock, *MUB* 37 (1961) 301–304 (*Essays* 2.922–924). Messengers: *Peregr.* 41.

54. *Peregr.* 36. Incense of the phoenix: Tac. *Ann.* 6.28.5. Sun worshiped by Greeks: Nilsson, *Gesch. gr. Rel.* 2² 508–509.

55. *Peregr.* 39.

56. *Philops.* 22; cf. Hermann, *RAC* 5 (1962) 1085–89.

is less usual, and he claims that it passed into the regular mythology of Peregrinus. Though this item has been taken as evidence for Peregrinus' Pythagoreanism, the vulture as a proverbially unpleasant bird seems likely to be Lucian's substitute for the eagle that was often believed to carry departed souls to heaven. There is no need to suppose that he was mocking the imperial cult at the same time, for the eagle was associated with the souls of private persons as well as of emperors and their families.[57] The words of the vulture are often thought to be his borrowing from a lost tragedy, but they could well be his own. When Apollonios of Tyana is accompanied to heaven with similar words in Philostratos' biography, that shows the sort of miraculous account ridiculed by Lucian.[58]

On returning to Elis, Lucian met a philosopher who claimed to have seen the transfigured Peregrinus dressed in white and "walking cheerfully about the Echo Colonnade, crowned with wild olive." Though this recalls passages of the Christian New Testament, the material is fully pagan. The closest parallel is in Plutarch's description of Romulus appearing after his death in shining armor and with cheerful face, while the crown of wild olive was the reward of Olympic victors.[59]

Peregrinus and Theagenes had therefore prepared the new cult far in advance. Besides selecting certain of his companions to be his "messengers of the dead" after his decease, Peregrinus was also alleged to have sent ambassadors to almost all the well-known cities carrying "dispositions, exhortations and laws." Similar messengers were dispatched by Alexander of Abonuteichos to advertise the new god Glycon, and such religious propaganda is found in other new or foreign cults.[60] Peregrinus' efforts appear to have had some success, especially if, as is probable, Lucian's predictions of his worship are really made after the event. He foresees that the Eleans and the other Greeks will set up statues in Peregrinus' honor, and that this was done at least in his native Parion is known from the Christian Ath-

57. The vulture Pythagorean: Pack, *AJPh* 67 (1946) 335–336. Proverbially unpleasant: Speyer, *RAC* 9 (1976) 452–454. Parody of imperial cult: e.g., Schwartz, *Lucien: Peregr.* 110. Eagle: Cumont, *Symbolisme funéraire,* index s.v. aigle; Schneider, *RAC* 1 (1950) 88–90.

58. Tragedy: Schwartz, *Lucien: Peregr.* 110, and Kannicht-Snell, *TrGF* 2.290a. Apollonios: Philostr. *VA* 8.30.

59. *Peregr.* 40. Romulus: Plut. *Rom.* 28, cf. Oepke, *RAC* 1 (1950) 931. For wild olive as the Olympic crown, references in Jones, *HSCPh* 85 (1981) 118.

60. Ambassadors and messengers: *Peregr.* 41. Alexander: *Alex.* 24, 36. On the propaganda of Egyptian gods, Nock, *Gnomon* 21 (1949) 225–228 (*Essays* 2.708–711).

enagoras.[61] The statue there was believed to give oracles and to heal the sick, and this confirms another of Lucian's predictions: that Peregrinus would be supposed to cure his devotees of quartan fever.[62] All this is well within the bounds of ordinary belief. Statues were thought to be invested with all kinds of numinous power, but particularly with the cure of fevers, a belief mocked by Lucian elsewhere.[63] Similarly it was not unusual to treat statues as oracles, particularly when the person represented was known for piety or virtue. Thus Athenagoras also mentions a contemporary citizen of Alexandria in the Troad, a city closely linked to Parion, whose statue was credited with the same powers as that of Peregrinus, and this man too may be presumed to have been of outstanding virtue or generosity.[64] It is again in accordance with normal reverence for a "holy man" that relics of Peregrinus were highly prized. Lucian mentions in this work embers from his pyre and, in another where he had no motive to invent, his stick which an admirer bought for a talent and displayed "as the Memphites display the locks of Isis' hair." He employs no such sarcasm, however, when discussing the honors paid by the Athenians to the stone chair on which Demonax used to sit.[65]

Lucian also predicts that Peregrinus' "accursed disciples" will establish a regular shrine beside his pyre, with oracle, priests, horrid rites of endurance, and torchlit mysteries. This recalls the cult of Glycon instituted by Alexander of Abonuteichos, which involved mysteries of a similar description, and it may merely be Lucian's malicious fantasy.[66] Peregrinus and his followers seem to have been far less successful than other religious innovators like Alexander, and though his memory lived on for centuries the cult is only mentioned within a few years of his death. This hybrid of Cynicism and popular religion was perhaps too monstrous to survive.

In making the death of Peregrinus the subject of satire, Lucian is not merely picking out an amusing item of news.[67] His pamphlet seems rather to belong to a whole debate of the period, as also does

61. *Peregr.* 41; Athenag. *Leg.* 26.3–5.
62. *Peregr.* 28.
63. *Philops.* 19, *Deor. Conc.* 12.
64. Athenag. *Or.* 26.3–5; see Jones, *CPh* 80 (1985) 40–45.
65. Embers: *Peregr.* 39. Stick: *Adv. Ind.* 14. Demonax' chair: *Demon.* 67. Pfister's classic study, *Reliquienkult*, is concerned mainly with cults of the ancient heroes.
66. *Peregr.* 28; *Alex.* 38–40.
67. "Un fait divers," Bompaire, *Lucien écrivain* 477.

the *Alexander*, even if the other participants can now be heard only faintly. The lead was presumably given by the protagonist's own writings. Lucian ascribes to him in his Cynic phase two Olympic speeches or tracts, the first being a defense *(apologia)* of his conduct at the previous Olympics, and the open letters sent just before his death.[68] A book list of the third century may preserve a reference precisely to *Apologies of Peregrinus*, though these could have been written in his defense by others.[69] Later in the same century his *Praise of Poverty* was still well enough known to be recommended by Menander the Rhetor.[70] Theagenes later became a celebrated preacher at Rome, and Galen preserves a curious account of his death there. He must have spread the gospel of the Master, and it is a reasonable guess that Lucian's work is aimed at him as much as at Peregrinus.[71]

Contemporary references to Peregrinus almost always have a combative tone, as if their authors were touching on a sensitive topic. Aulus Gellius, who had heard him at Athens, calls him "a man of gravity and courage" and reports his sermons with approval.[72] About the same time the elder Philostratos, the father of the biographer, wrote a work apparently entitled *Proteus, Cynic or Sophist:* its tendency can only be guessed, but it too seems to imply a continuing discussion.[73] In his description of Olympia already mentioned, Pausanias

68. *Peregr.* 20, 41: the speech against Herodes' nymphaeum (*Peregr.* 19) may also have been published.

69. Mitteis-Wilcken, *Chrestomathie* no. 155 i 15; *P. Ross. Georg.* 1 no. 22, [. . .] . . γρίνου ἀπολογίαι. The generally accepted reading is [Νε]ιγρίνου (thus, implicitly, Pack² no. 2089), but Wilcken thought it too short and not in accordance with the traces: [Πε]ρεγρίνου was apparently proposed by Praechter, cf. Schwartz, *Lucien: Peregr.* 101.

70. Men. Rh. p. 346.18–19, with the commentary of Russell-Wilson. However, alleging that "there is no evidence for written works," they implausibly suggest that the work mentioned is really the *Proteus* of the Elder Philostratos.

71. Theagenes: the evidence was first assembled by Bernays, *Lucian* 14–21 (an excellent summary by Dessau, *PIR*¹ T 110). His death: Galen, *Meth. Med.* 13.15 (10.909–916 Kühn). As Lucian's target: Bernays, *Lucian* 4–14. Lucian presumably refers to the same person in *Catapl.* 6, mischievously alleging that he killed himself for love of a *hetaira:* thus Dessau *PIR*¹ T 110 against Bernays, 90.

72. A. Gell, 12.11, cf. 8.3. It is debated whether Gellius outlived Peregrinus, but this passage, especially *constantem*, seems to imply it: cf. Marshall, *CPh* 58 (1963) 148–149.

73. *Suda* φ 422, Πρωτέα κύνα ἢ σοφιστήν. It is sometimes thought that two works are meant, a *Proteus* and a *Cynic or Sophist*, thus Solmsen, *RE* 20 (1941) 135: for the more probable view, Russell-Wilson, *Menander Rhetor* 249.

digresses to discuss an Olympic victor who burned himself alive when he found his strength gone, and comments that such actions are signs of madness rather than courage. The periegete, it seems clear, had the opposite view of Peregrinus to that of Gellius.[74] In the next generation too the younger Philostratos shows no sympathy with Peregrinus' attacks on Herodes Atticus.[75]

Christian writers also had mixed feelings about Peregrinus. Tatian refers to him in a way that has been thought to indicate respect, though the more probable interpretation is that he considers him a hypocrite and a parasite.[76] The passage of Athenagoras about his statue at Parion is by contrast neutral, and the same tone is preserved by later Christians such as Eusebios.[77] Near the end of pagan antiquity, however, Ammianus Marcellinus describes how Simonides, a philosopher condemned to the flames for practicing theurgy, was inspired by the example of Peregrinus.[78]

Lucian's account of Peregrinus gives an impression of less involvement and less ferocity than his attacks on personal enemies like the Mistaken Critic and Alexander. He does not claim greater acquaintance than a voyage they once shared from Alexandria in the Troad to Greece and their encounters at Olympia.[79] He must have observed Peregrinus at Athens and had perhaps even made inquiries about him in Parion, as his lay figure had done, but for that his general dislike of impostors was a sufficient motive. Lucian's comparatively detached tone, however, and the evident malice of some of his charges do not make his pamphlet literary or scholastic. Peregrinus was not a minor figure whom he plucked from obscurity to be the butt of a learned joke, but a Cynic on whose philosophical, political, and religious pretensions no cultivated man could fail to have an opinion.

74. Paus. 6.8.4; see, most recently, Habicht, *Pausanias* 11. However, the view that Arr. *Anab.* 7.3.6 is another anonymous reference to Peregrinus (e.g., Bompaire, *Lucien écrivain* 478 n. 1) implies far too late a date for the *Anabasis*.

75. Philostr. *VS* 71.10–22 K.

76. Tat. *Orat.* 25.1. The question turns on whether κατὰ τὸν Πρωτέα means "according to" or "like": the former is assumed by Bernays, *Lucian* 63, but the latter is surely right: Whittaker, *Tatian* 47.

77. Athenag. *Leg.* 26.4–5; Eusebios-Jerome on Ol. 236. 1 (p. 204 Helm).

78. Amm. Marc. 29.1.39 (Praechter, *RE* 3 A [1927] 197–198; *PLRE* 1.843).

79. *Peregr.* 43–45. For πάλαι in 43, Ch. 2 at n. 64.

12 Alexander of Abonuteichos

THE LONGEST and most elaborate of Lucian's personal satires is the *Alexander or the False Prophet*. The subject is Alexander of Abonuteichos in Paphlagonia, the self-proclaimed "interpreter" *(prophetes)* of the snake-god Glycon, a reincarnation of Asclepios. Eighty years ago it was possible to dismiss Alexander as a minor sham, a measure of the insignificance of the persons Lucian dared to attack.[1] As usual the social and cultural background provides the corrective. Alexander was the most formidable of Lucian's enemies, with powerful supporters in the court at Rome and wide religious influence throughout the Roman Empire.

The work purports to be written at the request of Lucian's friend Celsus, who had written his own attack on magicians *(magoi)* and was an Epicurean. This is a known person, though probably not the Celsus against whom Origen wrote his defense of Christianity.[2] The Epicureanism of Celsus helps to explain the great emphasis which Lucian places on Alexander's war against the sect, and his warm encomium of the Master at the end of the work. He begins with a show of reluctance, but appeals to a precedent: "Arrian, the pupil of Epictetos, a man among the first of the Romans, who consorted with culture all his life," had written a life of the bandit Tillorobos, and so Lucian will do the same for a bandit who ravaged "practically the whole

1. Wilamowitz in *Die gr. und lat. Litt. und Sprache*[1] 173 (ed.[3] 248), "der kleine Winkelprophet." For the contrary view, Robert, *Asie Mineure* 393–421, to which the present chapter is much indebted. The study of Branham, *Classical Antiquity* 3 (1984) 143–163, though interesting, suffers from its neglect of Robert's discussion.

2. *Alex.* 21 (*Against Magicians*: cf. Or. *Cels.* 1.68), 61 (Epicurean). Cf. Ch. 2 at n. 78.

Roman Empire."[3] This hesitation need not be taken seriously: there is a nearby parallel in Origen, who pretends that he would not have written his vast refutation of Celsus without the prompting of his friend Ambrose.[4] Lucian's invocation of Arrian serves several purposes. It calls to mind Alexander of Macedon with whom Lucian sardonically compares the prophet of Abonuteichos.[5] Joined with that of Epictetos, it puts the work in a context of culture and philosophy which is to be important later. And it perhaps contrasts a wise Roman with the foolish ones who fell under the prophet's influence.

Though evidence from elsewhere can be used to correct, confirm, or supplement Lucian, particularly in what he says of Glycon, for an account of Alexander's career he is the inescapable, if heavily biased, source. Alexander was born between about 105 and 115 in Abonuteichos, a small port-city on the coast of the Black Sea roughly midway between the better known Sinope and Amastris. Geographically it lay within the backward region of Paphlagonia, administratively within the Roman province of Pontus and Bithynia.[6] Lucian calls Alexander's parents "insignificant," but since he says nothing worse, and Alexander claimed descent from Perseus, the mythical ancestor of the Achaemenids, the truth is probably that he was of the old aristocracy of the city.[7] Lucian concedes, since it suits his purpose, that Alexander was extraordinary in both physique and personality. Physically he was

3. *Alex.* 2. On this work of Arrian, Stadter, *Arrian* 162; for the name Tillorobos (rather than "Tilloboros") see also Robert, *Noms indigènes* 94.

4. Or. *Cels.* pref. 1–3. Caster, *Études* 7, who usually insists on the artificiality of the *Alexander,* here takes Lucian literally: "Quant à la rupture du silence, il s'explique justement par cette demande que Lucian reçut un jour de ses amis Épicuriens."

5. *Alex.* 1, 7, 16. For this observation, Vidal-Naquet, *Flavius Arrien* 371–373.

6. Alexander's birthdate: this ultimately depends on that of Lucian's visit to Abonuteichos (*Alex.* 55) and on the accuracy of various ages that he gives in the work. The visit must belong about 165 (above, Ch. 2 at n. 63). Before this date Alexander's daughter had already married (P. Mummius Sisenna) Rutilianus (*Alex.* 54, 55), who was sixty at the time of the marriage (*Alex.* 35). Rutilianus died at seventy (*Alex.* 34), and yet outlived Alexander (*Alex.* 60), who therefore cannot have died later than 175, and probably rather earlier. Since he was "not yet seventy" at his death (*Alex.* 59), he should have been born ca. 105–115. It should be noted that the reference in Athenag. *Leg.* 26 to an Alexander buried at Parion concerns the Homeric Paris, not Lucian's enemy: see Jones, *CPh* 80 (1985) 41. On Abonuteichos, Robert, *Asie Mineure* 395.

7. Parents: *Alex.* 11. Perseus: *Alex.* 11, 58, cf. Robert, *Asie Mineure* 411.

the image of the "godlike" man—tall, fair-skinned, with long hair and intense eyes—and behind an appearance of mildness and simplicity he had an intellect of which Lucian emphasizes the "intelligence and cunning."[8] Lucian represents him as using these gifts as mere instruments of self-aggrandizement, but it may rather be that they created in him a conviction of his divine mission, and that he was his own first victim. In a letter to his son-in-law Rutilianus he compared himself to Pythagoras, for whom he shared the widespread veneration of the time, and it has even been suggested that to portray Alexander, Lucian draws on legends about the sage of Samos.[9]

Lucian alleges that Alexander began his career as a prostitute, an allegation too common to be taken seriously. It is a more credible charge that he studied under a doctor from Tyana in Cappadocia, who in turn had been a pupil of his own townsman the Pythagorean Apollonios. This association with a doctor explains Alexander's knowledge of medicine, which is conceded even by Lucian and contributed powerfully to the success of his oracle, just as his spiritual descent from Apollonios explains his attachment to Pythagoreanism.[10] The connection with Apollonios and with Pythagoreanism brought Alexander's oracle directly into the philosophical debates of the day, in which the reputations of Apollonios and Pythagoras, and the reliability of oracles, were hotly contested, and Lucian's essay can be understood partly as a volley in such an intellectual battle.[11]

The next stage in Alexander's career (again, according to Lucian) involved a partnership with a professional writer of choruses, a Byzantine to whom Lucian attributes the nickname, probably indecent, of "Cocconas." Together the pair set up as traveling "frauds," by which Lucian probably means that they told fortunes and sold medicines.

8. *Alex.* 3 (looks), 4 (intelligence). For these as features of the divine man, Bieler, ΘΕΙΟΣ *ANHP* 1.50–51, 54, 73–80. Compare the *Dictionary of American Biography* (17.312) on Joseph Smith, the founder of Mormonism: "in appearance he was tall, light-haired, blue-eyed, distinguished": similarly on his son of the same name (17.313), "he was of large frame, and his white hair and beard lent his unusual face impressiveness."

9. *Alex.* 4, cf. 25, 33, 40; note also Alexander's use of the doctrine of metempsychosis, 34, 43. For this theory, Lévy, *Légende de Pythagore* 141.

10. *Alex.* 5. On the medical activity of the oracle, cf. *Alex.* 22, 36, 53, 60; Robert, *Asie Mineure* 419 n. 137.

11. See below at n. 60.

In the course of their wanderings they were taken up by a Macedonian lady past her prime, whom they accompanied to Pella, and there they became acquainted with the large, tame snakes for which the region was famous.[12] They then hatched their plot, though not without disagreements. In the sanctuary of Apollo Pythaios at Chalcedon they buried bronze tablets which announced that Asclepios and his father Apollo would soon migrate to Abonuteichos, and these were duly discovered. Alexander went back to his native city, which had voted to build a temple to the new god, while Cocconas remained behind in Chalcedon, employing his skills as a poet in fabricating oracles. One of these announced that Alexander was the son of Podaleirios, and so himself the grandson of Asclepios. Another was a Sibylline oracle predicting that Abonuteichos would one day produce a prophet whose name, barely concealed by "isopsephs" (numerals equal in value to the letters of the name), was Alexander.[13]

These events probably occurred long before Lucian knew Alexander, and his account is no doubt distorted by malice. The view that Alexander "thought up" a life of deception when he could no longer support himself by prostitution accords with the color that Lucian puts upon the prophet's whole career. The story of the Macedonian woman similarly smacks of invective and may be due to Lucian's desire to contrast Alexander with Alexander of Macedon. The materials with which Lucian works, however, look genuine enough. The variety of snake which the swindlers used appears to be one frequently found as a domestic animal in the ancient world: Alexander's innovation was to supply it with a talking head.[14] The device of buried tablets is a well-known one, though it is not necessary to suppose with Lucian that it was a cold-blooded forgery. It may rather have been self-delusion, or a fabrication designed to serve higher ends.[15] The claim of divine parentage is not surprising for a "godlike" man: so also Apollonios of Tyana was rumored to be the son of the marine god

12. *Alex.* 6–7. On "Cocconas," Robert, *Noms indigènes* 138–139.

13. *Alex.* 8–11. On the sanctuary of Apollo at Calchedon, Robert, *Asie Mineure* 395 n. 6.

14. Caster, *Études* 15, citing Daremberg-Saglio, *Dictionnaire des antiquités* 1.695.

15. Weinreich, *NJbb* 47 (1921) 140 (*Ausg. Schr.* 1.535–536), adducing the parallel of Joseph Smith and the *Book of Mormon;* on this type of religious fabrication see now Speyer, *Bücherfunde* 99–110.

Proteus, and it will be seen that Alexander's own Glycon was alleged to have had mortal children.[16] Finally, the use of isopsephs was universal, especially favored in prophecies made up after the event, and there is no need to suppose that this one is Lucian's parody.[17]

Lucian next describes Alexander's return to Abonuteichos and the establishment of the oracle. The essential contrivance was to show to the citizens the god newly born in the foundations of the temple, so that not long after he could be displayed fully grown and already equipped with his miraculous head.[18] For the purpose Lucian accuses Alexander of resorting to a number of "devices," a word which recurs in his account.[19] One is that of the linen mask which Alexander fitted on the snake's head. It had a "vaguely human appearance," the jaws and tongue were manipulated by strings of horsehair, and later Lucian describes how the creature was made to appear to talk by means of a tube fashioned from the windpipe of a crane. His description of the mask is now corroborated by a statue of Glycon found at Tomi on the Black Sea, in which the god is shown with long hair, human ears, and a face more canine than anthropomorphic. The Christian Hippolytos describes how magicians used similar pipes to convey messages to their assistants or to make skulls appear to speak.[20] Lucian has probably drawn his description from a similar work, perhaps the book *Against Magicians* of his friend Celsus. Alexander's other alleged "device" is that of the goose egg in which he concealed a newborn snake: Hippolytos gives a detailed recipe for emptying eggs and sealing the perforations, and again Lucian may have drawn his description from some treatise.[21]

From this point on Lucian articulates his narrative in stages, in which there is a counterpoint between the geographical spread of the

16. Philostr. *VA* 1.4; cf. Nock, *Gnomon* 33 (1961) 586 (*Essays* 2.934–935).

17. Caster, *Études* 24–25. The best known prophetic isopseph is *Rev.* 13.18; on isopsephs in general, Robert, *CRAI* 1982, 130–132.

18. For swift growth as a supernatural sign, Weinreich, *NJbb* 47 (1921) 142 (*Ausg. Schr.* 1.539); Bieler, ΘΕΙΟΣ ΑΝΗΡ 38.

19. *Alex.* 13, μηχανᾶται; cf. 17, 19, 20, 26, 32, 38.

20. *Alex.* 12, 26, cf. Hippol. *Ref.* 4.28, 31. Statue at Tomi: below at n. 27. On most of the coins Glycon appears with a short beard; on ones from Nicomedeia under Caracalla, the head is fully human: Waddington-Babelon-Reinach, *Recueil* 545 nos. 225–227.

21. *Alex.* 13; Hippol. *Ref.* 4.29.

oracle and the elaboration of the cult. The first stage is the gradual adherence of the nearby regions, Bithynia, Galatia, and Thrace,[22] and there are two marks of the crystallization of the cult: the dissemination of a canonical image and the naming of the new god as Glycon. It is possible that Lucian's articulation is artificial and designed to make the growth of the cult seem planned rather than spontaneous, but his basic facts are corroborated by the material evidence. The image and name of Glycon are first found on coins of Abonuteichos under Antoninus Pius, where they continue until the end of the city's coinage in the mid-third century.[23] Still in the reign of Pius, the image appears on coins of Tieion some hundred and fifty kilometers to the west.[24] Further away, it appears at Germanicopolis in inner Paphlagonia, near the Galatian border, on its brief coinage of the years from 208 and 210,[25] and at Nicomedeia in Bithynia under Caracalla's sole reign and Maximus Caesar.[26] Although the representations in three dimensions are not dated, they too suggest a radiating influence. The chief one is the great marble statue at Tomi, but there are also two small statuettes in bronze, both probably from Athens.[27] Inscriptions from Apulum in Dacia show vows being paid to Glycon "at the god's behest," whereas one from near Scupi in southern Illyria is less clear, but seems to be a dedication to the snake, its otherwise unknown mate, and Alexander himself.[28] The god's name was announced in an

22. κατ᾽ ὀλίγον (*Alex.* 18) must be "gradually," not "in a short time," as Robert, *Asie Mineure* 399; see LSJ s.v. ὀλίγος IV 7. Lucian uses the phrase in this sense over twenty times, cf. e.g., *Herod.* 1.

23. Waddington-Babelon-Reinach, *Recueil* 166–170 nos. 7–9, 11, 12, 15–18. Cf. Robert, *Asie Mineure* 395, 400–402.

24. Waddington-Babelon-Reinach, *Recueil* 616 n. 2, 623 no. 54; *SNG* Deutschland 940. Cf. Robert, *Asie Mineure* 397, 399, and on the situation of Tieion, 176–190.

25. *SNG* Deutschland 6820; Robert, *Asie Mineure* 397. On the situation and coinage of Germanicopolis, Robert 204–219.

26. Waddington-Babelon-Reinach, *Recueil* 545 nos. 225–227, 562 no. 353; cf. Robert, *Asie Mineure* 395.

27. Tomi: Robert, *Asie Mineure* 397, 398 figs. 7–8. Bronze statues: Robert, *CRAI* 1981, 513–535. However, a headless bronze snake found at Ephesos is probably a tutelary god, Robert, *CRAI* 1982, 126–130. Note also two gems: Drexler in Roscher, *Lexicon* s.v. Glycon; Caster, *Études* 98; the example in the Louvre is now Delatte-Derchain, *Les intailles magiques* 68 no. 82.

28. Apulum: *CIL* 3.1021 (*ILS* 4079), 1022. Scupi: *Inscriptions de la Mésie supérieure* 6.10 (*CIL* 3.8238; *ILS* 4080), with the discussion of Weinreich, *NJbb* 47 (1921) 143–144 (*Ausg. Schr.* 1.540–542).

oracle which following his general interpretation Lucian ascribes to Alexander: "I am Glycon, the third in descent from Zeus, a light to mankind." These are well-known religious formulas, and though the line might be Lucian's invention, it is much more probably a genuine piece of propaganda, like the Sibylline oracle which announced the ascension of Peregrinus.[29]

The next stage in Lucian's narrative corresponds to the first and essential part of the new god's oracular activity, his replies to questions written in advance on sealed rolls of paper. To these Alexander replied as Glycon's interpreter in an underground chamber *(adyton)*.[30] The "cue," according to his biographer, was given by the celebrated oracle of Amphilochos in Cilicia, in which the mode of consultation was again by means of sealed paper.[31] Since this was one of the most popular oracles of the day, and Alexander cultivated friendly relations with it, Lucian's interpretation may well be correct. However, the use of an underground chamber seems to be drawn from Apolline oracles such as Delphi and Claros, with which Alexander was also on good terms. The underground chamber at Claros, of which the appearance is precisely known, gives an idea of that at Abonuteichos.[32]

Alexander's ruse for learning the questions was another one described by Hippolytos and probably by Celsus, whereby a seal could be broken and replaced without detection.[33] His answers, when he consented to give them, were sometimes ambiguous or unintelligible, though to medical questions he gave replies of which even Lucian acknowledges the expertise, often recommending a special ointment of his own devising made from bear's fat.[34] As a result Alexander and the large staff which the sanctuary now required made large sums, since each oracle cost one drachma and two obols, and about seventy or eighty thousand were submitted a year. If these figures are accurate, this would have amounted to about four hundred thou-

---

29. Weinreich, *NJbb* 47 (1921) 145–146 (*Ausg. Schr.* 1.543–545); Caster, *Études* 35–36; for Peregrinus, Ch. 11 at n. 47.

30. *Alex.* 19. On the technical terms in this passage, Festugière, *REG* 52 (1939) 232.

31. On this oracle, Ch. 4 at n. 17.

32. On the adyton at Claros, Robert in Delvoye and Roux, *Civilisation grecque* 1.309–312.

33. *Alex.* 20–21; Hippol. *Ref.* 4.34; cf. Caster, *Études* 38–40.

34. *Alex.* 22, cf. 53. See Robert, *Asie Mineure* 415, illustrating the frequency of bears in Paphlagonia.

sand Roman sesterces, ample to maintain a hundred or so persons in comfort.[35]

Lucian now proceeds to a new stage in Alexander's career, which he associates with a campaign of religious propaganda embracing the established oracles of Ionia and Cilicia. This section includes several new developments. The first is Alexander's war on "atheists," primarily Epicureans, and Christians. The Epicurean opposition was led by a certain Lepidus of Amastris, who is attested in inscriptions. He and his colleagues are probably the same as Lucian's later allies against Alexander, the pupils of a famous philosopher of Heraclea on the Pontus, Timocrates, and from these local opponents Lucian must have gathered at least some of his information about Alexander. The Christian community of Pontus and Bithynia existed already in apostolic times and was sizeable enough to disturb the younger Pliny in the early second century; the church in Amastris is attested in the reign of Marcus Aurelius, precisely the time described by Lucian.[36]

These struggles involved not only intellectual issues but also the traditional rivalries among Greek cities. Amastris had been formed about the year 300 by an amalgamation of several smaller cities including the Dorian Cytoros, while Abonuteichos was linked in the propaganda of Alexander with Ionia and the Milesian colony of Sinope to the east. When, therefore, Alexander refused to give responses to any citizen of Amastris, he was influenced by his war against opponents of the oracle and also by the local pride of Abonuteichos. The Amastrians, no doubt, desired to humble the claims of their upstart neighbors.[37]

The other important development which Lucian attributes to this stage is the creation of "autophones" (oracles spoken by the god himself). For these Alexander used the hidden pipes, and they were issued only to persons of high standing. One such was an eminent

35. *Alex.* 23. In the mid-second century a Roman legionary made 1,200 sesterces a year: cf. Duncan-Jones, *Economy*[2] 12.

36. *Alex.* 24–25. Lepidus: *CIG* 3.4149–50, cf. *PIR*[2] C 910. Pupils of Timocrates: *Alex.* 57. Christians in Pontus: *Ep. 1 Pet.* 1. 1; Pliny, *Ep.* 10.96; Dion. Cor. in Eus. *HE* 4.23.6, cf. Harnack, *Mission*[4] 754.

37. Robert, *Asie Mineure* 148, 414 (synoecism), 412–414 (Doros), 411–412 (Abonuteichos, Sinope). Cf. Robert, 412: "Alexandre était ainsi le porte-parole d'un mouvement très ample dans tout le monde grec et sans rapport avec Glycon."

Roman consular, M. Sedatius Severianus, who consulted the oracle before his disastrous invasion of Armenia in 161. The author claims that the encouraging response given to Severianus was afterward replaced in the "records" by a more suitable one, and gives other examples of such recantations, but he does not explain how he learned of the earlier versions.[38] The date of this incident, some years after the beginning of the cult under Pius, tends to confirm Lucian's picture of its growing fame and elaboration. He may also be right to place here Alexander's cultivation of the great oracles of Claros and Didyma in Ionia and of Amphilochos in Cilicia, for it is natural that a cult now reaching maturity should seek cordial relations with the senior establishments.[39]

The next phase described by Lucian involves the spread of Alexander's influence to the very capital. The chief of his supporters there was the influential consular P. Mummius Sisenna Rutilianus, who had been consul as long ago as 146 and since then had governed Upper Moesia and Asia. Lucian claims to have known him personally and praises his public character while deploring his superstitiousness. Rutilianus spread the oracle's fame at Rome, and Alexander began to receive many consultations from the capital, some so treasonable as to put the consultants in his power. One of Glycon's oracles persuaded Rutilianus to marry Alexander's daughter, whom Alexander had allegedly fathered on the Moon-goddess. This myth is clearly a counterpart to that of the prophet's own birth from Podaleirios, and both were later dramatized in Alexander's "mysteries." The marriage set the seal on his reputation, and is further proof that Lucian has not exaggerated his social importance.[40]

At this point Lucian claims for the second time that Alexander's influence extended over the whole empire. The oracle began to send apparently unsolicited "oracle carriers" to cities, advising them to beware of plagues and fires and promising them its help, a campaign which recalls the "infernal messengers" of Peregrinus, sent to prepare

38. Autophones: *Alex.* 26. Severianus: *Alex.* 27. On Severianus' defeat at Elegeia, Birley, *Marcus Aurelius* 161–162.

39. *Alex.* 29. Cf. Robert, *Asie Mineure* 403–405.

40. *Alex.* 30–35. On Rutilianus see Alföldy, *Senatorenstand* 87 (birth date), 151 (consulate), 215 (Asia), 234 (Moesia). Groag's article, *RE* 16 (1933) 529–533, is now out of date.

his own posthumous cult. Lucian singles out one oracle sent "to all the provinces in the plague," which promised the help of Glycon's grandfather Apollo. This was to be seen everywhere set up on gateways, but "by chance" the houses where it was inscribed were those most afflicted: here Lucian's malice is checked by his Epicureanism, since to allege that the oracle caused the misfortune would have been to suggest supernatural agency. His basic facts, however, must be correct. The great plague was brought by the victorious armies of Lucius Verus, returning from the east in 165 and 166. After first ravaging the eastern empire, it reached the capital about the time when the Marcomannic invasions across the Danube were beginning to spread great terror. Marcus was obliged to invoke strange rites and priests, and fanatics predicted the end of the world. In this atmosphere it was natural for the oracle of Glycon, now arrived at the summit of its power, to have exploited fears of "plagues and fires." What Lucian says of its intervention during the great plague may be confirmed by an inscription of Syrian Antioch, though inscribed on a plinth and not on a doorpost or gateway. It bears the oracle against the plague followed by the seven vowels, which had an apotropaic significance. It is not certain that the inscription is contemporary with the great plague, for the oracle is known to have continued in use for many centuries, but Antioch may well have made early use of it, since it was the headquarters of Verus' campaigns and must have been one of the first cities affected.[41]

After chronicling Alexander's successes in Italy and throughout the empire, Lucian reverts to Abonuteichos, and describes a new "device," the institution of secret rites or "mysteries." This was an era in which such mysteries pullulated, though the primacy still rested with those of Eleusis, which Lucian may be right in seeing as Alexander's chief model. As in those, the rite was preceded by a ritual prohibition, though not of murderers and barbarians as at Eleusis but of Christians and Epicureans. The celebration lasted for three days, again in imitation of Eleusis. The first commemorated the birth of Apollo and Asclepios, the second that of Glycon, the third that of

41. *Alex.* 36–37. Plague: Ch. 6 at n. 6. Effect in Rome: *HA* Marcus 13. Inscription of Antioch: Perdrizet, *CRAI* 1903, 62–66; Weinreich, *MDAI(A)* 38 (1913) 66–67 (*Ausg. Schr.* 1.201–202); Caster, *Études* 60; Robert, *Asie Mineure* 404. Later use of the oracle: Mart. Cap. *De Nupt. Philol. et Merc.* 1.19; the script also seems more suited to the third or fourth century, cf. Robert, *Asie Mineure* 404, n. 42.

Alexander and of his daughter. In the last the role of Alexander was taken by himself and that of the Moon-goddess by a certain Rutilia, the wife of an imperial steward, whose name suggests a client of the family of Rutilianus.[42]

Lucian follows his account of the mysteries with a series of items only loosely connected. One of the first concerns Alexander's female admirers, whose claim to have had children by him was corroborated by their husbands. This has been thought sheer malice, but an inscription from Caesarea Troketta in northwestern Lydia appears to confirm it. It records an oracle of Apollo of Claros and a statue of Apollo the Savior paid for by his priest, a Paphlagonian named Miletos son of Glycon. The conjunction of Glycon, Paphlagonia, and Apollo of Claros, whom Alexander assiduously cultivated, suggests that the man's alleged father was not a human one, but the snake-god of Abonuteichos. As for his name, "Miletos" refers to the Ionian origin claimed by Abonuteichos and skillfully exploited in the propaganda of Alexander. If this is right, Lucian has as usual started with a concrete fact but interpreted it maliciously. Whereas the deluded mothers claimed to have had intercourse with the god (a claim all the more easily made because of his serpentine form), Lucian conforms to his usual manner of treating Glycon as a mere puppet and affixes the paternity to the god's manipulator.[43]

Similar doubt has been cast on Lucian's next item, an inscription which he had seen in the house of a certain Sacerdos of Tieion. In gilded letters this recorded a dialogue between Sacerdos and Glycon in which the god answered questions about his origin and nature and the relation of his oracles to those of Didyma, Claros, and Delphi; Sacerdos was also told of his future existences and warned not to trust the Epicurean Lepidus. These questions closely resemble the so-called theological oracles of Claros, issued in reply to the question, "Who is God?" An inscription from Talmis in Nubia similarly shows a visitor asking the local god Mandulis whether he is the Sun-god.

---

42. *Alex.* 38–40. Alexander's mysteries: Weinreich, *NJbb* 47 (1921) 146–148 (*Ausg. Schr.* 1.545–547); Caster, *Études* 61–64; Nilsson, *Gesch. gr. Rel.* 2² 474. On mysteries generally in this period, Nilsson, 345–372.

43. *Alex.* 42. Doubted by Caster, *Études* 87; for this interpretation, Robert, *Asie Mineure* 405–408, discussing the inscription published by Buresch, *Klaros* (Keil-Premerstein, *Bericht* no. 16; *IGR* 4.1498). Lucian's identification of Glycon with Alexander: *Alex.* 18, 25, 29, etc.

In addition, the popularity of Glycon in Tieion is proved by his appearance on its coins already in the reign of Pius.[44]

One of the stories told by Lucian in this section of the work involves an "effrontery" *(tolmema)* against the emperor Marcus. Enjoying access to the court through Rutilianus, Alexander issued an oracle "when the divine Marcus was already grappling with the Marcomanni and Quadi," ordering that two lions be thrown into the Danube. It was obeyed, and the Romans suffered a great defeat. The incident, which probably occurred in 170 or so, reveals the extraordinary influence exerted by Alexander towards the close of his career, and like the oracle issued against the plague, it also shows him exploiting or at least answering the religious needs of a desperate time.[45]

Lucian also puts into this miscellaneous section one more "device" of Alexander, the so-called night-oracles. In these the prophet took the sealed questions and received in his sleep the answers given by the god. Expounders explained them for a fee, and allegedly paid him an Attic talent apiece, or about a quarter of a million sesterces. This figure, if at all accurate, indicates that the income of the sanctuary had increased hugely since its beginnings under Pius. The practice whereby the prophet himself "incubated" in the shrine seems unique, though the oracle of Amphilochos at Mallos seems to have combined the intervention of the prophet with responses given directly to the consultant in sleep, and Alexander's system may be an adaptation of practices there.[46]

The last major section of the work involves the author. The first part of it describes a number of questions which he put to the oracle by means of servants sent to Abonuteichos before his own visit there about 165. He does not indicate where he was, but it may have been the province of Asia. Most of the questions were tricks designed to show Alexander up as a fraud, but one reveals Lucian entering into

44. *Alex.* 43. Doubted by Caster, *Études* 66; for this interpretation, Robert, *Asie Mineure* 399–400, citing for the inscription of Mandulis Nock, *HThR* 27 (1934) 53–104 (*Essays* 1.357–400), esp. 70 (370–371). Coins of Tieion: above at n. 24.

45. *Alex.* 48, with Caster's discussion, *Études* 68–70. For a date in 170 or 171, Birley, *Marcus Aurelius* 223–224.

46. *Alex.* 49. On the procedure of the oracle at Mallos, Luc. *Philops.* 38; Cass. Dio 72.7.1; Bouché-Leclercq, *Histoire de la divination* 3.341–345 (it is not certain that the anecdote in Plut. *De Def. Orac.* 434 C–F concerns the same oracle). The oracles of Claros were also given at night: Robert in Delvoye and Roux, *Civilisation grecque* 1.310.

the local rivalries between Abonuteichos and its neighbors. The question of Homer's birthplace was hotly debated by scholars and rival cities, and the inquisitive Hadrian had consulted Apollo of Delphi on the subject. When Lucian put the same question to Alexander, he was thinking both of the familiar puzzle and also of the city of Amastris, which was the center of opposition to the oracle. For Amastris was one of the many cities which claimed to be the poet's birthplace, and it proudly displayed his portrait on its coins. Lucian's campaign against the oracle belongs to an ancient tradition of skeptical polemics, but is also characteristic of the author. In particular it recalls the forged works of Heracleitos which, according to Galen, he sent by means of friends to an eminent philosopher.[47]

The second stage in Lucian's duel with the prophet involves Rutilianus, whom he tried to warn against Alexander's influence. He also reports an oracle given by Glycon to Rutilianus in which he himself was accused of immorality. Though he nowhere else mentions an acquaintance with Rutilianus, it fits the little that is known about his friends in the upper class of Rome.[48]

These skirmishes are only a prelude to the main part of this section, which can also be seen as the climax of the work: Lucian's narrative of his direct encounter with the prophet. He arrived at Abonuteichos with two soldiers provided as an escort by his friend the governor of Cappadocia, a casual detail which again suggests a man who had his own influence with eminent Romans. After greeting Alexander by giving his hand a hearty bite (a claim which need not be taken seriously),[49] he was admitted to a private interview and emerged pretending to be the prophet's friend. He agreed to continue his journey on a ship provided by Alexander and only escaped being thrown overboard when the pilot was struck with repentance and confessed all. After disembarking at Aegialoi, he joined ambassadors from King Eupator of the Pontic Chersonese who were sailing to Bithynia, and

47. *Alex.* 53–54. For this interpretation of the question about Homer, Robert, *Asie Mineure* 414–419. Question posed by Hadrian: *Certamen* 32; *AP* 14.102; Parke-Wormell, 2.188 no. 465.

48. *Alex.* 54. The implication of the oracle that Lucian was a pederast suggests that he had access to Rutilianus' household: cf. *Merc. cond.* 12.

49. Branham, *Classical Antiquity* 3 (1984) 159–160, is perhaps right to connect this with the bite "as the signature of the poet of blame": but it seems excessive to say that "the most *geloios* character in the narrative is suddenly the narrator."

so arrived safely in Amastris. Enlisting the help of many supporters, notably the pupils of Timocrates of Heraclea, he approached the governor of Bithynia, Lollianus Avitus, intending to charge Alexander with attempted murder. The governor, however, urged the influence of Rutilianus and persuaded him to desist. In this account Lucian is both narrator and sole witness, and the charge of attempted murder may come from the common stock of invective. What else is fabricated can only be guessed, but it does not seem likely to include the fact of his friendship with Rutilianus and the governor of Cappadocia, or of his meeting Pontic ambassadors and the governor of Bithynia.[50]

After this account of his own contacts with Alexander, and before narrating his death, Lucian inserts another "effrontery" involving Marcus; that is, Alexander's request that Abonuteichos be renamed "Ionopolis" and his striking a novel coinage with Glycon on one side and himself, shown with the attributes of Asclepios and Perseus, on the other. The change to Ionopolis is first attested by coins struck between 161 and 169, and it has persisted in the modern name of the town, Ineboli. It was designed to obliterate the old name, suggestive of a garrison town of barbarian origin, and replace it with one proclaiming its full civic status and Hellenic culture. No example of the coin supposedly showing Alexander has survived, though Glycon already appears under the emperor Pius, and though this may be sheer invention, it is perhaps a misreading, intentional or not, of a type no longer attested.[51]

Lucian closes his narrative with Alexander's painful death and the competition among his followers for his succession. The allegation that he was gnawed by maggots, like the attempt on Lucian's life, is an item drawn from the common stock of invective and was perhaps never meant to be taken literally.[52] The dispute for the succession was settled by Rutilianus, who preserved it for the deceased Alexander. Lucian is indignant that one of the claimants was a doctor, but

50. *Alex.* 55–57. On the reference to Aegialoi and the ambassadors of King Eupator, Robert, *Asie Mineure* 417 with n. 125. For Avitus, highly praised by Apuleius in his *Apology, PIR*[2] H 40. On charges of murder in invective, cf. *I. trag.* 52, *Peregr.* 10, Caster, *Études* 87–88.

51. *Alex.* 58. For this interpretation, Robert, *Asie Mineure* 408–411. A coin struck under Severus Alexander shows Glycon being fed, not by Alexander as has been proposed, but by the personified Ionopolis: Robert, 400–402.

52. *Alex.* 59, cf. Robert, *Asie Mineure* 420.

that accords with the great importance of medicine in Alexander's own training and in the success of the oracle. Although public functions were often held after death by a benefactor who had left a foundation to cover the expenses, some religious fabrication must have been necessary to make Alexander continue to act as prophet, and a kind of formal heroization may have been arranged for him as for Peregrinus.[53]

In closing, Lucian reverts to the dedicatee and to the subject of Epicurus. His work, a mere sample of the facts,[54] is a present to Celsus, whom he depicts as the perfect Epicurean. It is also a vindication of Epicurus, "a man truly holy and divine in nature, who alone rightly recognized and recorded what is desirable and was the liberator of his followers." Earlier Lucian praises his *Chief Doctrines* with similar hyperbole. This enthusiasm is in part a polite gesture to Celsus, since the Epicureans habitually used such language of the Master,[55] but it also has a function in the work. As Alexander played on the hopes and fears that tyrannize mankind, so Epicurus brought liberation from them and was therefore "truly holy" by contrast with the sham holiness of Alexander.

Whatever Lucian's true feelings about Epicurus, his own actions and words put him in a long tradition of anti-oracular activity to which the Epicureans had contributed generously. There was also a corresponding literature of divine intervention and miraculous conversions. The *Exposure of Frauds* of the Cynic Oenomaos recounted the author's personal deception by Apollo of Claros and also cited historic oracles of Delphi to expose the god's cruelty and immorality.[56] On the other side, Plutarch records how a skeptical governor of Cilicia, egged on by his Epicurean associates, tested the oracle of Mopsos by means of a servant, and when the god proved his powers "fell down and worshiped"; Lucian's account of his sudden conversion to friendship with Alexander is a parody of this kind of tale.[57] In the generation after Lucian, the sophist Aelian composed works entitled *On Providence* and *On Divine Manifestations,* both of which recounted the

53. *Alex.* 60, cf. Robert, *Asie Mineure* 419–420.
54. This is another commonplace: cf. *Ev. Jo.* 21.25, Luc. *Demon.* 67.
55. *Alex.* 61, cf. 47. Epicureans on the Master: Caster, *Pensée* 95.
56. Ch. 4 at n. 55.
57. Plut. *De Def. Orac.* 434 C–F; cf. Weinreich, *NJbb* 21 (1921) 130–131 (*Ausg. Schr.* 1.523).

discomfiture of Epicureans who profaned the Eleusinian mysteries and committed other impieties. Like Alexander, Aelian recommended the burning of Epicurus' books and branded his followers as "atheists" and "incorrigibles" *(atenctoi)*.[58]

Like oracles, "divine men" were also liable to excite a literature of attack and defense. Lucian refers to such attacks on Pythagoras and, in fact, may be indebted to them.[59] Much closer than Pythagoras, however, was the figure of Apollonios of Tyana, at one remove the teacher of Alexander. The biography of Philostratos is carefully designed to neutralize the effect of earlier attacks on Apollonios which are now mainly lost, though they still echo in Eusebios' tract *Against Hierocles*. Apollonios' chief enemy, attacking him both in act and in writing, was the Stoic philosopher Euphrates, and it may be more than coincidence that Euphrates was the teacher of Timocrates of Heraclea, whose own pupils in turn formed the core of opposition to Alexander.[60]

The question whether Alexander was "really" fraudulent or sincere is unanswerable, and perhaps beside the point.[61] Nature had given him charismatic qualities and set him in an age thirsting for oracles and cures. But it was also an age of intense controversy, which could produce a Lucian no less than an Alexander. It is clear that Lucian's pamphlet would have been seen as an example of a familiar type, the literature of exposure. The only question is why he resorted to the type when he did, in the latest of his datable works. The reason may follow partly from the date. Rutilianus, whom the author had known personally, was now dead as well as Alexander. More important, so was Marcus, whom Alexander had counted among his victims. Lucian may have felt it discreet to delay his exposure until Marcus too had gone to join the gods.

58. Aelian, ed. Hercher, fr. 12, 58, 143, 344 (mysteries), 39 (books), 39, 111 (atheists), 143 (incorrigible).

59. *Alex.* 4, cf. above at n. 9.

60. On Euphrates, *PIR*² E 121, Follet, *Athènes* 123–124. Euphrates and Apollonios: e.g., Philostr. *VA* 1.13, 2.26, 5.39. Timocrates: Philostr. *VS* 46.30ff. K.

61. Note the excellent remark of Nock, in *Conversion* 270, cited by Caster, *Études* 100 n. 1: "If we cannot estimate the exact measure of honesty in the leaders of certain movements in our own times, how can we judge precisely how far Alexander of Abonutichus was charlatan and how far by his own lights prophet?"; also Robert, *Asie Mineure* 421.

13   Culture and Society

FOR ALL THE VARIETY of his writings, there is one word to which Lucian constantly resorts when discussing himself and his acquaintances: "culture" *(paideia)*, with its related verb usually in the participle, "cultured" *(pepaideumenos)*.[1] The class to which he refers as the arbiter of correctness in taste or manners is the cultured, the "best people," "those interested in literature *(logoi)*."[2] These are the people who laugh or sigh at Lexiphanes and the Uncultured Man; it is at their praise that the historian should aim.[3] This class includes the emperors and also literary men conspicuous in public life, such as Arrian and Herodes Atticus.[4] To lack culture implies ignorance not only of classics such as Homer, but of the behavior expected of civilized beings, and makes a Greek no better than a Paphlagonian.[5]

In this exaltation of culture Lucian is, as so often, a man of his time. Like him, contemporary authors place it at the very summit of the social pyramid, the emperor. Such language might be expected from Aelius Aristides, eager to gain imperial favor for the Greek heritage and for himself, but Christian apologists speak in the same

1. Throughout this chapter I translate *paideia* as "culture" and *mimesis* as "imitation" rather than using transliteration. Cf. Nock, *HThR* 57 (1964) 261 (*Collected Essays* 2.944), "Greek words are protean, and to transliterate them is liable to involve what Whitehead is quoted as calling 'the fallacy of misplaced concreteness.' " For Lucian's claims, note especially *Harm.* 4, and cf. *Patr. enc.* 8.

2. *Pisc.* 26 (ἄριστοι), *VH* 1.1 (οἱ περὶ τοὺς λόγους ἐσπουδακότες).

3. *Lex.* 17, 24; *Ind.* 28; *Hist. conscr.* 44.

4. Emperors: Marcus, *Ind.* 22; note also the emphasis on culture in Lucian's description of Pantheia, *Im.* 11, 16. Arrian: *Alex.* 2. Herodes: *Peregr.* 19.

5. *Gall.* 2 (Homer); *Merc. cond.* 4 (civilized behavior); *Alex.* 17 (Paphlagonians uncultured).

vein.[6] Just as Lucian refers to Herodes Atticus as a man "outstanding in culture and esteem," so also Marcus writing to the Athenians praises his "renowned zeal for culture," while Galen uses exactly the same phrase as Lucian to describe those whom he impressed by his skill at Rome.[7] Inscriptions from widely differing parts of the Greek world—the isle of Myconos, Boubon locked in the mountains of Lycia, Ancyra the capital of Galatia—attest the high value placed on "culture" not only by an elite in the intellectual capitals but by the educated classes of the whole eastern empire.[8]

Culture implies above all an acquaintance with the literary and artistic achievements of the past. It can scarcely be doubted that Lucian was very well read.[9] Though he has evident biases, they suggest a personal selection from a range of authors, and not the random emphases of one whose culture is at second hand. Just as he agrees with his contemporaries in the high value he assigns to culture, so the range of his reading resembles that of his age. It is especially instructive to compare his tastes with those of contemporary Egypt, insofar as the papyri permit a census of preferences there.[10] He draws on a stock very similar to that available in a town like Oxyrhynchos, and where he differs in his selection the reason can almost always be found in his own personality.

The major author, both for Lucian and in the papyri, is naturally Homer.[11] In preferring the *Iliad* to the *Odyssey,* and the first two

6. Aristid. *Or.* 23.73, 27.23, 35.12, 18 (for the ascription of *Or.* 35, above Ch. 8 at n. 29); Athenag. *Leg.* 6.2; Justin, *Apol.* 1.2.2 (the reigning emperors ἐρασταὶ παιδείας).

7. Luc. *Peregr.* 19, ἄνδρα παιδείᾳ καὶ ἀξιώματι προὔχοντα; *SEG* 29.127 l. 89, τῇ εὐκλεεῖ περὶ παιδείαν σπουδῇ; Galen, *De Praecog.* 2.25, οἱ ἀξιώματί τε καὶ παιδείᾳ ωπροὔχοντες.

8. *Bull.* 1971.463 (Myconos), 1973.455 (Boubon), 1939.438 no. 2 (Ancyra: all these appear to be of the late first or the second century). Cf. Robert, *Hellenica* 13.47–54 on cultural aspirations expressed in inscriptions of the central Anatolian plateau.

9. Cf. Helm, *RE* 13 (1927) 1766: "Lukianos ist zweifellos zu seiner Zeit eine der gebildetsten Persönlichkeiten gewesen." Anderson, *BICS* 23 (1976) 59–68 and *BICS* 25 (1978) 97–100, holds that Lucian's culture was meager and superficial, but the argumentation is thin: e.g., "I am not convinced that we have proof that Lucian ever read a single tragedy from cover to cover" (*BICS* 23 [1976] 66). For statistics and discussion of Lucian's quotations, Householder, *Literary Quotation.*

10. For statistics of reading in Egypt, Willis, *GRBS* 9 (1968) 205–241; Montevecchi, *Papirologia* 337–394.

11. For Lucian and Homer, Bouquiaux-Simon, *Lectures homériques de Lucien* esp. 352–354; on Homer in the papyri, Montevecchi, *Papirologia* 366–367.

books of the *Iliad* to the others, Lucian shares the general verdict of antiquity. Though his admiration for the poet is clear, he nevertheless subjects him to playful mockery as the chief source of received views about religion and the gods.[12] This double attitude of admiration and disrespect is even more marked in his treatment of Hesiod, whose *Theogony* was a particular irritation.[13] A similar bias colors his treatment of the three classic tragedians. Lucian's liking for Euripides was shared by many others, but not his neglect of Aeschylos and Sophocles.[14] At first sight it seems strange that he should quote Pindar with approval, but here he perhaps felt, as with Homer, that the beauty of the language compensated for the doctrines expressed.[15]

Other types of poetry had a direct influence on Lucian's own prose. The iambographers are cited in those invectives which involve questions of culture, clearly in order to affirm the author's own, and Lucian's preference for Archilochos agrees with the papyri.[16] Among the writers of old comedy, he favors Aristophanes, and among his plays, the *Clouds,* and here again the papyri concur.[17] In attacking the Uncultured Man, Lucian shows his familiarity with Eupolis' *Baptai,* a play used by Juvenal for similar purposes. For Lucian, as for Galen, Old Comedy was recommended both by its subject matter and as a canon of Attic diction.[18] The same two qualities probably explain his liking for Menander, and the discovery of the *Dyscolos* now provides a lesson in his "imitation" of his models. Without naming his source he adapts just enough to give the cultured reader the pleasure of recognition.[19]

Among writers of prose, Lucian's tastes seem even more severely

12. Bouquiaux-Simon, *Lectures homériques de Lucien* 38–39.

13. Note esp. *Hes.,* and also *Sacr.* 5.

14. For the references, Householder, *Literary Quotation* sub vv.; note esp. *Pseudol.* 32, "the fine Euripides," and contrast the mocking reference to Sophocles and Aeschylos, *Peregr.* 3.

15. *Gall.* 7, *Hipp.* 7, *Im.* 8.

16. Archilochos, with Hipponax (twice) and Semonides (spelled "Simonides," as often) once, *Ind.* 27, *Pseudol.* 1–2. In the papyri also, Archilochos is much better represented than Hipponax, Semonides not at all.

17. For Lucian, Householder, *Literary Quotation* 4; for the papyri, Montevecchi, *Papirologia* 375–376.

18. *Baptai: Ind.* 27–28, cf. Juv. 2.91–92, with Courtney's commentary. Galen: *De Libr. propr.* 17 (*Scr. min.* 2.124).

19. On Lucian's use of the *Dyscolos,* see Schmid, *RhM* 102 (1959) 157–158; note also *I. trag.* 1 (cf. Men. fr. 722), *Pseudol.* 4 (Men. fr. 717).

classical than among poets. Despite his praise of Thucydides in the treatise *On Writing History,* Herodotos is his clear favorite. He provides the subject of one of the prefaces, and the essay *On the Syrian Goddess* is a sustained pastiche of his manner and style.[20] Lucian had also read Ctesias, but shared the common view of his unreliability.[21] Of the successors of Thucydides, he names only Xenophon, and ignores such lesser masters as Philistos, Ephoros, and Theopompos. In these preferences, as the papyri and the manuscripts suggest, Lucian shares the general verdict of late antiquity.[22]

His classicism can also be observed in his selection of orators, and again two stand out. Demosthenes is "the fine rhetor" and one of the giants of literature, but Lucian also appreciated the driving style of Aeschines, especially the invective of the speech against Timarchos. Isocrates makes a poor third, and the others, even Lysias, fail to receive even a mention.[23] In this preference for Aeschines over Isocrates, Lucian's own affinities are apparent, and he dissents from the verdict suggested by the ancient and medieval manuscripts.

Philosophers formed a special class, since style could overcome an antipathy to content, and content to style. For Lucian, as for ancient culture in general, Plato was the supreme exponent and one of the strongest influences on his manner and style; his doctrines, however, are often the target of gentle mockery.[24] Lucian cares little for other philosophical authors, with two notable exceptions. His high opinion of Epicurus cannot be due to style, but rather to a sympathy for his teachings.[25] The other is the Cynic Menippos, whom he pretends to have "dug up" and uses as a character in several of his best dialogues. It is now generally agreed that Menippos was still well known in Lucian's day, and that his influence on him is much less than was

20. *Herod.* (cf. also *Dom.* 20), *Syr. D.* He is twice linked with Ctesias, however, on the traditional charge of mendacity, *Philops.* 2, *VH* 2.31.

21. *Hist. conscr.* 39 (with Homeyer's commentary), *Philops.* 2, *VH* 1.3, 2.31.

22. Xenophon: *Hist. conscr.* 39, *Im.* 10, *Somn.* 17.

23. Demosthenes "fine," *Merc. cond.* 5, cf. 25; *I. trag.* 15, *Rh. Pr.* 9, 10, 17, 21. Aeschines: *Ind.* 27, *Pseudol.* 27, *Rh. Pr.* 10, *Somn.* 12. Isocrates: *Rh. Pr.* 17.

24. Generally, Tackaberry, *Lucian's Relation to Plato* 62–85; Householder, *Literary Quotation* 34–36; for Lucian's praise, note esp. *Ind.* 27, *Laps.* 4, *Merc. cond.* 25, *Pisc.* 22–23, *Rh. Pr.* 9. Doctrines: *Bis acc.* 34, *Dom.* 4, *VH* 2.17–18, *Vit. Auct.* 17. Lucian praises two other Socratics for their styles, Aeschines and Antisthenes (*Im.* 17, *Ind.* 27).

25. *Alex.* 47, 61.

believed in the heroic age of reconstruction.[26] Nonetheless, Menippos is the only Hellenistic writer apart from Menander who is known to have had a literary influence on Lucian. Other writers of the centuries after Alexander fare poorly. The author of travelers' tales, Iamboulos, seems to be Lucian's chief target in the *True Histories,* and for Hellenistic poets, even Callimachos, he usually expresses aversion.[27] One work of recent date influenced him strongly, though he may have accepted its attribution to a pupil of Plato. This is the still extant *Picture of Cebes,* an allegorical discourse on the search for wisdom, which perhaps dates from the century before Lucian.[28]

To this informed conservatism in matters of literature Lucian joins a similar attitude towards style. Like most Greek stylists of the imperial period, he is an Atticist, who looks to Athens of the fifth and fourth centuries for his linguistic models.[29] Yet his ideal is not a rigid imitation, but the elegance, wit, and above all clarity of his favorite authors, Aristophanes, Menander, Plato, Demosthenes. Of the two lexicographers who are known to be his contemporaries, he is much closer to Phrynichos than to Pollux. Whereas Pollux admits to his lists of acceptable words anything sanctioned by the ancients, Phrynichos defends his selections with wit and gusto, and like Lucian he comments bitingly on the slips of recent and contemporary authors, notably the sophists Favorinus and Lollianus.[30] Just as Aelius Aristides can produce a string of witnesses to excuse his "remark in passing" (a passage of self-praise introduced in a moment of inspiration), so Lucian summons up a similar host to excuse a slip made in saluting an eminent Roman. So fluent is his defense that, as he admits, it seems rather to be offered as an exercise in linguistic virtuosity than required by the occasion.[31] His attack on the Mistaken Critic has its immediate

26. *Bis acc.* 33; for this playful use of ἀνορύττειν, cf. *Rh. Pr.* 10. The classic refutation of Helm's thesis was made by McCarthy, *YClS* 4 (1934) 3–55; the arguments are rehearsed by Hall, *Lucian's Satire* 64–150.

27. For Iamboulos in the *VH,* Ch. 5 at n. 38. Poets: *Lexiph.* 25 (Dosiades, Lycophron), *Hist. conscr.* 57 (Parthenios, Euphorion, Callimachos). There is however a neutral reference to Nicander at *Dips.* 9.

28. Cited in *Merc. cond.* 42 and *Rh. Pr.* 6; its influence is also palpable at *Herm.* 24, *Pisc.* 12, and in the *Somnium.* There is a recent edition and commentary by Fitzgerald and White.

29. See the summary of Deferrari, *Lucian's Atticism* 80–82.

30. Phr. *Ecl.* ed. Fischer, 140, 141, 152, 161, etc.

31. Arist. 28 K; Luc. *Laps.* esp. 19.

origin in another supposed slip, his use of the feminine noun *apophras* for a masculine person, on which the Critic had seized as a mark of barbarism and ignorance. The ferocity of Lucian's reply shows how keenly such charges were felt and how purity of language was seen as a mark of culture and status. Curiously, he does not allege in his defense an example of the same usage from Eupolis, but this does not prove his knowledge of the poet superficial, for even professional grammarians sometimes admitted to oversight.[32]

Another branch of culture in which Lucian again shows his conservatism is the visual arts, where his sensitivity has long been recognized as exceptional for a writer of antiquity. This is connected with his early training as a sculptor, but also with his literary profession.[33] Many writers of the Second Sophistic favor the device of the *ecphrasis* or verbal depiction of an object in art or nature, and whole collections of such descriptions survive from two of the Philostratoi and Callistratos. Though Lucian uses the device, he does not make the visual object a mere excuse for rhetoric, but tries to interpret the intention of the artist.[34] In both sculpture and painting his tastes, as in literature, are largely confined to masters of the fifth and fourth centuries, several of whom worked in Athens. The latest that he names are approximately of the time of Alexander, and his description of Apelles' *Calumny* and Aetion's *Marriage of Alexander and Rhoxane* were to inspire Botticelli and Sodoma in the Italian renaissance to attempt a recreation.[35] Here again Lucian's tastes coincide, apart from differences of emphasis, with those of his age. Several of the works that he singles out were reproduced to adorn Hadrian's villa at Tivoli,

32. *Pseudol.*, esp. 8–9, 16; Eupolis, fr. 309 K. Cf. Phrynichos' confession of oversight, *Ecl.* 231 Fischer.

33. This subject has been extensively canvased. The classic treatment is that of Blümner, *Archäologische Studien zu Lucian;* a good general survey in Le Morvan, *REG* 45 (1932) 380–390; almost every discussion of individual works mentioned by Lucian involves his powers of observation and description, for example Hartswick, *AJA* 87 (1983) 345.

34. For Lucian's *ecphrases,* e.g., *Dom.* 22–31, *Herc.* 3, *Herod.* 5–6, *Zeux.* 4–6.

35. *Calumny* of Apelles: *Cal.* 2–5: for Botticelli's version in the Uffizi, Horne, *Botticelli* 256–263. Aetion's *Marriage: Herod.* 5–6; for Sodoma's version in the Villa Farnesina, Hayum, *Il Sodoma* 167–168 with pl. 42. The statue of Kombabos by the otherwise unknown Hermocles of Rhodes (*Syr. D.* 26) is not really an exception, since Lucian only mentions it as an object in the shrine of the goddess at Hierapolis.

and others are noticed by Pausanias.[36] When in the *Portraits* he summons up writers, painters and sculptors of the past, and borrows
features of their works in order to depict Pantheia, the effect resembles those Roman matrons portrayed in the attitude of classical prototypes, for example the "Olympias" or the "Grande Herculanaise."[37]

In architecture Lucian departs from his conservatism to praise two
buildings in modern style. One is the "bath" built by a certain Hippias:
with its lofty construction and use of colored marbles, this resembles
extant thermal establishments such as those of Roman Ephesos and
Sardis.[38] Curiously, Lucian extols the architect in language that recalls
his famous homonym, the sophist from Elis, as if he tried to blend
the two figures together and thus to give the building an aura of
antiquity, rather as he uses the Herodotean manner when describing
the great temple of Syrian Hierapolis.[39] The *Hall* is an even more
elaborate encomium than that of the bath, and though Lucian does
not indicate the age of the building its sumptuous decoration again
suggests a modern one.[40] In both works his purpose is perhaps to be
explained by the circumstances, since a graceful way to flatter his
hearers was to emphasize their public buildings.

Lucian's culture therefore resembles that of his contemporaries,
even when they lived in a town like Oxyrhynchos. As one who had
his own contribution to make to literature, however, he had to define
his position toward the authors of the past. For this purpose, it has
been held, he adopted a doctrine of imitation *(mimesis),* whereby
almost all of his work can be seen as the product of literary recreation.
On this view, Lucian draws heavily on the work of his classic predecessors, especially Aristophanes, Plato, and Menippos, fusing it into
something that is at once derivative and original. Culture is thus

36. Hadrian's Villa: thus the Venus of Cnidos (Luc. *Im.* 4, 6, *I. trag,* 10, *Pro Im.*
23, Aurigemma, *Villa Adriana* 44–45); also the *Tyrannoctonoi* of Critias and Nesiotes,
the *Discobolos* of Myron, and perhaps the *Amazon* of Pheidias (Luc. *Philops.* 18, *Im.*
4, Aurigemma, pls. 197, 198, *EAA* 3 fig. 798). Paus. 1.8.5 (the *Tyrannoctonoi*), 1.19.2
(Alcamenes' *Aphrodite in the Gardens:* cf. Luc. *Im.* 4, 6), 10.26.3 (Cassandra in Po-
lygnotos' *Iliou Persis* at Delphi: cf. Luc. *Im.* 7).

37. Bieber, *Ancient Copies* 96 ("Olympias": on the identification of the original,
Delivorrias, *MDAI[A]* 93 [1978] 1–23), 148–162 (Herculaneum women).

38. Ginouvès, *Balaneutikè,* esp. 135 n. 4, 149, 220 n. 5.

39. Cf. Apuleius' encomium of the original Hippias, *Flor.* pp. 11–13 Helm.

40. *Dom.,* esp. 8 on the χρύσωσις.

everything in Lucian's art, while society, in the sense of contemporary manners and institutions, contributes little more than the fashion for archaism which led Lucian to turn his back on the present.[41]

Certainly, Lucian regards the "imitation" of the ancients as essential to his task. Lexiphanes will only be notable in literature when he has culled (apanthisamenos) all the best from antiquity. "Above all," Lucian advises him, "I beg you to remember not to imitate (mimeisthai) the worst things of the sophists who lived a little before us . . . but to rival (zeloun) ancient examples."[42] Disguised as Parrhesiades, Lucian claims that his work is nothing but a bouquet culled from the ancient philosophers; similarly, his True Histories will give amusement to the learned public because "everything in them alludes not without mockery to certain of the ancient poets, historians and philosophers." Even his portrait of Pantheia is built up by combining examples (paradeigmata) from ancient literature and art.[43] Yet allowance must be made for Lucian's characteristic irony and evasiveness. The claim that his works are nothing more than an anthology of the ancient philosophers is in part a device to disarm his philosophic critics. The True Histories may be a tissue of allusions and recondite jokes, but at the same time it constitutes a work apparently unique in ancient literature, with its own progeny of imitators.[44] There is no evidence that imitation is for Lucian some kind of program or doctrine,[45] still less that it was a general law governing all forms of expression, literary and otherwise.[46] Imitation is rather one dimension of culture, the way in which the educated artist displays his knowledge of his predecessors and pays them homage.

The view that Lucian's imitation implies an exclusive attachment

41. This view is particularly associated with Bompaire (Ch. 1 at n. 15).
42. Lex. 22–23. Cf. Rh. Pr. 9, "he will tell you to emulate those ancient men, setting before you outmoded examples of speeches, and ones not easy to rival."
43. Pisc. 6; VH 1.2; Im. 7–20, esp. 17.
44. Nicolson, Voyages to the Moon.
45. E.g. Bompaire, Lucien écrivain 137–138, on the Prometheus es and the Zeuxis: "deux courtes mises au point de sa doctrine littéraire . . . On conclura . . . à l'adoption de la Mimésis complète par Lucien." Lucian's readers are sometimes very solemn.
46. Bompaire, Lucien écrivain 93–97, "Mimésis et culture," followed by Reardon, Courants littéraires 10, and Vidal-Naquet, Flavius Arrien 365–366, "C'est le siècle de la mimésis. Chacun s'accordera à le dire ou à le constater . . ."; 367, "la mimésis est donc la loi générale de l'expression culturelle, politique, philosophique, voire artistique."

to ancient art and history sometimes has a corollary about the present: that he turns away from it in refined distaste for a world governed by Rome.[47] It is urged that many of his most characteristic works are dialogues set either in a vague past, such as those involving Menippos, or in no definite time at all, such as the *Cock* or the *Dialogues of the Courtesans*. The Menippean works in particular have been thought to prove Lucian's indifference to his own time. In the *Icaromenippos*, for example, the philosopher sights the Colossos of Rhodes on his ascent to heaven, and upon his arrival is asked by Zeus when the Athenians plan to complete the Olympieion. Since the Colossos had fallen down in 227, and the Olympieion had been completed by Hadrian, some have inferred that Lucian found these allusions in a work of Menippos and took them over unthinkingly.[48] These inferences suggest not so much Lucian's carelessness as modern insensitivity: such references might have been overtaken by events, but that made no difference to their effect.[49] Several passages in other works have been seized on to show his indifference to the passage of time, but the arguments are equally fragile.[50]

Far from being careless about time, Lucian exploits it in subtle ways, often by means of quotations from literature. Charon and Hermes are inspired by the text of Homer to pile Pelion on Ossa, and after doing so look down on a world of the sixth century that Lucian has

47. Thus Reardon, *Courants littéraires* 17, "une réaction aux grandes données de l'histoire contemporaine, et surtout à l'existence de l'empire romain; et cette réaction s'exprime sous la forme d'un manque d'intérêt pour ce qui est romain"; 179, on Lucian, "un artiste sérieux et . . . *par là même* désinvolte en ce qui concernait une époque qui n'était pas l'époque classique."

48. *Icar.* 12 (Colossos), 24 (Olympieion). For these inferences, Helm, *Lucian* 98–101, approved by Bompaire, *Lucien écrivain* 519 n. 3.

49. Contrast Helm, *Lucian* 99: "eine solche Frage . . . hatte für seine Hörer und Leser jeden Witz verloren"; in 99 n. 1, Helm even considers whether Lucian did not know that Hadrian had completed the Olympieion.

50. Thus Bompaire, *Lucian écrivain* 483 n. 2, on *Laps.* 6: Epicurus is distinguished from the παλαιοί and is therefore "le dernier cri de la nouveauté"; 494–495, on *Deor. Conc.* 12, because Momos complains that statues of Polydamas and Theagenes are "now" (ἤδη) used for cures, Lucian is treating practices five centuries old as "scandaleuses nouveautés"; 515–516, where τὰ τελευταῖα ταῦτα (*Herod.* 4) means not "lately" but "lastly," "finally," as in *Peregr.* 4; 516 n. 1 on *Pro Im.* 23, Lycinos "absurdly" says that Praxiteles carved the Venus of Cnidos "not many years ago." But Lucian is contrasting the eternity of "heavenly Aphrodite" with her embodiment in a work of art.

evidently peopled from Herodotos: Croesos converses with Solon, Milon of Croton is still alive, Nineveh has fallen but not Babylon.[51] While in the *Dialogues of the Gods* and the *Dialogues of the Marine Gods* Lucian humorously maintains the illusion of a time before literature, works which involve the gods in modern problems, for example the *Tragic Zeus* and the *Assembly of the Gods,* are full of quotations and pastiche.[52] The twin dialogues in which the author is put on trial, the *Double Indictment* and the *Fisherman,* exploit the contrast of ancient and modern: though the gods, the ancient philosophers, and Lucian's surrogates are all on stage together, the effect is not to blur distinctions of time, but to show that he sides with the old masters against their modern counterparts.

It is true that certain works are placed in a setting that seems vaguely Hellenistic, among them two of the most famous, the *Dialogues of the Dead* and the *Dialogues of the Courtesans.* But here nothing was to be gained by precision, and certain topics, such as that of legacy hunting, show Lucian thinking of his own time as much as of the past.[53] Other works with a modern setting have an antique patina: thus Lycinos and some companions in the *Ship* stroll down to Piraeos, like Socrates in the *Republic,* but the immense size of the ship and its destination in Italy betoken a world far different from Plato's.[54] As in the *Portraits,* the effect recalls sculptures in which modern Romans pose as antique gods or heroes. The cult of antiquity does not imply disrespect for the present: rather, it validates the present with the stamp of culture.

If culture and imitation are not expressions of an indifference to the present, the reason for the value placed on them by Lucian and his contemporaries must be sought elsewhere. Perhaps the chief one lies in the nature of his society. The Roman Empire had created the conditions whereby Greek art and literature had expanded over an area scarcely less than that conquered by Alexander. Unlike the empire of the Macedonian, however, the Roman Empire seemed by its stability to promise the Greek achievement an indefinite extension in time. Hadrian's creation of the Panhellenion, a union of Greek

51. *Cont.* 4 (Homer), 8 (Milon), 9 (Croesos and Solon), 23 (Nineveh and Babylon).

52. Note, however, the anachronistic reference to an oracle of Apollo on Delos (*Bis acc.* 1), an allusion to the Homeric Hymn to Apollo: thus Robert, *Asie Mineure* 402–403.

53. *Dial. Mort.* 5–11 (15–21): cf. Helm, *Lucian* 203–204.

54. For a good discussion of modern elements in the *Nav.,* Husson's commentary, in *Lucien: Navire* 1.14–15, 2.12–18.

cities with Athens as their capital, epitomized the Hellenic world and the respect paid to it by Rome. Greek culture expressed the cohesion of the educated elite of the empire; and for those not born into that elite, like Lucian and certain of the sophists, it offered unimagined avenues to social and economic advancement. A Commagenian settled and accepted in Athens might feel that he had penetrated the citadel of civilized society.

This feeling of solidarity may have been no less strong for the tokens of impending disruption. Outside the pale were forces threatening to break in. As early as the reign of Pius there appears in Greek literature the notion of the Roman Empire as a city walled against its adversaries.[55] In the succeeding reign the Costoboci crossed the Danube and carried their depredations within sight of the Acropolis, and the emperors had to go to war in the east against Parthians and in the north against tribes of eastern Europe. The plague brought back by Verus' troops added new disaster, which fell heaviest upon the cities of the Greek east, Athens among them.[56] The old order also had its enemies within. Impostors, some of them taking advantage of the troubles of the time, proclaimed new gods and burned the writings of the classic philosophers; votaries of an upstart religion denied the traditional religion and seemed to flaunt their lack of education.[57]

When Lucian imitated and praised the old masters, he was not encouraging his readers to turn their backs on the present, but was inviting them to join in the affirmation of a common heritage. No doubt like most authors he did not aim to reach a single audience only; he could hope that what pleased those who heard his recitals would also please those who read his works in Gaul or Commagene. His society consisted not only of those within his acquaintance but all those Greeks and Romans who shared a love of classical literature and of Attic refinement. For him and for them culture was not something apart from the world, indifferent to the present.[58] It was what made them a class allied in taste and feeling, a true society.

55. Aristid. 26.79–83; App. praef. 28.
56. Above, Ch. 6 at n. 6.
57. Christians and Greek gods: *Peregr.* 13. Christian ἀπαιδευσία: Celsus in Or. *Cels.* 4.36.
58. Gibbon's characterization is still worth remembering (*Decline and Fall* 2.58 Bury): "a philosopher who had studied mankind, and who describes their manners in the most lively colours."

APPENDIX A

Crepereius Calpurnianus

CREPEREIUS CALPURNIANUS of Pompeiopolis is one of the four historians of Lucius Verus' Parthian War whom Lucian names, the others being the doctor Callimorphos, Antiochianus son of Apollo, and Demetrios of Sagalassos.[1] He alleges that Crepereius combined servile imitation of Thucydides with the introduction of technical terms of Roman warfare, and some have suspected that Lucian invented him: "Crepereius," it is suggested, refers to the rare Latin word *creper* (which he is highly unlikely to have known).[2] Others have defended Crepereius' existence, and indeed attempted to reconstruct his career: perhaps he was a Paphlagonian, drafted into the legion *III Augusta* while on a visit to Africa, and then a soldier under Lucius in the east.[3]

Both sides have assumed with little compunction that Lucian refers to Pompeiopolis of Paphlagonia.[4] Yet there was another Pompeiopolis, the quondam Soloi on the coast of Cilicia, and homonymous cities are a notorious snare.[5] It was Moses Solanus (du Soul) who

1. Luc. *Hist. conscr.* 15.
2. Homeyer, *Lukian: Geschichte* 22. Cf. Anderson, *Lucian: Theme and Variation* 78, "Lucian enjoys collecting polysyllabic titles."
3. Baldwin, *QUCC* 27 (1978), 211–213, expanding his arguments in *Studies* 82–83.
4. Homeyer, *Lukian: Geschichte* 208, qualifies her opinion with a "wahrscheinlich": note the argument of Anderson, *Lucian: Theme and Variation* 78 n. 110, "Baldwin . . . argues that Pompeiopolis is in fact a real place. But it was in Paphlagonia, and Lucian tells us elsewhere what he thought of the fools who lived in that part of the world (*Alex.* 17)."
5. For problems of numismatic attribution involving these very cities, Klein, *GNS* 23 (1973) 47–55. Compare the two cities of Phrygia called Metropolis, Robert, *Asie Mineure* 257–299.

gave the decisive vote for the northern Pompeiopolis in the great edition of Lucian begun at Amsterdam in 1743, and since then only C. F. Hermann in his commentary of 1828 seems to have demurred.[6]

Pompeiopolis of Paphlagonia was founded by Pompey in 65 or 64, after his defeat of Mithradates of Pontos. It was situated at an important crossing of the river Amnias, and in the imperial period was the metropolis of the region.[7] In favor of ascribing Crepereius Calpurnianus to this city is the fact that it was the *patria* of Cn. Claudius Severus, son-in-law of Marcus Aurelius, *consul II ordinarius* in 173, and friend of several cultural luminaries of the day, such as Galen, Herodes Atticus, and Hadrian of Tyre. A compatriot of such a man might well have hoped to further his career by celebrating Lucius' victories in a work of history.[8] An argument might also be drawn from the city's coinage: most of the few types come from the joint reign of Marcus and Lucius, perhaps from the year 164.[9]

The name "Crepereius" has recently drawn attention because of its occurrence at Pisidian Antioch and Pamphylian Attaleia. It is associated both with commerce and with military settlements of the late republic. It is found early on Delos and in Narbonese Gaul, while many of the abundant Crepereii in Africa may have descended from followers of P. Sittius.[10] At present neither "Crepereius" nor "Calpurnius" occurs in the modest epigraphy of the two Pompeiopoleis. If either name, but particularly the former, were to do so in future, that would no doubt settle the question of Crepereius' origin and reality.[11]

The other Pompeiopolis was founded by the Rhodians as Soloi

6. Solanus in Hemsterhuis (Hemsterhusius) et al., *Luciani Opera* 2.22: "Duae huius nominis urbes memorantur, altera in Cilicia, in Paphlagonia altera . . . De posteriori intelligo." Contra, Hermann, *Luciani libellus, quomodo historia conscribi oporteat* 107–108: "quo argumento, equidem ignoro."

7. On the foundation and site of Pompeiopolis, modern Taş Köprü, Magie, *Roman Rule* 1.370, 372, 2.1083–84; Schneider, *RE* 21 (1952) 2044–45; on its title of metropolis, Robert, *Asie Mineure* 217–219.

8. Evidence in Halfmann, *Senatoren* 180–181. This argument is stressed by Baldwin, *Studies* 82–83, *QUCC* 27 (1978), 211–213.

9. Generally, Waddington-Babelon-Reinach, *Recueil* 194–196; Cahn in *Provincialia: Festschrift Laur-Belart* 62–63, esp. 62 n. 12; Klein, *GNS* 23 (1973) 47–55.

10. Levick and Jameson, *JRS* 54 (1964) 100–106; Levick, *Roman Colonies* 57–58; Pflaum, *CT* 15 (1967) 65–72 (*Scripta varia* 1.237–244).

11. It may be noted, however, that several ephebic lists of the second century are known from the northern Pompeiopolis (Mendel, *BCH* 27 [1903] 327–330; Jacopi, *Esplorazioni e studi in Paflagonia* 42, with the improvements of J. Robert and L. Robert,

about 700 B.C. Situated at the western extremity of level Cilicia, it possessed a fine harbor. Despite its reputation for bad Greek, it produced the astronomical poet Aratos and the Stoic Chrysippos. Depopulated by Tigranes I of Armenia to swell his new foundation of Tigranocerta, it was reconstituted by Pompey in 66 or 65 after his defeat of the pirates, who according to tradition formed a large part of the population. As Pompeiopolis it dated its era from the new foundation and never reverted to its previous name, even though "Soloi" is sometimes found in literature. In this it contrasts with cities like Arcadian Mantinea or Bithynian Cios, which dropped their Hellenistic styles (respectively Antigoneia and Prusias) in the Roman period. The ruins have been badly plundered to build the nearby Mersin, but enough remains, especially of the well-known colonnade leading up from the harbor, to suggest a place of great prosperity.[12]

The coinage of the Cilician city is distinguished by its large variety of types, most of them dated by the civic era. By far the greatest abundance comes from the year 229, of which the Julian equivalent is early 163 to early 164.[13] In a fundamental study, A. A. Boyce showed that these issues commemorated a visit made by Lucius Verus on his way to the Parthian War, when according to the *Historia Augusta* "he lingered to enjoy himself in all those maritime cities which are conspicuous for their pleasures in Asia, Pamphylia and Cilicia."[14] Pompey appears on three different types of this year, and it is natural that the city should have remembered its founder when another Roman

---

Bull. 1939.437), so that a much larger number of Roman names is known from this city than from the southern one.

12. Essential discussion in Ruge, *RE* 3 A (1927) 935–938, with additions by Schneider, *RE* 21 (1952) 2043–44; Magie, *Roman Rule* 1.273–274, 300, 2.1148–49, 1180 n. 43; cf. also Dreizehnter, *Chiron* 5 (1975) 239–240. For the site, du Loup, *BCTH* 1930–31, 711–716 (very evocative); Verzone, *Palladio* 7 (1957) 62–64; Boyce, *AJA* 62 (1958) 67–78; Peschlow-Bindokat, *MDAI(I)* 25 (1975) 373–391. The principal publications of inscriptions known to me are: *CIG* 4434–36, 4436 b; Lebas-Waddington, 1471–73; Davis, *Life in Asiatic Turkey* 20–28; Beaudoin and Pottier, *BCH* 4 (1880) 75–76; Duchesne, *BCH* 5 (1881) 316–318; Kontoleon, *MDAI(A)* 12 (1887) 258 nos. 30 and 31; Hicks, *JHS* 11 (1890) 242–243; Radet and Paris, *BCH* 14 (1890) 587–589 (*OGIS* 230); Heberdey and Wilhelm, *Reisen in Kilikien* 43–44 nos. 101–109; von Gladiss, *MDAI(I)* 23–24 (1973–74) 175–181. The Hellenistic epigram copied at Mersin by Paribeni and Romanelli, *Monumenti Antichi* 23 (1914) 86–87 (Peek, *GVI* no. 502) must also be from Soloi.

13. Full bibliography in Klein, *GNS* 23 (1973) 48 n. 3; for a survey of the known issues, Klein, 52–55, with addenda in *GNS* 33 (1983) 63–64.

14. Boyce in *Hommages Renard* 3.87–103, esp. 102–103, citing HA *Verus* 6.9.

general was leading an expedition to the east. Writing to Marcus Aurelius in 161 or 162, Fronto sends him a copy of Cicero's *Pro Lege Manilia:* there Marcus will find Pompey praised to the full, and also "many paragraphs closely fitting your present interests, about the choice of leaders for armies, the welfare of our allies, the protection of the provinces."[15]

Another of the types struck by Pompeiopolis in this year leads back to Lucian, though not directly to Crepereius. Copied from the imperial coinage of 161–62, it shows Marcus and Lucius clasping hands and bears the legend Ὁμόνοια Σεβαστῶν.[16] Though similar types are found in many cities of the eastern empire, they are particularly characteristic of Cilicia, where they are found in five or six cities beside Pompeiopolis.[17] Louis Robert has given the explanation. The legend, "Concord of the Augusti," refers not merely to their brotherly unanimity but also to their joint care for the security of the empire. In Cilicia, as in Lucian's own Commagene, the power of Parthia was dangerously near: "aussi célébrait-on avec ferveur, dans la vie publique et dans le monnayage, les succès et les paix, mêmes précaires, obtenues par l'empereur."[18] Robert has recently evoked this political context to illustrate another chapter in this same essay of Lucian. Here he makes fun of a historian who, writing near the end of the war, had undertaken to anticipate events of the future, including "a city in Mesopotamia of the greatest size and the finest beauty; but he is still deliberating whether to call it Nicaea after the victory or Concord (Ὁμόνοιαν) or Eirenias."[19]

It seems safe to conclude that, like the unnamed historian, Crepereius Calpurnianus of Pompeiopolis is a real person and, since the

15. Fronto, *Parth.* 10; on the date, Champlin, *JRS* 64 (1974) 155. It is curious, however, that Polyaenos, who wrote his *Strategemata* expressly to help Marcus and Lucius in their conduct of the war, mentions Pompey only for his losses to Julius Caesar (*Strat.* 8.23).

16. *BMC Lycaonia, Isauria, and Cilicia,* lxxv; Boyce, *Festal and Dated Coins* pl. III 22, cf. Boyce, *Hommages Renard* 3.103, Klein, *GNS* 33 (1983) 58–59.

17. For Cilicia, see the references given by Robert in *Déesse de Hiérapolis* 76 no. 37; for addenda, Klein, *GNS* 33 (1983) 61–62.

18. Robert in *Déesse de Hiérapolis* 77–78; Robert, *Asie Mineure* 425–426, whence the quotation in the text. Polyaenos, though he does not use the word ὁμόνοια, talks of the two emperors' conduct of the war without ever mentioning their physical separation, *Strat.* 1. pref. 1; 3 pref., etc.

19. Luc. *Hist. conscr.* 31; see the full discussion of Robert, *Asie Mineure* 423–426, and cf. Ch. 6 at n. 18.

attribution of him to the northern Pompeiopolis rests on nothing but psittacism, to attribute him to the southern one. In his opening words he advertised his Roman citizenship and his city. As Soloi this had been distinguished in Greek literature, and as Pompeiopolis was connected with an earlier Roman victor and had recently been visited by Lucius Verus. His Thucydidean history glorified a campaign which assured the security of Pompeiopolis, Cilicia, and all the eastern empire.

LIKE CREPEREIUS HIMSELF, the circumstances under which Lucian heard him and the other historians he discusses can perhaps be made more concrete by documentary evidence. He claims to draw all his examples from recitations he had recently attended in Corinth (which seems to be where he wrote the work) and in Ionia not long before.[20] Since Lucius Verus is the focus of these histories and to some extent of Lucian's own essay, it may be asked whether the emperor's presence had something to do with this frenzy of historiography. This would be excluded if the prevailing view of his return were correct, that is, that he took the usual overland route from Syria across the Taurus and through Cappadocia and Galatia to Bithynia.[21] The only evidence seems to be an inscription from Aezanoi in northern Phrygia which has drawn attention for other reasons. It honors a benefactor of the city who "provided the lord Caesar with a *diogmites* at his own expense in the proconsulate of Quintilius Maximus." The *diogmitai* were a kind of rural police, and it has been supposed that this one was to serve as a gendarme to Lucius during his passage. The older view, that the inscription refers to Marcus Aurelius' emergency measures for the impending German wars, is now confirmed by a milestone which dates the tenure of Quintilius Maximus to 168–69 or more probably 169–70.[22]

20. *Hist. conscr.* 14, 17, 29. Cf. also 3, the comparison between Lucian and Diogenes the Cynic in Corinth.

21. Magie, *Roman Rule* 1532 n. 6, followed by Keil, *AAWW* 92 (1955) 162.

22. Lebas-Waddington 3 no. 992 (*OGIS* 511; *IGRR* 3.580). For the correct interpretation, adducing HA *Marcus* 21.7, Waddington on no. 992 followed by Dittenberger and Cagnat. However, by assigning Quintilius Maximus to 165–66, Waddington misled others into referring the inscription to Lucius' return from the Parthian War (see previous n.): the correct date follows from the milestone published by D. French, *ZPE* 21 (1976) 77–78 (*Bull.* 1977.380; *L'année épigraphique* 1976.652; *SEG* 26.1335). Cf. also Jones, *GRBS* 13 (1971) 47 n. 8.

Lucius went out to Syria in 162 by way of Corinth, Athens, Ephesos, and the southern coast of Asia Minor.[23] He returned to Ephesos in the course of the war to marry Lucilla, and inscriptions attest that part of his army stayed in the city on its way home. Another inscription mentions "visits" of the emperor there. Although these might be only two, his outward journey and his marriage, it might rather be suspected that this pleasure-loving emperor took the same route back as he had taken going out. Though the rejoicing over the Parthian victories was widespread, it was conspicuous in Ephesos. The city held splendid *Epinicia* and erected a great monument, the so-called *Partherdenkmal*, which has been shown by recent discoveries to have been begun about 166 and completed after 169.[24] Lucius may have been present at some of the recitations heard by Lucian in Ionia and Achaea, just as Pompey after defeating Mithradates lingered in cities of the Greek east, listening to poetic encomia of his achievements and to other learned discourses.[25] And just as Lucian had written the treatise *On the Dance*, the *Portraits* and the *Defense of the Portraits* to please Lucius in Antioch, so he may have written, and even recited, a version of the work *On Writing History* while the emperor was in Corinth.

23. HA *Verus* 6.9.

24. Marriage with Lucilla: HA *Verus* 7.7. Armies: *I. Ephesos* 3.672 ll. 7–10 (Heberdey, *JOAEI* 15 [1912] Beibl. 164–165); *I. Ephesos* 3.672 b; *I. Ephesos* 7.1.3080 ll. 7–10 (Keil, *Forsch. in Ephesos* 3 no. 80); cf. also Alföldy and Halfmann, *ZPE* 35 (1979) 195–212. "Visits": *I. Ephesos* 3.728 l. 23 (Miltner, *JOEAI* 44 [1959] Beibl. 257–259 no. 3), cf. *I. Ephesos* 7.1.3072 ll. 19–20 (Keil, *Forsch. in Ephesos* 3 no. 72). *Epinicia: I. Ephesos* 5. 1605 l. 8 (Hicks, *GIBM* 3.605), with the commentary of Robert in *RPh* 4 (1930) 40–41 (*OMS* 2.1140–41); *I. Ephesos* 3.671 (Knibbe, *JOEAI* 49 [1968–1971] Beibl. 74 no. 12); *I. Ephesos* 3.721 (Knibbe, *JOEAI* 50 [1972–1975] Beibl. 29–33 no. 2); perhaps *I. Ephesos* 4.1146. "Partherdenkmal": see Oberleitner in *Funde aus Ephesos* 66–94, esp. 92–93 on the date; cf. also J. Robert and L. Robert, *Bull.* 1977.417 no. 2, discussing the inscription now *I. Ephesos* 3.721.

25. Plut. *Pomp.* 42.7–11; on his stay in Mitylene, Robert, *CRAI* 1969, 47.

Chronology

THE LIST BELOW is confined to those works whose date is more or less assured by references to Lucian's own time of life, to other of his works, or to external events. I have not dated works by their resemblances to one another, nor by making assumptions about his literary development. One criterion which might seem reliable is best discussed separately. The "Syrian" states (*Bis acc.* 32) that he gave up "accusing tyrants and praising heroes" at about the age of forty, and in the same work he is accused by Dialogue of having joined him with Comedy and Menippos (33). It can be inferred that the four surviving declamations (*Abd., Phal.* I, II, *Tyr.*) belong to a time before Lucian was forty, and that his two dialogues in which Menippos is a character *(Icar., Nec.)* belong to a later one. To this later period should belong also *Zeux.* and *Prom. es,* which are prefaces to readings of his comic dialogues. Nonetheless, since it is not clear how many of Lucian's works he would have classified as comic dialogues (for example, *Nav.*), and since his birthdate is not exactly known, I have assigned a date to works not on the ground of their form alone, but only on the basis of other evidence. The dialogues which I have omitted, though thinking them likely to be from a later period, are: *Anach., Cont., Dear. Iud., D. Deor., D. meretr., D. mar., D. Mort., Gall., Hes., Icar., I. conf., I. trag., Nec., Philops., Pisc., Prom., Sat., Symp., Tim.* For some works there is not even this criterion of date: *Cal., Dips., Dom., Electr., Hipp., Iud. Voc., Luct., Musc. Enc., Nigr., Pod., Syr. D., Sacr., Tox., VH.*

Lucian's birthdate can only be fixed approximately between about 115 and 125: Ch. 2 at n. 10. I have therefore listed his datable works in alphabetical order, since to attempt a listing by date would only confuse: for example, the *Bis acc.*, written when he was past forty, might be earlier or later than the *Hist. conscr.*, written in 166.

Alex. After 180, since Marcus Aurelius has been deified (θεός, 48).

Apol. After 180 (?). Lucian has "one foot on [Charon's] ferry" (1); he is "in extreme old age and practically over the threshold [of Hades]" (4: this last evidently an exaggeration); there seems to be only one emperor ruling (13), who might be Marcus (cf. on *Ind.*) but should rather be Commodus.

Bacch. Lucian is an old man (γέρων, 7–8).

Bis acc. The "Syrian" is past forty (32).

Cat. 165 or later. "The philosopher Theagenes" (6) is probably the Cynic who appears in *Peregr.* and was therefore alive in 165: Ch. 11 at n. 71. The many dead "in Media" (6) might refer to Lucius Verus' Parthian War.

Demon. Later than ca. 174, perhaps than 177: Ch. 9 at n. 5.

Deor. Conc. Ca. 165 (?). Perhaps refers to political struggles of the mid-160's at Athens: Ch. 4 at nn. 23–24.

Eun. After 176. The work presupposes the existence of the imperial chairs of philosophy at Athens, established by Marcus in that year (Cass. Dio 72.31.3).

Fug. 165 or later. After the death of Peregrinus (1–3), on which see s.v. *Peregr.* It is unclear which of the two works came first.

Harm. The language of 3–4 suggests that Lucian, though "already famous," has yet to make his career.

Herc. Lucian old and with a gray beard (7–8).

Herm. "Lycinos" is forty (13).

Herod. Lucian appears to be young: Ch. 2 at n. 27.

Hist. conscr. 166. See Ch. 6 at n. 3.

Im. 163 or 164. Apparently written while Lucius Verus was in Antioch and before his marriage to Lucilla: Ch. 7 at nn. 2, 38.

Ind. Between 161 and 180, perhaps between 169 and 176. The "king" described as a "wise man" (22–23) should be Marcus. Since Lucian speaks as if there was only one "king," the work may belong between the death of Lucius Verus and the elevation of Commodus to the rank of Augustus.

Laps. Lucian an "old gentleman"(πρεσβύτης ἀνήρ, 1, cf. 15).

Merc. cond. Probably not much earlier than the *Apol.*, q.v.: Ch. 8 at n. 24.

Nav. Mid-160's (?). The reference to imaginary campaigning in

Mesopotamia (34) might glance at Lucius Verus, but see Ch. 2 at n. 10. At several points there may be allusions to Herodes Atticus (13, 20, 24), but these are of little help for the date.

Patr. Enc. Lucian seems to have "become famous" (8).

Peregr. 165 or later. Probably not much time has elapsed since Peregrinus' death in 165: Ch. 11 at n. 14.

Pro Im. Published with or shortly after *Im.,* q.v.

Pseudol. Ca. 160–170 (?). If the target is Hadrian of Tyre, he was in Ephesos (where Lucian met the Mistaken Critic) approximately in the 160's: Ch. 10 at n. 67.

Rh. Pr. If the target is Pollux of Naucratis, perhaps after 180, though preferably under Marcus Aurelius: Ch. 10 at nn. 33–34.

Salt. 163 or 164. Probably written in Antioch to gratify Lucius Verus' taste for pantomimes: Ch. 7 at n. 2.

Scyth. Lucian apparently young: Ch. 2 at n. 26.

Somn. Lucian's career is well launched (18).

Vit. Auct. Precedes the *Pisc.* (*Pisc.* 4).

Disputed Works

THERE WILL NEVER BE agreement on a canon of Lucian's works. I have tended to exclude those about which there is strong suspicion, but give here a list of doubtful cases, briefly indicating my reasons for or against authenticity and some recent bibliography. The following are agreed to be spurious and are not noted: *Am., Charid., Cyn., Halc., Macr., Nero, Ocyp., Philop.*

Asin. The linguistic arguments seem decisive against authenticity (Helm, *RE* 13 [1927] 1749; henceforth cited as "Helm"), but the work has had many defenders, thus Macleod in the Loeb translation (8.47–51, esp. 50, "Lucian's own hand had some share in the composition"), Anderson, *Studies* 34–49; against, Hall, *Lucian's Satire* 354–367.

Astr. This defense of astrology seems incredible in Lucian: authenticity is argued by Hall, *Lucian's Satire* 381–388.

Dem. Enc. The extreme artificiality of construction and the vocabulary seem to exclude Lucian as the author (Helm, 1736). But for a defense, Baldwin, *Antichthon* 3 (1969) 54–62; Hall, *Lucian's Satire* 324–331.

Epigr. Some of these may well be genuine: Baldwin, *Phoenix* 29 (1975) 311–335.

Paras. This curious pastiche of Plato seems excluded by its language (Helm, 1754), though it is defended by Anderson, *Phoenix* 33 (1979) 59–66 and by Hall, *Lucian's Satire* 331–339.

Patr. Enc. This has been supposed a sketch or fragment (Helm, 1754), but without good reason: Bompaire, *Lucien écrivain* 278.

Pod. This could be genuine, Hall, *Lucian's Satire* 368–370.

Salt. In favor of authenticity, Ch. 7 at n. 3.

Sol. The difficulties of interpretation tell against attributing it to a master of clarity: in favor, Macleod, *CQ* 6 (1956) 102–111; against, Hall, *Lucian's Satire* 298–307. I have not seen the monograph reviewed by Vidalis, *REG* 93 (1980) 600–602.

Syr. D. In favor of authenticity, Ch. 4 at n. 37.

Bibliography

The following bibliography contains all books and articles (except those in encyclopedias and the like) referred to in the notes; since they are there cited summarily, by supplying full bibliographical details this list should aid the reader who does not recognize an item. I have given the full titles of periodicals, except for those listed in the Abbreviations. I have included commentaries and annotated editions, and bare texts when they have been especially useful.

Alföldi-Rosenbaum, E. Review of C. C. Vermeule, *Roman Imperial Art in Asia Minor, Phoenix* 25 (1971) 179–186.

Alföldy, G. *Konsulat und Senatorenstand unter den Antoninen; Prosopographische Untersuchungen zur senatorischen Führungsschicht.* Antiquitas, Reihe 1, 27. Bonn 1977.

Alföldy, G., and H. Halfmann. "Iunius Maximus und die Victoria Parthica," *ZPE* 35 (1979) 195–212.

Allinson, F. G. "Pseudo-Ionism in the Second Century A.D.," *AJPh* 7 (1886) 203–217.

——— *Lucian: Satirist and Artist.* New York, 1926.

Ameling, W. *Herodes Atticus, 1: Biographie, 2: Inschriften-katalog.* Hildesheim, 1983.

Anderson, G. *Lucian: Theme and Variation in the Second Sophistic. Mnemosyne* Suppl. 41. Leiden, 1976.

——— *Studies in Lucian's Comic Fiction. Mnemosyne* Suppl. 43. Leiden, 1976.

——— "Lucian's Classics: Some Short Cuts to Culture," *Bulletin of the Institute of Classical Studies* (London) 23 (1976) 59–68.

——— "Lucian and the Authorship of the *De Saltatione*," *GRBS* 18 (1977) 275–286.

—— "Patterns in Lucian's Quotations," *Bulletin of the Institute of Classical Studies* (London) 25 (1978) 97–100.

—— "Motifs and Techniques in Lucian's *De Parasito*," *Phoenix* 33 (1979) 59–66.

Astarita, M. L. *Avidio Cassio.* Rome, 1983.

Aurigemma, S. *Villa Adriana.* Rome, 1961.

Avenarius, G. *Lukians Schrift zur Geschichtsschreibung.* Meisenheim am Glan, 1956.

Avotins, I. "The Holders of the Chairs of Rhetoric at Athens," *Harvard Studies in Classical Philology* 79 (1975) 313–324.

Bagnani, G. "Peregrinus Proteus and the Christians," *Historia* 4 (1955) 107–112.

Baldwin, B. "Lucian as Social Satirist," *CQ* 11 (1961) 199–208.

—— "The Authorship and Purpose of Lucian's *Demosthenis Encomium*," *Antichthon* 3 (1969) 54–62.

—— *Studies in Lucian.* Toronto, 1973.

—— "The Epigrams of Lucian," *Phoenix* 29 (1975) 311–335.

—— "Crepereius Calpurnianus," *Quaderni Urbinati di Cultura Classica* 27 (1978) 211–213.

Balsdon, J. P. V. D. *Romans and Aliens.* London and Chapel Hill, 1979.

Barigazzi, A., ed. *Favorino di Arelate: Opere.* Florence, 1966.

Barnes, T. D. "Hadrian and Lucius Verus," *JRS* 57 (1967) 65–79.

Beaudouin, M., and E. Pottier. "Inscriptions de Pompéiopolis," *BCH* 4 (1880) 77–78.

Becker, O. *Das Bild des Weges und verwandte Vorstellungen im frühgriechischen Denken. Hermes* Einzelschrift 4. Berlin, 1937.

Bellinger, A. R. "Lucian's Dramatic Technique," *Yale Classical Studies* 1 (1928) 3–40.

Bernays, J. *Lucian und die Kyniker.* Berlin, 1879.

Betz, H. D. "Lukian von Samosata und das Christentum," *Novum Testamentum* 3 (1959) 226–237.

—— *Lukian und das Neue Testament: Religionsgeschichtliche und paränetische Parallelen.* Texte und Untersuchungen 76. Berlin, 1961.

Bieber, M. *Ancient Copies: Contributions to the History of Greek and Roman Art.* New York, 1977.

Bieler, L. ΘΕΙΟΣ ANHP: *Das Bild des "göttlichen Menschen" in Spätantike und Frühchristentum.* 2 vols. Vienna, 1935–1936.

Billerbeck, M. *Epictet: Vom Kynismus.* Philosophia Antiqua 34. Leiden, 1978.

—— *Der Kyniker Demetrios.* Philosophia Antiqua 36. Leiden, 1979.

Birley, A. R. *Marcus Aurelius.* London, 1966.

Bloch, R. "De Pseudo-Luciani Amoribus," *Dissertationes Philologicae Argentoratenses* 12, 3. Strasbourg, 1907.

Blümner, H. *Archäologische Studien zu Lucian*. Breslau, 1867.

Bol, R. *Das Statuenprogramm des Herodes-Atticus-Nymphäums,* Deutsches Archäologisches Institut, Olympische Forschungen 15. Berlin, 1984.

Boll, F. "Das Eingangstück der Ps.-Klementinen," *Zeitschrift für die Neutestamentliche Wissenschaft* 17 (1916) 139–148.

Bompaire, J. *Lucien écrivain: Imitation et création*. Bibliothèque des Écoles Françaises d'Athènes et de Rome 190. Paris 1958.

―――― "Travaux récents sur Lucien," *REG* 88 (1975) 224–229.

Bonner, C. *Studies in Magical Amulets, Chiefly Graeco-Egyptian*. Ann Arbor and London, 1950.

Bouché-Leclercq, A. *Histoire de la divination dans l'Antiquité*. 4 vols. Paris, 1879–1882.

Boulanger, A. "Lucien et Aelius Aristide," *RPh* n.s. 47 (1923) 144–151.

Bouquiaux-Simon, O. *Les lectures homériques de Lucien*. Académie Royale de Belgique, Classe des Lettres. Mémoires, Collection in-8o, 2nd ser., 59, 2. Brussels, 1968.

Bowersock, G. W. *Greek Sophists in the Roman Empire*. Oxford, 1969.

―――― "Greek Intellectuals and the Imperial Cult in the Second Century A.D.," in *Le culte des Souverains dans l'empire romain*, Entretiens Hardt 19. Geneva, 1973, 177–206.

―――― *Julian the Apostate*. London and Cambridge, Mass., 1978.

Bowie, E. L. "Greeks and Their Past in the Second Sophistic," *Past and Present* 46 (1970) 3–41 (M. I. Finley, ed., *Studies in Ancient Society*. London and Boston, 1974, 166–209).

―――― "The Importance of Sophists," *Yale Classical Studies* 27 (1982) 29–59.

Box, H. "Philo: *In Flaccum* 131 (M. 2. p. 536)," *CQ* 29 (1935) 39–40.

Boyce, A. A. "The Harbor of Pompeiopolis," *AJA* 62 (1958) 67–78.

―――― *Festal and Dated Coins of the Roman Empire: Four Papers*. Numismatic Notes and Monographs 153. New York, 1965.

―――― "The Foundation Year of Pompeiopolis in Cilicia: The Statement of a Problem," in *Hommages à Marcel Renard* 3, Collection Latomus 103. Brussels, 1969, 87–103.

Branham, B. "The Comic as Critic: Revenging Epicurus—a Study of Lucian's Art of Comic Narrative," *Classical Antiquity* 3 (1984) 143–163.

Bruns, I. "Lucian's philosophische Satiren," *Rheinisches Museum* 43 (1888) 86–103, 161–196.

―――― "Lucian und Oenomaos," *Rheinisches Museum* 44 (1889) 374–396.

Burckhardt, J. *Die Zeit Constantin's des Grossen*². Leipzig, 1880.

Buresch, K. *Klaros: Untersuchungen zum Orakelwesen des späteren Altertums*. Leipzig, 1889.

Cadoux, C. J. *Ancient Smyrna: A History of the City from the Earliest Times to 324 A. D*. Oxford, 1938.

Cahn, H. A. "Münzen aus fernen Gegenden in Augst," in *Provincialia: Festschrift für Rudolf Laur-Belart*. Basel and Stuttgart, 1968, 57–69.

Camelot, P. T., ed. *Ignace d'Antioche, Polycarpe de Smyrne: Lettres, Martyre de Polycarpe*⁴. Sources Chrétiennes 10. Paris, 1969.

Cameron, A. "The Date and Identity of Macrobius," *JRS* 56 (1966) 25–38.

——— *Circus Factions: Blues and Greens at Rome and Byzantium*. Oxford, 1976.

Capelle, W. Review of Helm, *Lucian, Berliner Philologische Wochenschrift* 34 (1914) 260–276.

——— "Lukian: Spötter von Samosata," *Socrates: Zeitschrift für das Gymnasialwesen* 2 (1914) 606–622.

Caster, M. *Lucien et la pensée religieuse de son temps*. Paris, 1937.

——— *Études sur Alexandre ou le faux prophète de Lucien*. Paris, 1938.

Castorina, E., ed. *Tertulliani De Spectaculis*. Biblioteca di Studi Superiori 47. Florence, 1961.

Chadwick, H. *Origen: Contra Celsum*. Cambridge, 1953.

Champlin, E. "The Chronology of Fronto," *JRS* 64 (1974) 136–159.

——— *Fronto and Antonine Rome*. Cambridge, Mass., 1980.

Chapman, J. J. *Lucian, Plato and Greek Morals*. Boston, 1931.

Cheesman, G. L. *The Auxilia of the Roman Army*. Oxford, 1914.

Clinton, K. *The Sacred Officials of the Eleusinian Mysteries*. Transactions of the American Philosophical Society, n.s. 64, 3. Philadelphia, 1974.

Coenen, J. *Lukian: Zeus Tragodos*. Beiträge zur klassischen Philologie 88. Meisenheim am Glan, 1977.

Cormack, J. M. R. "The Nerva Inscription in Beroea," *JRS* 30 (1940) 50–52.

Courtney, E. *A Commentary on the Satires of Juvenal*. London, 1980.

Cova, P. V. *I principia historiae e le idee storiografiche di Frontone*. Naples, 1970.

Croiset, M. *Essai sur la vie et les oeuvres de Lucien*. Paris, 1882.

Cumont, F. *Recherches sur le symbolisme funéraire des Romains*. Paris, 1942.

Cureton, W. *Spicilegium Syriacum: Containing Remains of Bardesan, Meliton, Ambrose and Mara bar Serapion*. London, 1855.

Daremberg, C., and E. Saglio, eds. *Dictionnaire des antiquités grecques et romaines*. 5 vols. in 10. Paris, 1877–1919.

Daris, S. "Ricerche di papirologia documentaria, II," *Aegyptus* 63 (1983) 117–169.

Datsuli-Stavridis, A. "Συμβολὴ στὴν Εἰκονογραφία τοῦ Πολυδεύκη," *Athens Annals of Archaeology* 10 (1977) 126–148.

——— "Συμβολὴ στὴν Εἰκονογραφία τοῦ Ἡρώδη τοῦ Ἀττικοῦ," *Athens Annals of Archaeology* 11 (1978) 214–231.

Davis, Rev. E. J. *Life in Asiatic Turkey*. London, 1879.

Deferrari, R. J. *Lucian's Atticism: The Morphology of the Verb*. Princeton, 1916.

Deininger, J. *Die Provinziallandtage der römischen Kaiserzeit*. Vestigia 6. Munich, 1965.

Delatte, A., and P. Derchain. *Les intailles magiques gréco-égyptiennes*. Paris, 1964.

Delivorrias, A. "Das Original der sitzenden Aphrodite-Olympias," *MDAI(A)* 93 (1978) 1–23.

Delz, J. *Lukians Kenntnis der athenischen Antiquitäten*. Freiburg, 1950.

——— Review of Bompaire, *Lucien*, *Gnomon* 32 (1960) 756–761.

Dillon, J. *The Middle Platonists: A Study of Platonism 80 B.C. to A.D. 220*. London, 1977.

Dimitsas, M. G. Ἡ Μακεδονία ἐν Λίθοις φθεγγομένοις καὶ Μνημείοις σωζομένοις. Athens, 1896.

Dodds, E. R. *Pagan and Christian in an Age of Anxiety*. Cambridge, 1965.

Döring, Kl. *Exemplum Socratis: Studien zur Socratesnachwirkung in der kynischen-stoischen Populärphilosophie der frühen Kaiserzeit und im frühen Christentum*. Hermes Einzelschrift 42. Wiesbaden, 1979.

Dörner, F. K., ed. *Kommagene, Antike Welt*. Sondernummer 6 (1975).

Dörner, F. K., and R. Naumann. *Forschungen in Kommagene*. Istanbuler Forschungen 10. Berlin, 1939.

Downey, G. *A History of Antioch in Syria from Seleucus to the Arab Conquest*. Princeton, 1961.

Dreizehnter, A. "Pompeius als Städtegründer," *Chiron* 5 (1975) 213–245.

Duchesne, L. "Inscriptions de Pompéiopolis," *BCH* 5 (1881) 316–318.

Dudley, D. R. *A History of Cynicism*. London, 1937.

Dunant, C., and J. Pouilloux. *Recherches sur l'histoire et les cultes de Thasos 2*. Études Thasiennes 5. Paris, 1958.

Duncan-Jones, R. P. *The Economy of the Roman Empire: Quantitative Studies*[2]. Cambridge, 1982.

Dupont-Sommer, A. "Un anthroponyme anatolien dans une inscription phénicienne archaïque récemment trouvée à Kition en Chypre," in *Proceedings of the Tenth International Congress of Classical Archaeology*. Ankara, 1978, 1.287–292.

Dupont-Sommer, A., and L. Robert. *La déesse de Hiérapolis Castabala (Cilicie)*. Bibliothèque Archéologique et Historique de l'Institut Français d'Archéologie d'Istanbul 16. Paris, 1964.

Edelstein, E. J., and L. Edelstein. *Asclepius: A Collection and Interpretation of the Testimonies*. 2 vols. Baltimore, 1945.

Edelstein, L. *Ancient Medicine: Selected Papers of Ludwig Edelstein*. Baltimore, 1967.

Ehlers, B. *Eine vorplatonische Deutung des sokratischen Eros: Der Dialog Aspasia des Sokratikers Aeschines*. Zetemata 41. Munich, 1966.

Eitrem, S. "Daulis in Delphoi und Apollons Strafe," in ΔΡΑΓΜΑ *Martino P. Nilsson dedicatum.* Lund, 1939, 170–180.

Elderkin, G. W. "An Athenian Maledictory Inscription on Lead," *Hesperia* 5 (1936) 43–49.

Ellis, R. S., and M. M. Voigt. "1981 Excavations at Gritille, Turkey," *AJA* 86 (1982) 319–332.

Euzennat, M. "Grecs et Orientaux en Mauritanie tingitaine," *Antiquités Africaines* 5 (1971) 161–178.

Festugière, A. J. Review of Caster, *Études sur Alexandre, REG* 52 (1939) 230–233.

Fitzgerald, J. T., and L. M. White, eds. *The Tabula of Cebes.* Chico, Calif., 1983.

Flacelière, R. "Hadrien et Delphes," *CRAI* 1971, 168–185.

Follet, S. *Athènes au IIe et IIIe siècle: Études chronologiques et prosopographiques.* Paris, 1976.

———— "La datation de l'Archonte Dionysos (*IG* II², 3968); Ses conséquences archéologiques, littéraires et philologiques," *REG* 90 (1977) 47–54.

———— "Lettre de Marc-Aurèle aux Athéniens (*EM* 13366): Nouvelles lectures et interprétations," *RPh* 53 (1979) 29–43.

Forbes, C. A. "Οἱ ἀφ' Ἡρακλέους in Epictetus and Lucian," *AJPh* 60 (1939) 473–474.

Fowler, H. W., and F. G. Fowler, trans. *The Works of Lucian of Samosata.* Oxford, 1905.

Fraser, J. G. *Pausanias's Description of Greece.* 6 vols. London, 1898.

Fraser, P. M. *Ptolemaic Alexandria.* 3 vols. Oxford, 1972.

———— "The Kings of Commagene and the Greek World," in *Studien zur Religion und Kultur Kleinasiens* 1. Études Préliminaires aux Religions Orientales dans l'Empire Romain 66, 1. Leiden, 1978, 359–374.

French, D. "S. Quintilius Maximus, Proconsul (of Asia)," *ZPE* 21 (1976) 77–78.

Friedländer, L. *Darstellungen aus der Sittengeschichte Roms*[10]. 4 vols. Leipzig, 1921–1923.

Funk, K. *Untersuchungen über die lucianische Vita Demonactis. Philologus* Supplementband 10 (1907) 558–674.

Gajdukevic, V. F. *Das Bosporanische Reich.* Berlin, 1971.

Gallavotti, C. *Luciano nella sua evoluzione artistica e spirituale.* Lanciano, 1932.

Geffcken, J. *Zwei griechische Apologeten.* Leipzig and Berlin, 1907.

Gigon, O. "Antike Erzählungen über die Berufung zur Philosophie." *Museum Helveticum* 3 (1946) 1–21.

Gil, J. "Lucianea." *Habis* 10–11 (1979–1980) 87–104.

Gilliam, J. F. "The Plague under Marcus Aurelius," *AJPh* 82 (1961) 225–251.

Ginouvès, R. *Balaneutikè: Recherches sur le bain dans l'antiquité grecque.* Bibliothèque des Écoles Françaises d'Athènes et de Rome 200. Paris, 1962.

Gladiss, A. von. "Ein Denkmal aus Soloi," *MDAI(I)* 23–24 (1973–1974) 175–181.

Graindor, P. *Un milliardaire antique: Hérode Atticus et sa famille.* Cairo, 1930.

Grandjouan, C. *Terracottas and Plastic Lamps of the Roman Period. The Athenian Agora* 6. Princeton, 1961.

Habicht, C. *Die Inschriften des Asklepieions. Altertümer von Pergamon* VIII 3. Berlin, 1969.

——— *Pausanias' Guide to Ancient Greece.* Berkeley, 1985.

Habrich, E., ed. *Iamblichi Babyloniacorum Reliquiae.* Leipzig, 1960.

Hägg, T. *The Novel in Antiquity.* Oxford, 1983.

Halfmann, H. *Die Senatoren aus dem östlichen Teil des Imperium Romanum bis zum Ende des 2. Jahrhunderts n. Chr.* Hypomnemata 58. Göttingen, 1979.

Hall, J. A. Reviews of Anderson, *Lucian* and Anderson, *Studies, JRS* 100 (1970) 229–232.

——— *Lucian's Satire.* New York, 1981.

Harnack, A. von. *Die Mission und Ausbreitung des Christentums in den ersten drei Jahrhunderten*[4]. 2 vols. Leipzig, 1924.

Harris, H. B. *The Newly Recovered Apology of Aristides: Its Doctrine and Ethics.* London, 1891.

Hartswick, K. J. "The Athena Lemnia Reconsidered," *AJA* 87 (1983) 335–346.

Hayum, A. *Giovanni Antonio Bazzi. "Il Sodoma."* New York and London, 1976.

Heberdey, R. "IX. Vorläufiger Bericht über die Ausgrabungen in Ephesos 1907–1911," *JOAEI* 15 (1912) Beibl. 157–182.

Heberdey, R., and A. Wilhelm. "Reisen in Kilikien," *Oesterreichische Akademie der Wissenschaften, Wien, Philos.-Hist. Kl.* Denkschriften 44, 6. Vienna, 1894.

Heitsch, E. *Die Griechischen Dichterfragmente der römischen Kaiserzeit.* 2 vols. Göttingen, 1961–1964 (1[2], 1963).

Hellenkamper, H. "Der Limes am nordsyrischen Euphrat. Bericht zu einer archäologischen Landesaufnahme," in *Studien zu den Militärgrenzen Roms, 2: Vorträge des 10. Internationalen Limeskongresses in der Germania Inferior, Bonner Jahrbücher* Beiheft 38. Bonn, 1977, 461–471.

Helm, R. *Lucian und Menipp.* Leipzig and Berlin, 1906.

——— ed. *Die Chronik des Hieronymus*[2]. Die Griechischen Christlichen Schriftsteller der ersten Jahrhunderte 47. Berlin, 1956.

Hemsterhuis, T, ed. *Lucianus Samosatensis: Opera.* 4 vols. Amsterdam, 1743–1746.

Hermann, C. F., ed. *Luciani Samosatensis libellus, quomodo historia conscribi oporteat*. Frankfurt, 1828.

Herrmann, P. *Der Römische Kaisereid. Untersuchungen zu seiner Herkunft und Entwicklung*. Hypomnemata 20. Göttingen, 1968.

Heyman, C. "Homer on Coins from Smyrna," in *Studia Paulo Naster oblata*. 1: *Numismatica Antiqua*. Louvain, 1982, 161–174.

Hicks, E. L. "Recent Discoveries in Eastern Cilicia," *JHS* 11 (1890) 231–254.

Hirdt, W. *Gian Giorgio Trissinos Porträt der Isabella d'Este: Ein Beitrag zur Lukian-Rezeption in Italien*. Studien zum Fortwirkung der Antike 12. Heidelberg, 1981.

Hirzel, R. *Der Dialog: Ein literarhistorischer Versuch*. 2 vols. Leipzig, 1895.

Homeyer, H., ed. *Lukian: Wie man Geschichte schreiben soll*. Munich, 1965.

Honoré, T. *Ulpian*. Oxford, 1980.

Horne, H. P. *Botticelli: Painter of Florence*, introd. J. Pope-Hennessy. Princeton, 1980.

Hornsby, H. M. "The Cynicism of Peregrinus Proteus," *Hermathena* 48 (1933) 65–84.

Householder, F. W. *Literary Quotation and Allusion in Lucian*. New York, 1941.

Howell, P. A. *A Commentary on Book One of the Epigrams of Martial*. London, 1980.

Husson, G., ed. *Lucien: Le navire ou les souhaits*. 2 vols. Paris, 1970.

Jacopi, G. *Esplorazioni e studi in Paflagonia e Cappadocia: Relazione sulla seconda campagna esplorativa, agosto-ottobre 1936*. Rome, 1937.

Jebb, R. "Lucian," in *Essays and Addresses*. Cambridge, 1907, 164–192.

Jones, C. P. *Plutarch and Rome*. Oxford, 1971.

——— "Two Enemies of Lucian," *GRBS* 13 (1972) 475–487.

——— "Aelius Aristides, Εἰς Βασιλέα," *JRS* 62 (1972) 134–152.

——— *The Roman World of Dio Chrysostom*. Cambridge, Mass., 1978.

——— "Three Foreigners in Attica," *Phoenix* 32 (1978) 222–234.

——— "Two Inscriptions from Aphrodisias," *Harvard Studies in Classical Philology* 85 (1981) 107–129.

——— "Tarsos in the *Amores* Ascribed to Lucian," *GRBS* 25 (1984) 177–181.

——— "Neryllinus," *CPh* 80 (1985) 40–45.

Keil, J. "Ephesos und der Etappendienst zwischen der Nord- und Ostfront des Imperium Romanum," *Oesterreichische Akademie der Wissenschaften, Wien, Philos.-Hist. Kl.* Anzeiger 92 (1955) 159–170.

Keil, J., and A. von Premerstein. "Bericht über eine Reise in Lydien und der südlichen Aiolis," *Akademie der Wissenschaften, Wien, Philos.-Hist. Kl.* Denkschriften 53, 2. Vienna, 1910.

Keller, O. *Die Antike Tierwelt.* 2 vols. Leipzig, 1909–1913.

Kindstrand, J. F. "Sostratus-Hercules-Agathion—The Rise of a Legend," *Annales Societatis Litterarum Humaniorum Regiae Upsaliensis* 1979–1980, 50–79.

—— *Anacharsis: The Legend and the Apophthegmata.* Acta Universitatis Upsaliensis, Studia Graeca Upsaliensia 16. Uppsala, 1981.

Klein, U. "Pompeiopolis in Paphlagonien und in Kilikien," *Gazette Numismatique Suisse (Schweizer Münzblätter)* 23 (1973) 47–55.

—— " Ὁμόνοια Σεβαστῶν und Faustina Augusta: Zwei rara oder inedita von Mark Aurel und Faustina II," *Gazette Numismatique Suisse (Schweizer Münzblätter)* 33 (1983) 57–67.

Kleiner, D. E. E. *The Monument of Philopappus in Athens.* Archaeologica 30. Rome, 1983.

Klose, D. O. A. "Homer—ΟΜΗΡΟΣ," *Gazette Numismatique Suisse (Schweizer Münzblätter)* 34 (1984) 1–3.

Knibbe, D. "Neue Inschriften aus Ephesos III," *JOEAI* 49 (1968–1971) Beibl. 57–88.

—— "Neue Inschriften aus Ephesos V," *JOEAI* 50 (1972–1975) Beibl. 27–56.

Knoepfler, D. "Contributions à l'épigraphie de Chalcis," *BCH* 103 (1979) 165–188.

Koenigs, W. *Die Echohalle.* Deutsches Archäologisches Institut, Olympische Forschungen 14. Berlin, 1984.

Kontoleon, A. E. " Ἐπιγραφαὶ τῆς ἐλάσσονος Ἀσίας," *MDAI(A)* 12 (1887) 245–261.

Kraiker, W. *Das Kentaurenbild des Zeuxis.* Winckelmannsprogramm der Archäologischen Gesellschaft zu Berlin 106. Berlin, 1950.

Labriolle, P. de. *La réaction païenne: Étude sur la polémique antichrétienne du Ier au VIe siècle.* Paris, 1948.

Lambert, R. *Beloved and God.* London and New York, 1984.

Lanckoroński, K. *Städte Pamphyliens und Pisidiens.* 2 vols. Prague, Vienna, Leipzig, 1890.

Laum, B. *Stiftungen in der griechischen und römischen Antike.* 2 vols. Leipzig, 1914.

Lenaerts, J. "Fragment de parchemin du *Lucius* ou l'Âne: P. lit. Lond. 194," *Chronique d'Égypte* 49 (1974) 115–120.

Lepper, F. A. *Trajan's Parthian War.* Oxford, 1948.

Levi, D. *Antioch Mosaic Pavements.* 2 vols. Princeton, London, The Hague, 1947.

Levick, B. M. *Roman Colonies in Southern Asia Minor.* Oxford, 1967.

Levick, B. M., and S. Jameson. "C. Crepereius Gallus and His *Gens,*" *JRS* 54 (1964) 98–106.

Lévy, I. *La légende de Pythagore de Grèce en Palestine*. Paris, 1927.

Loup, G. du. "Excursions aux ruines de Pompéiopolis (Cilicie)," *Bulletin Archéologique du Comité des Travaux Historiques* 1930–1931, 711–716.

Love, I. C. "A Preliminary Report of the Excavations at Knidos, 1969," *AJA* 74 (1970) 149–155.

———— "A Preliminary Report of the Excavations at Knidos," *AJA* 76 (1972) 61–76.

Macleod, C. W. "The Poetry of Ethics: Horace, *Epistles* I," *JRS* 69 (1979) 16–27 (*Collected Essays*. Oxford, 1983, 280–291).

Macleod, M. D. " ᾿Aν with the Future in Lucian and the *Solecist*," *CQ* 6 (1956) 102–111.

———— "Lucian's Activities as a μισαλάζων," *Philologus* 123 (1979) 326–328.

———— ed. *Luciani Opera*. 3 vols. Oxford, 1972–.

Magie, D. *Roman Rule in Asia Minor*. 2 vols. Princeton, 1950.

Marshall, P. K. "The Date of Birth of Aulus Gellius," *CPh* 58 (1963) 143–149.

Martin, J. *Symposion: Die Geschichte einer literarischen Form*. Paderborn, 1931.

Marx, K., and F. Engels. *The German Ideology*. Collected Works 5. London, 1976, 19–539.

Mattioli, E. *Luciano e l'Umanesimo*. Istituto per gli studi storici in Napoli. Naples, 1980.

Mayor, J. E. B., ed. *Thirteen Satires of Juvenal*. 2 vols. London, 1900–1901.

McCarthy, B. P. "Lucian and Menippus," *Yale Classical Studies* 4 (1934) 3–55.

Mendel, G. "Inscriptions de Bithynie et de Paphlagonie," *BCH* 27 (1903) 314–333.

Mengis, K. *Die Schriftstellerische Technik im Sophistenmahl des Athenaios*. Paderborn, 1920.

Mesk, J. "Des Aelius Aristides verlorene Rede gegen die Tänzer," *Wiener Studien* 30 (1908) 59–74.

———— "Lucian's Nigrinus und Juvenal," *Wiener Studien* 34 (1912) 372–382, 35 (1913) 1–33.

Michell, H. *Sparta*. Cambridge, 1952.

Millar, F. "Paul of Samosata, Zenobia and Aurelian: The Church, Local Culture and Political Allegiance in Third-Century Syria," *JRS* 61 (1971) 1–17.

Miltner, F. "XXII. Vorläufiger Bericht über die Ausgrabungen in Ephesos," *JOEAI* 44 (1959) Beibl. 243–378.

Misch, G. *Geschichte der Autobiographie* 1: *Das Altertum*³. 2 vols. Berne, 1949–1950.

Momigliano, A. D. Review of Peretti, *Luciano*, *Rivista Storica Italiana* 60

(1948) 430–432 (*Quarto contributo alla storia degli studi classici*. Rome, 1969, 641–644).

Montevecchi, O. *La papirologia*. Turin, 1973.

Le Morvan, A. "La description artistique chez Lucien," *REG* 45 (1932) 380–390.

Müller, A. "Das Bühnenwesen in der Zeit von Constantin d. Gr. bis Justinian," *Neue Jahrbücher für das klassische Altertum* 23 (1909) 36–55.

Nicolson, M. H. *Voyages to the Moon*. New York, 1948.

Nilsson, M. P. *Geschichte der griechischen Religion 2: Die Hellenistische und Römische Welt²*. Munich, 1961.

Nisbet, R. G. M., ed. *M. Tulli Ciceronis in L. Calpurnium Pisonem oratio*. Oxford, 1961.

Nisbet, R. G. M., and M. Hubbard. *A Commentary on Horace: Odes Book 1*. Oxford, 1970.

Nock, A. D. "A Vision of Mandulis Aion," *Harvard Theological Review* 27 (1934) 53–104 (*Essays* 1.357–400).

——— *Conversion: The Old and the New in Religion from Alexander the Great to Constantine*. Oxford, 1933.

——— "Conversion and Adolescence," in Th. Klauser and A. Rücker, eds., *Pisciculi: Studien zur Religion und Geschichte des Altertums. Antike und Christentum* Ergänzungsband 1. Münster, 1939, 165–177 (*Essays* 1.469–480).

——— Review of Harder, *Karpocrates von Chalkis, Gnomon* 21 (1949) 221–228 (*Essays* 2.703–711).

——— "Deification and Julian," *JRS* 47 (1957) 115–123 (*Essays* 2.833–846).

——— Review of Schoeps, *Paulus, Gnomon* 33 (1961) 581–590 (*Essays* 2.928–939).

——— "Nymphs and Nereids," *Mélanges de l'Université Saint Joseph (Beyrouth)* 37 (1961) 297–308 (*Essays* 2.919–927).

——— "Gnosticism," *Harvard Theological Review* 57 (1964) 255–279 (*Essays* 2.940–959).

——— *Essays on Religion and the Ancient World*, ed. Z. Stewart. 2 vols. Oxford, 1972.

Norden, E., ed. *P. Vergilius Maro: Aeneis VI⁴*. Darmstadt, 1957.

——— *Die Antike Kunstprosa⁵*. 2 vols. Darmstadt, 1958.

Nutton, V., ed. *Galen: On Prognosis (De Praecognitione). Corpus Medicorum Graecorum* 5, 8, 1. Berlin, 1979.

Oberleitner, W. *Funde aus Ephesos und Samothrake*. Kunsthistorisches Museum, Wien, Katalog der Antikensammlung 2. Vienna, 1978.

Oden, R. A., Jr. *Studies in Lucian's De Syria Dea*. Harvard Semitic Monographs 15. Missoula, Mont., 1977.

Ogilvie, R. M. *The Library of Lactantius*. Oxford, 1978.

Oliva, P. *Pannonia and the Onset of Crisis in the Roman Empire*. Prague, 1962.

Oliver, J. P. *Marcus Aurelius: Aspects of Civic and Cultural Policy in the East.* *Hesperia* Supplement 13. Princeton, 1970.

——— "The Actuality of Lucian's *Assembly of the Gods,*" *AJPh* 101 (1980) 304–313 (*The Civic Tradition and Roman Athens.* Baltimore and London, 1983, 76–84).

Pack, R. "The 'Volatilization' of Peregrinus Proteus," *AJPh* 67 (1946) 334–345.

——— *The Greek and Roman Literary Texts from Greco-Roman Egypt².* Ann Arbor, 1965.

Page, D. L., ed. *Further Greek Epigrams.* Cambridge, 1981.

Palm, J. *Rom, Römertum und Imperium in der griechischen Literatur der Kaiserzeit.* Lund, 1959.

Pape, W., and G. E. Benseler. *Wörterbuch der griechischen Eigennamen.* 2 vols. Braunschweig, 1863–1870.

Paribeni, R., and P. Romanelli. "Studi e ricerche archeologiche nell'Anatolia meridionale," *Monumenti Antichi* 23 (1914) 5–274.

Parke, H. W. *The Oracles of Zeus: Dodona, Olympia, Ammon.* Oxford, 1967.

Parke, H. W., and D. E. W. Wormell. *The Delphic Oracle.* 2 vols. Oxford, 1956.

Penella, R. J., ed. *The Letters of Apollonius of Tyana. Mnemosyne* Supplement 56. Leiden, 1979.

Perdrizet, P. "Une inscription d'Antioche qui reproduit un oracle d'Alexandre d'Abonotichos," *CRAI* 1903, 62–66.

Peretti, A. *Luciano: Un intellettuale greco contro Roma.* Florence, 1946.

Perry, B. E. *The Ancient Romances: A Literary-historical Account of Their Origins.* Berkeley and Los Angeles, 1967.

Peschlow-Bindokat, A. "Zur Säulenstrasse von Pompeiopolis in Kilikien," *MDAI(I)* 25 (1975) 373–391.

Pfister, F. *Der Reliquienkult im Altertum.* Religionsgeschichtliche Versuche und Vorarbeiten 5. 2 vols. Giessen, 1902–1912.

Pflaum, H. G. "Lucien de Samosate, *archistator praefecti Aegypti,* d'après une inscription de Césarée de Mauritainie," *Mélanges de l'École Française de Rome* 17 (1959) 281–286 (*Afrique romaine: Scripta varia* 1. Paris, 1978, 155–160).

——— "Les Crepereii et les Egrilii d'Afrique," *Cahiers de Tunisie* 15 (1967) 65–72 (*Afrique romaine: Scripta varia* 1. Paris, 1978, 237–244).

des Places, E., ed. *Oracles Chaldaïques, avec un choix de commentaires anciens.* Paris, 1971.

——— ed. *Eusèbe de Césarée: La préparation évangélique livres V, 18–36, VI.* Sources Chrétiennes 266. Paris, 1980.

Plassart, A. "Fouilles de Thespies: Inscriptions," *BCH* 50 (1926) 383–462.

Polman, G. H. "Chronological Biography and *Akmé* in Plutarch," *Classical Philology* 69 (1974) 169–177.

Prawer, S. S. *Heine: The Tragic Satirist.* Cambridge, 1961.

Preisshofen, F. "Kunsttheorie und Kunstbetrachtung," in H. Flaschar, ed., *Le classicisme à Rome aux Iers siècles avant et après J.-C.* Entretiens Hardt 25. Geneva, 1979, 263–277.

Quacquarelli, A. *La retorica antica al bivio (L'Ad Nigrinum e l'Ad Donatum).* Rome, 1956.

Rabe, H. "Die Überlieferung der Lukianscholien," *Königliche Gesellschaft (Akademie) der Wissenschaften, Göttingen, Philol.-Hist. Kl.* Nachrichten, 1902, 718–736.

—— "Die Lukianstudien des Arethas," *Königliche Gesellschaft (Akademie) der Wissenschaften, Göttingen, Philol.-Hist. Kl.* Nachrichten, 1903, 643–656.

—— ed. *Scholia in Lucianum.* Leipzig, 1906.

Radermacher, L. "Lucian, *Philopseudes* Cap. 11 und 24," *Rheinisches Museum* 60 (1905) 315–317.

—— "Cyprian der Magier," *Archiv für Religionswissenschaft* 21 (1922) 233–235.

—— "Griechische Quelle zur Faustsage," *Akademie der Wissenschaften in Wien, Philos.-Hist. Kl.* Sitzungsberichte 206, 4 (1927).

Radet, G., and P. Paris. "Inscription relative à Ptolemée fils de Thraséas," *BCH* 14 (1890) 587–589.

Reardon, B. P. *Courants littéraires grecs des IIe et IIIe siècles après J.-C.* Paris, 1971.

Reitzenstein, R. *Hellenistische Wundererzählungen².* Darmstadt, 1963.

Robert, J., and L. Robert. "Inscriptions de l'Hellespont et de la Propontide," *Hellenica* 9 (1950) 78–97.

Robert, L. "Pantomimen im griechischen Orient," *Hermes* 65 (1930) 106–122 (*Opera minora selecta* 1.654–670).

—— "Études d'épigraphie grecque," *RPh* ser. 3, 4 (1930) 25–60 (*Opera minora selecta* 2.1125–60).

—— *Études anatoliennes: Recherches sur les inscriptions grecques de l'Asie Mineure.* Études Orientales Publiées par l'Institut Français d'Archéologie de Stamboul 5. Paris, 1937.

—— "Hellenica," *RPh* sér. 3, 13 (1939) 97–217 (*Opera minora selecta* 2.1250–1370).

—— *Les gladiateurs dans l'orient grec.* Bibliothèque de l'École des Hautes Études, IVe Section, Sciences Historiques et Philologiques. Paris, 1940.

—— "La bibliothèque de Nysa de Carie," *Hellenica* 1 (1940) 144–148.

—— "Épitaphes métriques de médecins à Nicée et à Tithorée," *Hellenica* 2 (1946) 103–108.

—— "Épigrammes relatives à des gouverneurs," *Hellenica* 4 (1948) 35–114.

—— "Un juriste romain dans une inscription de Beroia," *Hellenica* 5 (1948) 29–34.

—— "Les boules dans les types monétaires agonistiques," *Hellenica* 7 (1949) 93–104.

—— *Les fouilles de Claros.* Limoges, 1954.

—— "Inscriptions des Dardanelles," *Hellenica* 10 (1955) 266–282.

—— "Épigrammes," *Hellenica* 11/12 (1960) 267–349.

—— *Noms indigènes dans l'Asie-Mineure gréco-romaine, première partie.* Bibliothèque Archéologique et Historique de l'Institut Français d'Archéologie d'Istanbul 13. Paris, 1963.

—— *D'Aphrodisias à la Lycaonie (Hellenica 13).* Paris, 1965.

—— "Inscriptions de l'antiquité et du bas-empire à Corinthe," *REG* 79 (1966) 733–770.

—— *Monnaies grecques: Types, légendes, magistrats, monétaires et géographie.* École Pratique des Hautes Études, IVe Section, Centre de Recherches d'Histoire et de Philologie, Hautes Études Numismatiques 2. Paris, 1967.

—— "L'oracle de Claros," in C. Delvoye and G. Roux, *La Civilisation grecque de l'antiquité à nos jours* 1. Brussels, 1967, 305–312.

—— "Enterrements et épitaphes," *L'Antiquité Classique* 37 (1968) 406–448.

—— "Les épigrammes satiriques de Lucillius sur les athlètes: Parodie et réalités," in *L'épigramme grecque.* Entretiens Hardt 14. Geneva, 1969, 181–295.

—— "Théophane de Mytilène à Constantinople," *CRAI* 1969, 42–64.

—— *Opera minora selecta.* 4 vols. Amsterdam, 1969–1974.

—— "Documents d'Asie Mineure," *BCH* 101 (1977) 43–132.

—— "Deux poètes grecs à l'époque impériale," in Στήλη: Τόμος εἰς Μνήμην Νικολάου Κοντολέοντος. Athens, 1977, 1–20.

—— "Sur un mois du calendrier bithynien," Ἀρχαιολογικὴ Ἐφημερίς 1979, 231–236.

—— *À travers l'Asie Mineure: Poètes et prosateurs, monnaies grecques, voyageurs et géographie.* Bibliothèque des Écoles Françaises d'Athènes et de Rome 239. Paris, 1980.

—— "Le serpent Glycon d'Abonouteichos à Athènes et Artemis d'Éphèse à Rome," *CRAI* 1981, 512–535.

—— "Amulettes grecques," *Journal des Savants* 1981, 3–44.

—— "Une épigramme satirique d'Automédon et Athènes au début de l'empire," *REG* 94 (1981) 338–361.

—— "Dans une maison d'Éphèse: Un serpent et un chiffre," *CRAI* 1982, 126–132.

Robertson, D. S. "The Authenticity and Date of Lucian *De Saltatione*," in

Essays and Studies Presented to William Ridgeway. Cambridge, 1914, 180–185.

Robinson, C. *Lucian and His Influence in Europe.* London and Chapel Hill, 1979.

Rohde, E. "Γέγονε in den Biographica des Suidas," *Rheinisches Museum* 33 (1878) 161–220 (*Kleine Schriften.* Tübingen and Leipzig, 1901, 1.114–184).

——— *Der Griechische Roman und seine Vorläufer³.* Leipzig, 1914.

Roscher, W. H., ed. *Ausführliches Lexikon der griechischen und römischen Mythologie.* 6 vols. Leipzig, 1884–1936.

Rostovtzeff (Rostowsew), M. I. *Scythien und der Bosporus.* Berlin, 1931.

Rotroff, S. I. "An Athenian Archon List of the Second Century after Christ," *Hesperia* 44 (1975) 402–408.

Russell, D. A., and N. G. Wilson, eds. *Menander Rhetor.* Oxford, 1981.

Şahin, S. "Griechische Epigramme aus dem südlichen Propontisgebiet," in *Hommages à Maarten J. Vermaseren* 3. Études Préliminaires aux Religions Orientales dans l'Empire Romain 68. Leiden, 1978, 997–1002.

Saller, R. P. *Personal Patronage under the Early Empire.* Cambridge, 1982.

Schmid, W. "Menanders Dyscolos und die Timonlegende," *Rheinisches Museum* 102 (1959) 157–182.

Schmid, W., and O. Stählin. *Geschichte der griechischen Litteratur* 1: *Die Klassische Periode.* 5 vols. Munich, 1929–1948. 2: *Die Nachklassische Periode.* 2 vols. Munich, 1920–1924.

Schuster, M. "Der Werwolf und die Hexen," *Wiener Studien* 48 (1930) 149–178.

Schwartz, J. *Lucien de Samosate: Philopseudès et De morte Peregrini².* Paris, 1963.

——— *Biographie de Lucien de Samosate.* Collection Latomus 83. Brussels, 1965.

Settis, S. "Il ninfeo di Erode Attico a Olympia e il problema della composizione della Periegesi di Pausania," *Annali della Scuola Normale Superiore di Pisa,* ser. 2, 37 (1968) 1–63.

Seyrig, H. "Antiquités syriennes 78: Les dieux de Hiérapolis," *Syria* 37 (1960) 233–252 (*Antiquités Syriennes* 6. Paris, 1966, 79–98).

Shackleton Bailey, D. R., ed. *Cicero's Letters to Atticus.* 7 vols. Cambridge, 1965–1970.

Sherwin-White, A. N. *The Letters of Pliny: A Historical and Social Commentary.* Oxford, 1966.

Sittig, E. *De Graecorum nominibus theophoris.* Dissertationes philologicae Halenses 20, 1. Halle, 1912.

Smith, M. F. "Eight New Fragments of Diogenes of Oenoanda," *Anatolian Studies* 29 (1979) 69–89.

Solin, H. *Die Griechischen Personennamen in Rom: Ein Namenbuch.* 3 vols. Berlin and New York, 1982.

Speyer, W. *Bücherfunde in der Glaubenswerbung der Antike.* Hypomnemata 24. Göttingen, 1970.

Stadter, P. A. *Plutarch's Historical Methods: An Analysis of the Mulierum Virtutes.* Cambridge, Mass., 1965.

—— "Flavius Arrianus: The New Xenophon," *GRBS* 8 (1967) 155–161.

—— *Arrian of Nicomedia.* Chapel Hill, 1980.

Stein, A. "Zu Lukians Alexandros," in *Strena Buliciana.* Zagreb and Split, 1924, 257–265.

Strohmaier, G. "Übersehenes zur Biographie Lukians," *Philologus* 120 (1976) 117–122.

Stucky, R. A. "Prêtres syriens II: Hiérapolis," *Syria* 53 (1976) 124–140.

Sullivan, R. D. "The Dynasty of Commagene," in H. Temporini and W. Haase, eds., *Aufstieg und Niedergang der römischen Welt* II.8. Berlin and New York, 1977, 732–798.

Süss, W. *Ethos: Studien zur alteren griechischen Rhetorik.* Leipzig and Berlin, 1910.

Tackaberry, W. H. *Lucian's Relation to Plato and the Post-Aristotelian Philosophers.* University of Toronto Studies, Philological Series 9. Toronto, 1930.

Tooke, W., trans. *Lucian of Samosata from the Greek, with the Comments and Illustrations of Wieland and Others.* 2 vols. London, 1820.

Travlos, J. *Pictorial Dictionary of Ancient Athens.* London, 1971.

Treadgold, W. T. *The Nature of the Bibliotheca of Photius.* Dumbarton Oaks Studies 18. Washington, D.C., 1980.

Turner, E. G. *Greek Papyri: An Introduction.* Oxford, 1968.

Vahlen, J. "Index lectionum hibernarum 1882/83 (Luciani de Cynicis iudicium; Lucianus de Peregrini Morte)," in *Opuscula Academica.* Leipzig, 1907, 1.181–197.

vander Leest, J. "Lucian in Egypt," *GRBS* 26 (1985) 75–82.

Verzone, P. "Città ellenistiche e romane dell'Asia Minore," *Palladio* n.s. 7 (1957) 54–68.

Vidal-Naquet, P. "Flavius Arrien entre deux mondes", in P. Savinel, trans., *Arrien: Histoire d'Alexandre.* Paris, 1984, 311–393.

Vidalis, A. M. Review of Sakalis, Ἡ Γνησιότητα τοῦ Ψευδοσοφιστὴ τοῦ Λουκιανοῦ, *REG* 93 (1980) 600–602.

Waddington, W. H., E. Babelon, and T. Reinach. *Recueil général des monnaies grecques d'Asie Mineure* 1. Paris, 1908–1925.

Wagner, J. *Seleuceia am Euphrat/Zeugma.* Beihefte zum Tübinger Atlas des Vorderen Orients B 10. Wiesbaden, 1976.

—— "Dynastie und Herrscherkult in Kommagene. Forschungsgeschichte und neuere Funde," *MDAI(I)* 33 (1983) 177–224.

Waites, M. C. "Some Features of the Allegorical Debate in Greek Literature," *Harvard Studies in Classical Philology* 23 (1912) 1–46.

Walker, S. "A Sanctuary of Isis on the South Slope of the Athenian Acropolis," *Annual of the British School at Athens* 74 (1979) 243–257.

Walzer, R. *Galen on Jews and Christians.* Oxford, 1949.

Weinreich, O. "Heros Propylaios und Apollon Propylaios," *MDAI(A)* 38 (1913) 62–72 (*Ausgewählte Schriften* 1.197–206).

———— "Alexandros der Lügenprophet und seine Stellung in der Religiosität des II. Jahrhunderts n. Chr.," *Neue Jahrbücher für das klassische Altertum* 47 (1921) 129–151 (*Ausgewählte Schriften* 1.520–551).

———— *Menekrates Zeus und Salmoneus: Religionsgeschichtliche Studien zur Psychopathologie des Gottmenschentums in Antike und Neuzeit.* Tübinger Beiträge zur Altertumswissenschaft 18. Stuttgart, 1933.

———— *Epigrammstudien 1: Epigramm und Pantomimus. Akademie der Wissenschaften, Heidelberg, Philos.-Hist. Kl.* Sitzungsberichte 1944–48, 1.

———— *Ausgewählte Schriften,* ed. G. Wille. 4 vols. Amsterdam, 1969–1979.

Whittaker, M., ed. *Tatian: Oratio ad Graecos and Fragments.* Oxford, 1982.

Wilamowitz-Moellendorff, U. von, et al. *Die griechische und lateinische Literatur und Sprache,* in P. Hinneberg, ed., *Die Kultur der Gegenwart* I 8. Berlin and Leipzig, 1905 (ed.³, 1912).

———— *Erinnerungen 1848–1914².* Leipzig, n.d.

———— *Der Glaube der Hellenen³.* 2 vols. Darmstadt, 1959.

Wilhelm, A. *Neue Beiträge zur griechischen Inschriftenkunde 5. Oesterreichische Akademie der Wissenschaften in Wien, Philos.-Hist. Kl.* Sitzungsberichte 214, 4 (1932) (*Akademieschriften* 1.245–293).

———— "Griechische Grabinschriften aus Kleinasien," *Preussische Akademie der Wissenschaften, Berlin. Sitzungsberichte* 1932, 792–865 (*Akademieschriften* 2.336–409).

———— "Das Epithalamion in Lukianos' Συμπόσιον ἢ Λαπίθαι," *Wiener Studien* 56 (1938) 54–89.

Williams, W. "Individuality in the Imperial Constitutions, Hadrian and the Antonines," *JRS* 66 (1976) 67–83.

Willis, W. H. "A Census of the Literary Papyri from Egypt," *GRBS* 9 (1968) 205–241.

Zetzel, J. E. G. *"Emendavi ad Tironem,"* Harvard Studies in Classical Philology 77 (1973) 225–243.

Zgusta, L. *Personennamen griechischer Städte der nördlichen Schwarzmeerküste.* Prague, 1955.

———— *Kleinasiatische Personennamen.* Prague, 1964.

Zimmermann, F. "Lukians *Toxaris* und das Kairener Romanfragment," *Philologische Wochenschrift* 1935, 1211–16.

Index

INDEX